Doug

Merry Christmas always, 12/92

Love
Susan

C U R R E N C Y

D O U B L E D A Y

The
REPUBLIC of TEA

Letters to a Young Zentrepeneur

MEL ZIEGLER·BILL ROSENZWEIG·PATRICIA ZIEGLER

CURRENCY

DOUBLEDAY

New York   London   Toronto   Sydney   Auckland

For Josh Mailman

A CURRENCY BOOK
PUBLISHED BY DOUBLEDAY
a division of Bantam Doubleday Dell Publishing Group, Inc.
666 Fifth Avenue, New York, New York 10103

CURRENCY and DOUBLEDAY are trademarks of
Doubleday, a division of Bantam Doubleday
Dell Publishing Group, Inc.

Book design by Tasha Hall

Library of Congress Cataloging-in-Publication Data
Ziegler, Mel.
The republic of tea : letters to a young zentrepreneur /
Mel Ziegler, Bill Rosenzweig, Patricia Ziegler. — 1st ed.
        p.   cm.
"A Currency book" — T.p. verso.
1. Tea trade — Management — Case studies.   2. Retail trade —
Management — Case studies.   3. New business enterprises — Management —
Case studies.   I. Rosenzweig, Bill.   II. Ziegler, Patricia.
III. Title.
HD9198.A2Z54   1992
658.8'7 — dc20   92-12990
                                                            CIP

ISBN 0-385-42056-0

ACKNOWLEDGMENTS

The authors gratefully thank and acknowledge Faye Rosenzweig for her gracious assistance and support, and for her warm, ever-steady, and always-open Tea Mind; Harriet Rubin for her incisive but gentle probes that captivated us and drove us to try to make more sense than we thought we could; Bruce Katz for his true friendship, his laserlike intelligence, and for being Bruce Katz; Morton Janklow for his masterful ways; Stephen Yafa for his early sensitive reading and great advice; Nancy Bauch and Vic Zauderer for their keen eyes and enthusiastic hearts; Paul Saffo, Doug Menuez, Elliot Hoffman, Michael Whitacre, Eric and Suzy Schuman, Paul Hawken, and Don Joseph for their encouragement and assistance; Michael Spillane and Brian Writer for their patient teaching about *camellia sinensis*; Samuel Twining for his spirited talk about the tea business and for blending some damned fine teas that educated our palettes; and finally Sam Rosenzweig and Zio Ziegler for showing us that our Tea Minds go all the way down to our toes.

A moment of thanks for the pot. It gives up its emptiness for the tea. Is there a greater sacrifice?

— The Minister of Leaves

REPUBLIC of TEA

DEAR FELLOW PEOPLE OF TEA:

I came to The Republic of Tea through a journey of many cups.

I had served nearly ten years as Prime Minister in another Republic, where the beverage of choice was brewed from roasted coffee beans. Fueled by the coffee, life moved very rapidly for me in that other Republic, so fast that I began to sense I was missing something quite grand along the way. The sensation grew until I could bear it no longer. I was compelled to defect. Fleeing the race-to-nowhere that had been my life, I tasted the joys of existence in a new way — sip by sip rather than gulp by gulp.

I wandered for nearly a year in a pathless land until one night I found myself staying at a lodge where coffee was not available. Its absence left me untroubled until a few hours after breakfast. It was then that a wrenching and furious storm unlike anything I had experienced before swept into my head. Lightning ripped from behind my eyes to the back of my skull. By evening the fury had dissipated and I was well again. Better than well, I should say. I found myself in a deep state of clarity and calm. It was while I was in that novel condition that I came to realize something I could never see before: *It wasn't I who was having the coffee all those years; rather, it was the coffee that was having me.* If one day without coffee could bring me into such wretched discomfort, then this beverage

I had assumed to be benign was in truth nothing but a dark, oily opiate. I vowed to myself then and there that never again would I be hostage to the black swill.

I switched to tea.

With all due respect to Sir Thomas Lipton, be he apocryphal or real, I sadly realized that to drink the beverage served under his name for the rest of my life would be a sentence too bleak to bear. A new mission had finally found me. I set out in search of true tea.

Little did I know what a staggering assignment I had taken on. In the Land of America, where I began my journey, it was all but impossible to find any tea whatsoever whose leaves had not been pulverized into tiny "tea" bags. I decided I would sooner take my hot water plain than allow myself to drink those sickly shavings passed off to the unwitting as "tea."

It was with supreme good fortune that The Minister of Progress appeared one fine day and graciously offered his services. He declared it his own personal charge to canvass the most prized tea gardens of the world for their worthiest leaves, and said he would not rest until he saw these teas steaming in the cups of men, women, and children everywhere. Inspired by his dedication, I, too, vowed that I would stand beside him and serve Tea, as its humble Minister of Leaves. I took upon myself the task of easing the worried, the frustrated, the stressed and the obsessed into the tranquil spell of the divine little *camellia sinensis* bush, where they would find themselves in the company of the immortal who, sipping himself into eternity, wrote, "Steam billows, the teapot fragrant. I enter a state of desires diminishing. Within the stillness, a further pleasure. Nothing coarse or superficial. This is drinking tea."

— THE MINISTER OF LEAVES

The First Sip

I WAS THREE THOUSAND MILES AWAY FROM MY TWO-YEAR-old son, attending a conference on business and social responsibility. I kept looking at his photo during breaks in the sessions until, finally, I could not bear being away from him a moment longer. I called the airline and booked myself out on the next flight home.

After checking out of the hotel, I found myself sharing a car to the airport with a young man who had been attending the conference and was leaving early to make a meeting in San Francisco. As it turned out, we were on the same flight. We struck up a conversation in the car to the airport, a conversation that became so quickly intense that it obliterated everything else around us as we negotiated through the check-in procedures and boarded the aircraft. We immediately rearranged our seats so that we could sit together. Strangers on a plane speeding at 35,000 feet across America, we found ourselves in the grip of an energy that was clearly overtaking us. Whatever the energy was, it had us spinning into the vortex of a creative zone. We were in a highly charged no-man's-land, outside space and time, where The Source of an Idea was revealing itself to us in its as yet unborn state. Time and space reappeared seven hours later when we looked up and saw that the plane, on the ground in San Francisco, was empty. By then it was apparent The Idea had been born — in us.

Creativity can leave people with the idea that they are "creative." Not so. This is the cultural hubris of the Western world — that *I create*. Interestingly, the ancient Sanskrit language has no equivalent of the word "creation" as we freely use it to mean "something coming out of nothing." The fact is that creation is a *projection* of what already exists. What I am saying is that The Idea existed but had not *manifested*. It was as a projection looking for a screen — and we were that screen. The great mystery we know as the "creative process" is, in fact, the stirring of the unborn in its search for a friendly place to be born. It is awesome enough to find oneself engaged alone with the process. But it is truly imposing when the process visits two or more people simultaneously. That is what happened to this young man and me. The Idea that had me was having him at the same time.

To best understand the particulars of The Idea that rode back with my seatmate and me, the reader should know a thing or two about us, and about the circumstances in which we came together. The conference we had both been attending was hosted by the Social Venture Network, a lively group of bright, idealistic entrepreneurs and investors committed to making business a force for positive social change. At the time, I was on the SVN board of directors. I had started my own business, Banana Republic, and seen it grow in the course of nine years from a $1500 investment to a large corporation. I was drawn to SVN after I had left my business, because in looking back I felt I had not done it quite right. I had not fully explored the potential of business as a force for positive social change on the planet, nor did I wind up in a business structure that welcomed such exploration. Moreover, I left my business with mixed feelings about the ultimate social value of what I had helped to create, and some real doubt as to whether business, rooted by its nature in self-interest and responsive to the ultimate demand of profit, could serve as a catalyst for fundamental change. I define "fundamental change" as a society where every individual comes to accept every social problem as a problem of his own making, and sees the wisdom of changing himself (into a happier and compassionate human being) as his way of changing the world. I had always had strong feelings about building a sane and equitable society, but I had found that integrating those feelings with the challenges of an explosively growing business was an exasperating experience. It would be easy to say that the source of my exasperation was the fact that I had sold my business to a larger corporation, but the truth is that whether I owned it or Amalgamated Gigantic owned it, the business had its own mind, a mind at least as strong as mine, and it was that mind, given to needs other than mine, with which I frequently found myself clashing. It might seem odd if not a little unnerving to some readers that a business tends to develop a mind of its own that is independent of its founder, but in fact it is quite a natural development. A business is a living thing, a confluence of energies, each of which wants to see its own self-interest served first. If you're a young, hungry entrepreneur, as I was when I started my business, you find it quite hard to make the distinction between you and your creation, but as a business grows, it becomes more concerned with its own survival than yours. This does not mean it is always smarter than its founder; it just means it doesn't always see things the way he does, and if he is unwilling to yield to its demands on him, it eventually grows willing to go on its own way.

I wasn't the first entrepreneur, and I won't be the last, who came to a point where he and his business decided it was time to part, but in my case the parting felt more like a coming home than a forced exile. I felt much truer to my nature out of business than in business. A former employee quoted anonymously in a magazine said of me and my wife, "They were in business, but not of business," and I could not have agreed more. I had no interest in going around the track again; life was much too pregnant with possibilities to bother with proving to anybody, especially myself, that given a second chance I could really do it right, but still . . . there was all that hard-earned knowledge, all that roughed-up experience, all that finely honed intuition — and there was no denying that business had become the dominant metaphor of our times. Much as I relished my retirement from business, and the time it gave me to write and to be with my child and garden and hike and bike and swim and explore my deep interest in various Eastern philosophies and yogas, it also seemed to me that my hopeful colleagues in the SVN may be on to something: The world had to change, something had to show the way, and that something, for better or worse, for now at least, looked like it was going to be business.

William Blake once characterized the human journey as one that takes us from innocence to experience to higher innocence. If that's the ride, then by the time I got on that plane to San Francisco on a sunny

April morning in 1990, I'd had (as much as any man can by his mid-forties) my romp in experience and was newly off on a meandering trek in search of higher innocence. My seatmate, as I discovered about him almost immediately, was just pulling out of innocence, looking for experience. Although he was younger than I by nearly a decade and a half, I could relate to him in many ways. When I was his age I shared his deeply conditioned need to succeed, his quick, curious, and restless mind. What I didn't share (having come to manhood on turbulent campuses in the late 1960s) was his natural affinity for business. He was careful but eager, astute but naive, and he was on a personal mission to find the medium in the real world that would give his essence fullest expression. It was almost too much to hope for that he could arrange a life in which *what he did* would be one with *who he was*, but he hoped for it anyway. Hopeful Bill Rosenzweig was a young man in search of a true calling, and as the gods would have it, the man sitting next to him on that United Airlines jet just happened to have one for him.

Tea.

I am mad about tea. I can't think of a commodity more inappropriately marketed in the United States. I can't think of a product that is less appreciated for its awesome history, less heralded for its stunning effects, less savored for the haunting boundlessness of its many tastes. For reasons best left to others to explain, tea, the "cup of humanity," civilization's oldest beverage, an ancient friend to body and mind alike, gets less respect than sweetened, artificially flavored canned bubbles in the United States and most Western countries.

I would not think of starting a business unless I was its first customer. And no matter what's been said or written to the contrary, all it takes to launch a business in which you are the first customer is to find a second customer and sell him the product. That's what I did. I sold Bill Rosenzweig on tea.

Although, I must say, it did not take much selling. Bill himself was already a tea drinker, and he himself had already begun to wonder how anybody can get away with pulverizing the detritus of the splendid *camellia sinensis* and peddling it by the ton in "tea" bags throughout the United States.

The possibilities of introducing new customers to a drink that is 5000 years old are endless. Green tea, loose tea, kids' tea, bottled iced teas, and all the stuff of tea — the pots, the cups, the books — yes, books, because tea is not just a beverage but a way of life, and what a way of life it is! Slow down. Pay attention. Be grateful. Enjoy what you have. Take pleasure in the wonder of being alive. Can you imagine a better prescription for our tense, overdriven, hyperacquisitive, uptight world?

Perhaps you are beginning to get the picture of how Bill and I started to cook on that airliner. By the time we landed, we were wholesaling, mail-ordering, and selling tea in 150 retail stores in the best locations in America, we were the premier merchants of green tea in the West, we were appealing to the public to throw away their tea bags in favor of loose tea, we were introducing people to notes they never thought possible in black tea, we were helping people to discover their own paths to longevity with herbal teas, and we were unleashing a new way of life in America. Our secret and subversive agenda was to bring Americans to an awareness of "Tea Mind," in which we would all come to appreciate the perfection, the harmony, the natural serenity, and the true aesthetic in every moment and in every natural thing. This was one of our more practical and realistic ideas. In other words, we were out *there*, spinning gleefully together in the vortex of the creative zone, giving ourselves fully to the dream that was having us.

When we parted at the airport, Bill, I later realized, had the upside-down impression that I was recruiting him for a job. It was one of the rare mistakes he's made in the nearly two years since I've known him. The fact is, I was recruiting him for a cause, and it was not *my* cause, but the cause of tea. And it wasn't a job. It was a life in which he, and I, would both work for tea.

The real surprise came several days later when he returned to his home, which was then in Sedona, Arizona. Just before he left the Bay Area he came to visit my wife and me in our home, and I took the occasion to whisper the name of the company I hoped would be started: The Republic of Tea.

The next day from Sedona came the first fax. It seemed Bill Rosenzweig was ready to put it all on the line. He wanted The Republic of Tea started. He wanted it started so badly, in fact, that he had appointed himself The Minister of Progress to be sure it was done. And as for the man who had sold him this wild idea of inventing a new way to sell the world's oldest commodity, he himself had no intention of ever stepping into an office again (if he could help it), but from the hills he vowed to serve The Republic as its Minister of Leaves.

Herewith, in the pages that follow, as it happened day by day over twenty months, is the record of how the business of The Republic of Tea created itself through our two chattering fax machines and the whimsical pen and eye of my wife and partner, The Minister of Enchantment. For me, as you will see when you rifle through our trunk of assorted jottings and inspirations and drawings, allowing The Idea to have its way has been a conscious (and not always easy) exercise. In a sense I am doing what I once swore I would never do: I am having yet one more go at business, hoping that this time, in the process of collaboration with sensitive partners, a new kind of enterprise might be brought to life — a business that holds no interest higher than using its products, its relationships, and its message to help people who see the wisdom in changing themselves as the first step to changing the world.

— MEL ZIEGLER
Mill Valley, California
January 14, 1992

THE MINISTER OF PROGRESS

April 7, 1990

To: The Minister of Leaves

If you have to boil it down into a single phrase, what is the *philosophy* behind The Republic of Tea?

- -

ZIEGLER   4157212171

THE MINISTER OF LEAVES

April 7, 1990

To: The Minister of Progress

To show, through the metaphor of tea, the lightness of taking life sip by sip rather than gulp by gulp.

What would you say is the *business* behind the philosophy?

THE MINISTER OF PROGRESS

April 7, 1990

To: Leaves

The business of The Republic of Tea is to sell (which means first we have to find) the best tea on Earth.

THE MINISTER OF PROGRESS

---

12 April 1990

Minister,

I like the idea of having a personal business with a visible *personality*. There's something charming and wonderful about "feeling" and sensing the human character behind the business. Leaves, you are clearly the "voice" of The Republic. It seems to me that the challenge of this business will be to retain the personality (and the clarity of the voice) as the organization grows beyond the founder(s).

Your "Dear People of Tea" letter sets the tone beautifully for a first transaction with our customer — a transaction when he or she not only *buys* tea, but *comes to* tea, just as you did. It's clear that tea is more than a beverage.

On to practical matters. Needless to say, I'm all fired up. I just got back from the health food store, where I purchased a variety of beverages to taste and discover. I want to become familiar with everything that's on the market — how it's made, presented, and distributed.

I'm going to keep a tasting journal too. I'd appreciate it if you would save me all tea boxes and packaging that you consume and collect. It will be a useful reference.

I'm working on a more formal research plan right now, sending letters of inquiry to about sixteen tea associations around the world, and searching the electronic databases for articles about guess what!

It's important for me now to get a true sense of the size of the tea market, how well different companies are doing, and how the distribution of the product is organized in the marketplace.

You tune the voice and I'll look for the ground to put our feet on.

— Progress

P.S. Can poetry make a business?

. . . .

12 April 1990

When I returned home to Sedona I was really obsessed with this tea idea. I didn't know what had gotten into me. (Neither did my wife.) My plate was already full of other work and responsibilities, but it all seemed to dim in light of the potential of a new business and the thrill of collaborating with Mel and Patricia. I couldn't stop thinking, talking, or drinking tea. I was exhilarated by the idea of forming The Republic of Tea and was motivated by some inexplicable energy to make it happen. Basically I didn't sleep. Everything became tea for me. The shelves in the supermarket took on a whole new meaning. I no longer saw tea as a product on the shelf to buy, but was now looking between the packages: What was missing? Where were the opportunities? Magazine and newspaper articles were suddenly speaking to me about the need for tea in our culture, and for the first time in my life I was noticing how many really weird teapots there were on the market. Honestly, I was feeling pretty woozy about this whole thing; I think I had fallen in love with an idea. — **Bill**

. . . .

THE MINISTER OF LEAVES

April 12, 1990

To: Progress

You ask: "Can poetry make a business?"

Not without the tea.

When it comes to creating a business, film is probably a better analogy than poetry. Starting a business is like making a movie. First there is the idea, and it gets worked into a treatment or screenplay. Next comes the money and the casting (often these two go hand in hand). Next you shoot the picture. So think of what we're doing as a production that we are going to call *The Republic of Tea*, written by The Minister of Leaves, designed by The Minister of Enchantment, produced and directed by The Minister of Progress, and starring its customers.

Do you know what a metaphor is all about? It has its roots in the Greek word *metaphero,* which means "to carry along from one place to another." Our task is to find a product and create a style of marketing that lures people who are living crazed coffee-style lives and then transports them through our metaphor of The Republic of Tea to a new place of calm and contentment. Tea Mind! That's what this project is all about for me. So at this early state it's important for us to continually noodle what the place we're calling The Republic of Tea is all about. Here's some of my random thoughts:

• The life of tea is the life of the moment. We have only Now, and we each sip it in our own cups.

• Imperfection itself is what we find to be perfect. In our land, a symphony is heard in the voices of frogs and a work of art is in the as-is-ness of what the Chinese call "the ten thousand things." All things have their own inner truth, no matter how "imperfect" they might *seem*. If a sip of tea brings me, no matter how briefly, to enter things as they are, I have been transported outside myself, into perfection itself. And I have known a cup of tea to do just this thing. The best of many good praises that can be sung for tea is that it creates Tea Mind.

•　　Life is impossible, and so what. It is in its very impossibility that we find our joy. Tea Mind allows life to live us. It frees us from the hubris of trying to *control* what cannot be controlled.

•　　Tea is Contentment. Tea Mind sees that contentment is love of content. The secret of happiness, you see, is in accepting (dare I say *wanting?*) what you already have.

I don't want to get all mystical about this, and I know this is not exactly the stuff that it is going to take to convince investment bankers that the world needs a new tea company, but I trust that if we enter the spirit of tea in the beginning, the business will end up putting you to work in a way that takes care of what's truly important. A good business wants to be, Progress. A good entrepreneur allows it.

— Leaves

THE MINISTER OF PROGRESS

12 April 1990

To:　　The Minister of Leaves

Leaves,

What's fascinating to me right now is how the ancient wisdom within this metaphor is so absolutely relevant to *today*. The spirit of tea, as you put it, can serve as a nurturing guide during these tough (getting tougher) times of adjustment in our country.

We're done with the greed, growth, and hollow glamour of the '80s. Life and business are different now. They've got to be. Our customers are looking for balance in their lives. They're trying to discover how to have fun without acquiring more material possessions. I see people beginning to express their personal values through their purchasing decisions.

There are many paradoxes about becoming a merchant in our consumer-laden society (at a time when I think we have too many merchants). This is why it made so much sense to me when you said on the plane "if I were ever to go back into business, the only thing I could sell is tea." We have an opportunity here to sell a suggestion for a healthy lifestyle through tea. I can recognize some other metaphors developing in the marketplace, mainly about environmental issues. But I see marketers running to extremes, selling "green this" and "green that," or this social value or that newly chic attitude. What most of these companies are missing is the true "spirit" within their product and what that truly represents to the customer.

That's where tea is so magnificent! It is in the natural makeup, history, and charm of tea where this spirit is alive. It's not something that either you or I have to invent or fabricate as "marketers." It's all there for real, penned in history. We just have to make it accessible, enjoyable, and meaningfully timely.

The Republic of Tea will be the new home for this present-day tea spirit, and our customers will become citizens of our little land. Perhaps The Minister of Enchantment could create some kind of Declaration of Citizenship that we could give to our customers to let them know how welcome they are (and how we value their business, ideas, and suggestions).

My desire is for our product and message to capture the imagination of our customers, to inspire them toward a peaceful and fulfilling lifestyle, and to provide them with a little dose of energy to persevere and adjust through any time, good or bad.

Finally, here's a small insight from your dedicated Minister of Progress:

This business is about *refreshment*.

— Progress

ZIEGLER   4157212171   14 April 1990

Dear Minister of Progress,
May I introduce
our mascot?

- The Minister
of Enchantment

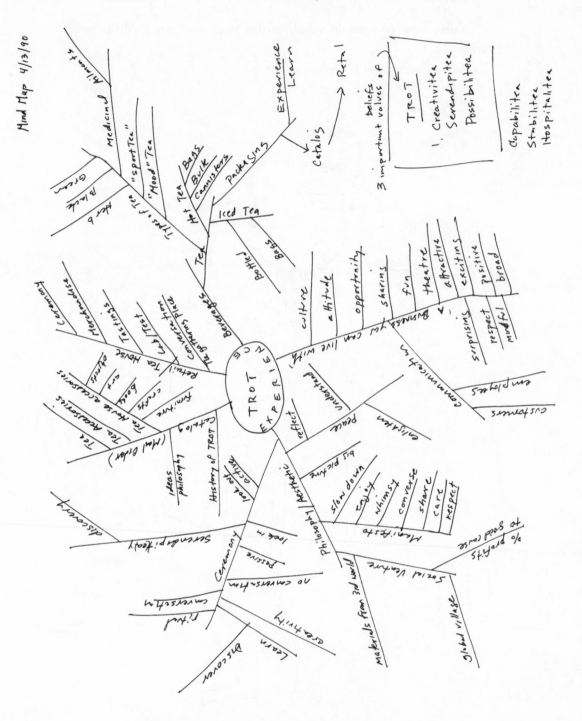

THE MINISTER OF LEAVES

April 13, 1990

To my dear Minister of Progress,

I am greatly enjoying your various missives, mind maps, and reflections on the future of our little republic.

I myself have been giving the subject considerable attention in the last few days, and so what I toss your way now are some random thoughts, impressions, hunches, hoping that you may find among them a few gems worthy of polishing:

- **We Are Inventing a Game.**

In the concrete world I recognize that it must be structured as a business, but in fact the power of the TRoT concept is that it is ultimately a game, a game that we get to play with the customers. In creating TRoT, we and the customers together begin to see and to give shape to a whimsical, reflective state where we all agree the highest goal is to get in touch with the wonder of our lives. Tea is the shared catalyst. Think of The Republic of Tea as having always been here. You and I and the customers did not create it. It has always been here. It's just that we've only recently found it.

(This is not dissimilar to Patricia's and my experience with Banana Republic, where the catalyst was clothing. The game we played through BR with the customers was to invent an imaginary place where together we transcended our everyday lives by fantasizing adventure in faraway places. We all got there through the metaphor of clothing. As I look back at it now, the difference between BR and TRoT is that the former uses fantasy to lighten up the customer's idea of reality, and the latter prods the customer to see that nothing is more gratifying or more purifying than surrendering to reality. Perhaps the exercise in moving from BR to TRoT is all only a projection of my own slow process of growing up, but as I wrote you earlier, Tea Mind shows the way to peace and happiness is not to have what you want but to want what you have. Tea Mind is the natural state; it's absolute fiction that peace and happiness are something on the outside to be attained; they are already here, inside each and every one of us, waiting to be welcomed.)

So as I see it, with TRoT we participate in the invention of a game that brings alive again the ancient culture of tea in a manner appropriate to today, a culture that takes us into the true adventure that is latent in our everyday lives, here and now. When I see how many people these days are stressed out and worried and lost in the *idea* of their lives, it really saddens me. If a cup of tea can bring them, however briefly, out of their woes and into a fuller appreciation of the gift of life (without which, they might begin to see, those woes would not be possible), we would in the very least be doing what the *I Ching* terms "no harm." I say you can trace the whole mess on this planet to the fact that we are living as if reality were a concept. Well, if they must see life through an idea, then what they need is a better idea! And what better idea is there than tea, the idea of which is that tea is not an idea? Are you still with me, Minister?

• There Can Be Nothing *Overtly* Spiritual About This Business. No Dogma, No New Age Lingo.

Our goal is to use the metaphor of tea (by promoting the culture of it, and presenting Tea Mind as a new kind of reverse kick for the Pepsi generation) to get as many people as possible to notice how stupendous life is in and of itself, no matter what you may think *it* is doing to *you*. So let's stay clear of Buddhism, Taoism, Catholicism, Existentialism, Rastafarianism, even Minister of Leaves-ism. In other words, let's let tea be without making it into Teaism. What's wrong with *all* belief systems is that by nature they are *exclusionary* — they create a barrier between believers and nonbelievers. There's nothing to believe here in TRoT. It's only about boiling water, preparing tea, and drinking it.

> Boil Water
> Prepare Tea
> Drink It

(Would we dare make that our slogan?)

• **Merchandising Possibilities Are Endless.**

1. Going to dinner at someone's home? Take tea, not wine.
2. A line of children's teas, where the names and the boxes and the tea bag wrappers are fanciful, playful, and educational. The herbs can be healthful, and children from an early age can be introduced to the magic of tea. The Minister of Enchantment loves this idea and is sketching up some possibili-teas.
3. Expand through licensing and joint venture into other packaged food product lines. One way TRoT could go as a business would be to model itself along the lines of, say, Nabisco, but with healthy, honest, and fun products without all that bad stuff like saturated fats, salt, and sugar.
4. Pocket packs. You're going out to dinner. Since the restaurant serves only poor tea, does that mean you have to drink it? In the world of TRoT, every moment counts. Who'd want to drink rotgut tea after the only dinner you are going to eat tonight?
5. The packaging is our greatest propaganda tool. What we do with it should enhance the effect of the tea through suggestion. The last thing we would want is for people to swill tea as they do coffee. If our graphics and our words are a true expression of our own inner experience of tea, the customer will *feel* for herself that the tea is a

door to the ineffable quality of Big Silence. A guideline here that would be useful to remember is the difference between Western and Oriental art. Western artists (Americans and Europeans) tend to regard themselves as separate from the object of their attention, and what they create, however inspired it might be, stands as something outside themselves. But going back thousands of years, Chinese artists have cultivated the quality of entering what they paint to a point where they themselves dissolve and the inner life of the object seems to express itself through their hands. If the packaging of our teas can reflect the inner life of the tea, can suggest the latent experience that is realized only by entering the tea, then we will have really done something exquisitely subtle, and damned useful.

One Essential Fact About The Republic of Tea

The Republic of Tea is a place that has never been spoiled. It's important to note this because we must be clear that we will not simply yield to the winds and become yet another socially responsible business in the same mold — social action, cause marketing, etc. For us, it's not about changing the planet. It's about changing *ourselves*, counting on the fact that if we as individuals truly change, sooner or later our planet must change with us. To address ourselves to seemingly more immediate social problems, environmental issues, etc., something others, like our friends Ben and Jerry and Anita Roddick, are already doing very well, would only confuse the metaphor, break the spell. In The Republic of Tea we embody Chuang Tzu's "time before history," when people were kind to one another but did not call it "being kind to one another," when people naturally looked out for each other and for the world around them but didn't see it as "being caring and responsible." Incidentally, the reason Chuang Tzu called this the "time before history" is because it was an era that came and went without leaving a trace of itself. Since nothing went "wrong," nobody had any reason to write anything down. It was *lived*, not recorded. That is until Messrs. Progress and Leaves appeared to tell everybody it still exists, and has all along in The Republic of Tea. So in light of this, our product *of course* reflects our own needs and tastes, our packaging *of course* reflects an awareness that we are custodians of the Earth, our service *of course* reflects an awareness that by helping others we are only helping ourselves, our relations with employee *of course* reflects that business is life and life is business and our understanding that anybody who separates the two is just looking for a way to rationalize his uncivil behavior in business. I could go on and on, but the point is made: TRoT is a comfortable place you fall into and realize you've *always* been here. It's the kind of place that reminds you of your own true nature, and it makes you wonder how it was you came to forget it.

A Word or Two About Our Ministries

In the fanciful world of TRoT, tea is *everything* — currency, medicine, you name it. The catalogue has the look of an Asian government publication at the beginning of the century, yellowing from age. Each department in the catalogue has a somewhat different "look," which is its own unique little refinement on the core "look." Items are sold by ministries: There's a Minister of Cups, a Minister of Pots, a Minister of Gardens, etc. Information *about* the effects of various teas comes from The Minister of Health, about special preparation procedures from The Minister of Brewing, tips about water quality from The Minister of Water, about ritual from The Minister of Ceremony. The order form is under the letterhead of The Ministry of Supply, and the customer is requested to make his check payable to "The Minister of Finance of The Republic of Tea," recognizing that it may take a few extra strokes of the pen to write that out, but is it not time well spent if the writer uses it to notice the pen and the pressure in the hand that moves it?

— Leaves

THE MINISTER OF PROGRESS

April 13, 1990

Dear Minister of Leaves,

I'm inspired!

The game, as you have so cleverly identified it, encompasses creativity and the process of being creative. We want to engage people to *imagine* and use their undernourished imaginations in this hard-edged, time-sliced world of ours. There's always too much to do (too many options) and not enough time. The options in TRoT are endless, but what makes them special is that they all require imagination (and a sense of

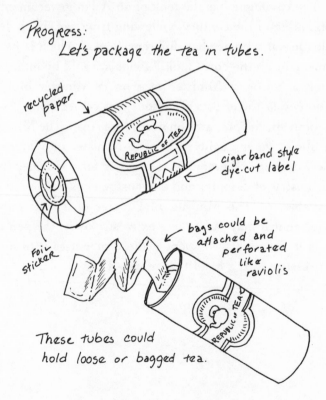

Progress:
Let's package the tea in tubes.

recycled paper

REPUBLIC OF TEA

cigar band style
dye-cut label

Foil sticker

bags could be
attached and
perforated
like
raviolis

REPUBLIC OF TEA

These tubes could
hold loose or bagged tea.

humor). Yes, you are right, the awareness of the wonder of our lives is elusive in a world consumed by impending doom.

In The Republic of Tea there is a peace and equilibrium — a momentary escape from the day-to-day. And *our* job is to get our customers to bring back a special part of our tiny nation and incorporate it into their everyday lives. And in some businesses, that's called merchandise. . . .

Merchandising Possibilities Are Endless, Continued

Tea Time in itself is a powerful idea. In The Republic of Tea we quietly keep pace with our inner clocks. Americans have never caught on to the tradition of the siesta, the prolonged break, the afternoon tea. Our culture is all about fifteen-minute *coffee breaks*. Grab it and go.

In The Republic of Tea the aesthetic of simplicity prevails. Things are neat, economical. We believe in "The Moment That Never Ends," so we build things to last. Quality exudes from every item we craft. We also believe in our future, and that is why our youngsters enjoy the healthy beverages we call tea.

The pocket pack is a wonderful idea. And what would you say to a special TRoT Blending Kit, full of fanciful ingredients and the encouragement to "brew your own . . ."

And do we have an entertaining board game that challenges our constituents to converse, to question, to learn more about each other?

Do we have a special chair, a love seat perhaps, designed for two, to sit together and sip their tea? And what about our beautifully illustrated books with inviting pictures of our little land that lull our little ones to sleep?

The Essential Republic of Tea

Our land has never been spoiled, because we've been creative enough to greet change and welcome it. We don't have crises because we look ahead and adjust so that we can enjoy the moment. (I love the way you wrote this section.)

The Republic of Tea is a place that encourages creativity. That's why our tiny nation hosts a variety of educational challenges that reward those who participate in an outstanding way. Imagine a grant for a children's book, a reward for a clever solution to a staggering problem, or a "What's So Great about The Republic of Tea" essay contest. . . .

Back to This Minister's Eminent Domain . . .

It has been a productive and progressive day here in the Progress Ministry. We've turned up some fascinating support in the form of newspaper and magazine articles. Most exciting is the discovery of the *Official Tea Buyers Guide* which I have ordered right away.
According to an old tea man I talked to,
this is *the* book. We also uncovered the
West Coast's largest tea broker and his
catalogue is on the way.

— Progress

Oh, Minister of Leaves,
Just one more thing:
In The Republic of Tea, the beverage
of choice after a successful day is:
Humili-Tea.

the
Tea
enters
me
slowly

warming
my
core

then
SLOWLY
spReading to my edges and beyond
until there are no edges

NO Tea

NO ME

ONLY MERGING

THE MINISTER OF PROGRESS

15 April 1990

To: The Minister of Leaves

Re: Can't stop these ideas from coming

Minister,

Now, I believe as much as the next person that the seventh day was made for resting, but my creative juices have been flowing even though it's five A.M. Sunday. I wanted to share a couple of new ideas with you today.

1. The Mother's Little Helper's idea for a line of children's teas is good. We need to couch it into the form of TRoT so that it integrates with the total concept. It needs to be expressed in a form and tone that is harmonious with the big picture we are painting for our little land. The names you came up with are unique and attention-getting. I suggest we release a line of children's and adult products concurrently to establish the identity of the brand and company. *Little People's Teas*. How does that sound?
2. I like INFUSIONs, too, but I think the name should be in TRoT lingo. I'm curious to see what portion of the tea market accounts for the medicinal area and if it is growing or still considered special-purpose.
3. The packaging-tube idea is clever and different. I wonder how these would stack up on the shelves or if that would be a problem for retailers. I've been playing around with a cube box (symmetry and simplicity in our land of tea). All other boxes I have seen are rectangular. I also think a triangular box would be interesting to play with.

4. In the middle of the night last night I woke up with ideas about the structure of our organization. I roughed them out on the attached sheet. I hope you can read the writing. Feel free to build on this and let me know your thoughts. And just for the challenge of it I took a stab at the first ten-year plan. This is a good exercise, even if it has nothing to do with what we end up doing, because it forces me to think about where we want to go.

5. As I roughed out that org chart last night I realized that we need to write a "product charter" that guides our product-development process. This should articulate the vision and purpose of our products in broad terms: They are healthy. They reflect the spirit of our land, etc. This will be a challenge, but it will provide the guide for all initial product development. I look forward to brainstorming this with you.

— Progress

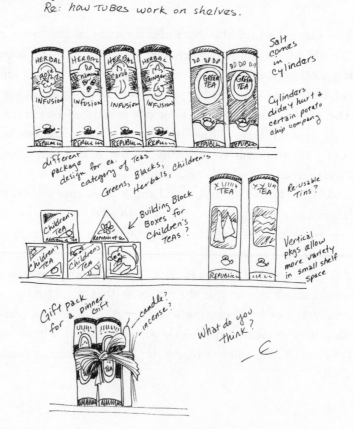

Progress:
Re: how TUBes work on shelves.

Salt comes in cylinders

Cylinders didn't hurt a certain potato chip company

different package design for ea. category of Teas
Greens, Blacks, Children's, Herbals,

Re-usable Tins?

← Building Block Boxes for Children's Teas?

Vertical pkgs allow more variety in small shelf space

Gift pack for a Dinner Gift

candle? incense?

What do you think?
— E

The REPUBLIC of TEA
CHILDREN'S TEAS

- MONKEYING AROUND
      TEA

   a fruity blend of
naturally sweet &
colorful herbs like
rose hips, hibiscus,
etc...

- CAT NAPPING TEA
      a blend of
calming herbs to
encourage naps like
chamomile, passion flower, etc...

We could call them
MOTHERS' LITTLE HELPERS

      (Too loaded?
            Too coded?)

☆
AND
FOR moms:

- Pregnancy TEA
(with Red Raspberry leaf)

- Patience TEA

   (there must be an herb!)

THE MINISTER OF LEAVES

April 13, 1990

To: The Minister of Progress

Re: Tao Te Tea & Other Fantasies

I see the good minister never sleeps, but be assured that what you send is hardly insomniac gibberish. Good thinking, sir.

A few desultory responses to your predawn musings:

1. I had the same reservations about MOTHERS and INFUSIONS, and I think the whole issue bears further discussion. One thing I learned in my prior incarnation was that one must be careful not to be too cute. By this I mean, if we shape TRoT too narrowly, we run the risk of tiring our customers with "republic"-oriented lingo. Remember, there's going to be plenty of TRoT lingo, simply because it arises *naturally* out of the concept. What we don't want to do is strangle ourselves with the lingo, because then we'll risk creating a fad, not the enduring business we both envision. Having said all that, I think LITTLE PEOPLE'S TEAS isn't a bad name for the line. Or maybe, CHILDREN OF THE REPUBLIC. I don't know what I think about INFUSIONS, which, incidentally, is the name the British, who are finicky about what grows on the *camellia sinensis* and what doesn't, use for herbal teas.

2. Yet another category might be LIFE IS BUT A DREAM teas, which I would define as the metaphysical category. Each box might contain a few lines to ponder while you sip. (One, from Lao Tzu, especially close to the heart of your humble Minister of Leaves is *"Practice not-doing, and everything will fall into place."*) Maybe this idea is off the

deep end, but you can't be afraid of swimming there when you're starting a business. Otherwise, you end up in the same old shallow waters as everybody else.

3. Lots to discuss about packages. In the end, practicality is our destination (your department), but why not be as wild and wacky as possible on our way there?

4. Can't imagine what prompted this thought, but DOES ANYBODY MAKE ANY MONEY IN THE TEA BUSINESS?!?!

5. Another item to research is powdered teas. These are sold in Europe, and the Japanese use a killer version of it in their tea ceremonies. We have a few here a friend brought from Germany, which we were giving to my son Zio until we discovered they were packed with fructose.

6. England is a great resource. There may even be a company there for us to buy to quick-start the project.

7. How about if we buy an L.A. radio station and name it KTEA.

8. And since we'll have a radio station, why not publish a magazine called *Tea Life* and write a book called *The Republic of Tea* too, and while we're at it produce a compact disk of tea music (it's playing in my brain right now), and, hey, why not produce a movie, and really show people what Life As Tea is all about? Can you handle it? We're not in the tea business, Progress, we're in the *phenomenon* business.

Oh, and I forgot: we should have a publishing venture (what goes better with tea than books), a retail venture, including teahouses, tea, tea accessories, and other merchandise including but not limited to tea clothing sold in THE REPUBLIC OF TEA's exclusive shops, as well as tea furnishings and a line of accoutrements for one's personal tea garden also sold exclusively in exclusive shops named LIFE AS TEA.

I think I'll sign off now and go brew a pot of something to calm me down.

Yours in solidari-tea,

— Leaves

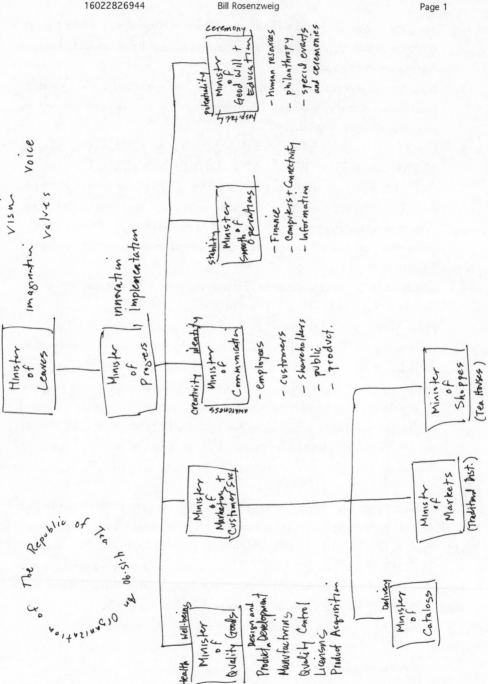

An Organization of The Republic of Tea 06-15-94

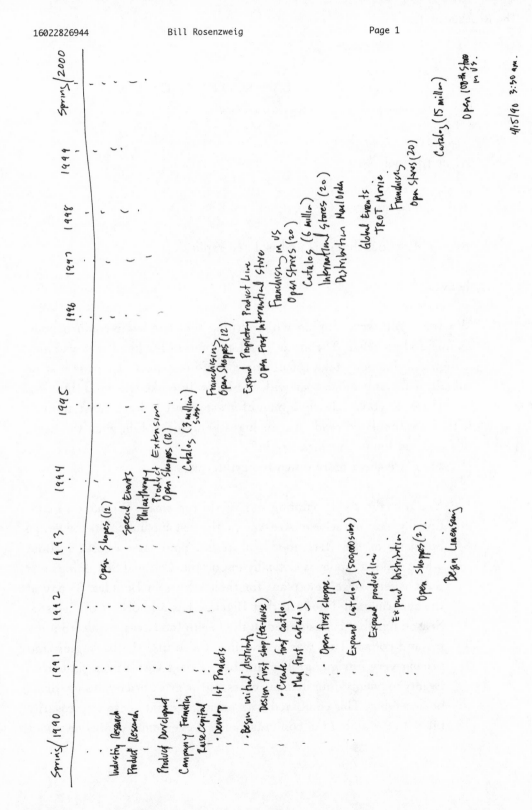

THE MINISTER OF PROGRESS

April 16, 1990

To: Leaves

Re: Random thoughts and isolated replies

Leaves,

Whatever you were sipping while writing that last letter could become an instant best seller. The more I read, the more I felt like I was watching a thousand balloons take off during a half-time show. There is just no substitute for unbridled, soar-with-the-birds, free-like-the-wind thinking.

(Leaves, you're clearly a man of great alibi-tea, but I must admit, I felt a bit intimidated reading your high-flying ideas. Oh, what the heck, this is a "no-limits" business, right?)

Here are some more down-to-earth replies:

1. You're right about painting our world too small. We have to continually ask ourselves: Are we in the tea business, the beverage business, or the "feel good" business? Your later question about who's making money is critically important. Celestial Seasonings just built a very large new plant for their efforts in Boulder. Today at the supermarket I noticed that Bigelow has a knockoff of Celestial Seasonings that is positioned in the health food area, away from the tea and coffee. That was interesting. I also find the packaging and pricing very intriguing. The number of bags varies from sixteen to twenty to twenty-four in many cases, so the gross price can sometimes be deceiving. This combined with packaging that doesn't necessarily relate to the amount of contents makes it even more confusing about

who's charging what per bag. Only an informed customer could figure it out.

2. I like Life Is But a Dream. I'm working on a new diagram for us that shows categories and distribution. I think this will help us figure out our product strategy. Hope to have it to you in the next couple of days. Waiting for some information to come in before I can complete it.

3. Industry research. I may need to spend a little money with a research firm that checks out private companies. I want to see what the top ten tea companies do in sales and profits. The category is big and new players are entering every day. It will be important for us to feel confident about our point of entry. I think the kids' teas are a winner. I haven't seen anything like this. Have you?

4. Enchantment's sketches are really nice. Clever and neat. It will be lots of fun to explore the whole packaging and communications challenges of the company.

Which brings me to a revelation I'm having: Communication, I'm convinced, is in the center of every successful business.

— Progress

THE MINISTER OF LEAVES

16 apr 90

Dear Progress,

Communications is the business. But there is nothing to communicate unless we've got great-tasting teas.

— L.

THE MINISTER OF PROGRESS

16 April 1990

To: The Minister of Leaves

Last night it struck me that maybe it's time for me to get somebody who's
a little less emotional about tea to take a look at the business, and so I've
appointed the other half of my brain as The Minister of Research, and
here for a start is what I want him to find out:

+ Size of Market
- Worldwide
- US
- Number of businesses
- Exporters, Manufacturers, Distributors   - Associations
- Publications
- Trade Shows and Conferences
+ Product Categories (perceived and actual)
- Caffeinated
- Decaffeinated
+ Families of Tea
- Black
- Green
- Herbal (encompasses organic materials)
+ Popular Flavors and Types
- Blends
- Pure, Original
+ Preparation
- Hot Tea
- Iced Tea
- Bottled Tea

+ Significant Marketers in the Tea Business
  - Twinings
  - Lipton
  - Bigelow
  - Stash
  - Celestial Seasonings
  - Yogi
  - Wisdom of the Ancients
+ Participating Company Profiles (to be completed for each significant company)
  - Product Line and Description (rank best-selling)
  - Positioning
  - Pricing
  - Annual Sales
  - Company History
  - Sales History
  - Distribution
  - Notes
+ Sources of Tea
  - Distributors
  - Private Labelers
  - Importers
  - Brokers
  - Growers
+ Packaging of Tea
  - bags
    - Cotton
    - Biodegradable
  - bulk blended
  - powder
  - bottled
  - canned
+ Master Packaging
  - Boxes
  - Canisters/Tins

+ Distribution of Tea and Beverages
  - Grocery Stores
  - Liquor Stores
  - Health Food Stores
  - Specialty Food Stores
  - Specialty Coffee/Tea Stores
  - Specialty Housewares Stores
  - Mail Order

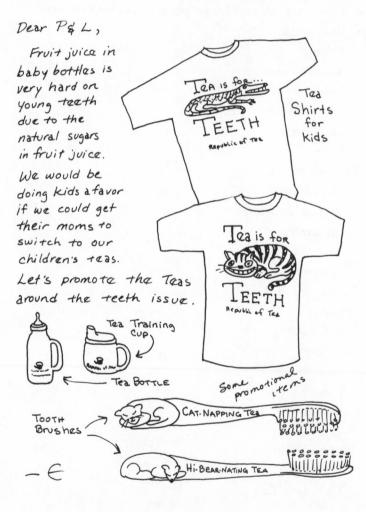

Dear P & L,

Fruit juice in baby bottles is very hard on young teeth due to the natural sugars in fruit juice.

We would be doing kids a favor if we could get their moms to switch to our children's teas.

Let's promote the Teas around the teeth issue.

Tea Shirts for Kids

Tea Training Cup

Tea Bottle

Some promotional items

Tooth Brushes

Cat-Napping Tea

Hi-Bear-Nating Tea

— E

THE MINISTER OF PROGRESS

16 apr 1990

To: Leaves

Fr: Progress

Re: Bounding along an inch at a time

I've contacted a reputable research firm to get a quote on what it would cost to get some inside financial info on the industry and its players. Should hear back later today or tomorrow. I'm also planning to query my own on-line sources later this week (as soon as I figure out how to do it).

I'm eager to dig in to sort out what this business is really like. It's definitely looked on as a little brother (an orphan brother) to coffee in this country. (An aside: I talked to the American Tea Association today. Asked them for any back issues of *Tea World* magazine. They said they didn't have any. They'd all been thrown out accidentally . . . could that say anything about the state of tea in the US?)

—Progress

THE MINISTER OF PROGRESS

16 April 90 evening

To: Minister of Leaves

Fr: Minister of Progress

Re: Do you believe in synchronici-tea?

This evening, after a refreshing cup of Oriental Lemon Tea (Long Life Teas), my mind opened up and out poured a couple of new ideas. Be advised, these aren't start-up ideas, nor are they necessarily viable or wise, but nonetheless, they are to be added to the heap.

1. "TEAS WITH A PURPOSE." After we get established we pick out a cause and create a special tea and a campaign to specifically address a certain cause. Solidari-tea, Equali-tea (all proceeds go toward the apartheid challenge), Individuali-tea (human rights) etc., purpose and story. Good tie-in with other socially venturesome companies. Good values are good business. Think on it. The package and the campaign could become a powerful vehicle for promoting understanding and awareness of issues dear to us. A portion of the profits are committed to the cause.

2. TEA CEREMONIES NEIGHBORHOOD STYLE. Check this one out. You know Tupperware, right. Well, imagine a woman (not to be sexist here, but it's probably more likely) organizes a tea party/ceremony at her house for a group of friends. She's learned the ceremony and how to put the party together from our guide and video that she has purchased. She gets ten of her friends together and they have a great

time. They order lots of stuff from the TRoT catalogue. Some want to become ceremony givers and host their own parties . . . not an original idea, but one that we haven't applied yet to this business. Might also work well with the Little People's Teas.

Leaves, you've obviously got a propensi-tea for good ideas and success. I look forward to the days when we share in the prosperi-tea of this rich idea. . . .

And now for a dunk in the hot tub. Good night.

THE MINISTER OF LEAVES

17 apr 90

DEAR PROGRESS,

I am going to advise the TDA (Tea & Drug Association) to put Oriental Lemon on the restrict-use list. If it continues to spawn any more ideas like Tuppertea, I fear for our children.

— Leaves

THE MINISTER OF PROGRESS

17 apr 1990

To: Minister of Leaves

Fr: Minister of Progress

Re: I've found a tea expert

So, Leaves, you didn't like the Tuppertea idea, huh? I have to admit it is astray from our previous directions, but what I'm getting at is promoting the idea of bringing back a new kind of tea ceremony for the 1990s. I think that is in harmony with your original idea about sip by sipping rather than gulp by gulping.

Anyway, the big news today is that I've found a tea expert. Bill McMellville has been in the business since 1938. He's a founding member of the U.S. Tea Association and was at the first tea conference in 1947.

We talked for a half an hour. He seems to know the world tea market. Told me about Lipton's foray into herbal and flavored markets. Said they tried to buy Celestial Seasonings a couple of years ago, but just before the deal went through, the feds intervened and prevented the acquisition for trade/monopoly reasons. Kraft ended up buying CS, not Lipton, which enabled CS to really grow in the supermarket category. A couple of years later the CS management did a leveraged buyout with a venture firm to regain their independence. When the LBO went through, CS picked off the head of specialty products from Lipton. They gave him lots of money, equity, and a place on the board of directors.

Told me that it was almost impossible to compete with the big boys . . . but that there were lots of niche opportunities. He really knows import/bagging/manufacturing, etc. He told me that the tea association shunned the herbal guys originally because they didn't consider it tea. If tea doesn't have caffeine, it isn't tea. He also mentioned that the FDA has chemical guidelines for the tea business. I'll follow this up.

We talked about green tea. He said that after WWII, many soldiers came back from Asia with a taste for the green stuff, but it wasn't widely available, and so they soon forgot about it. He told me we weren't going to find a big market for green tea.

What was interesting about this guy was he really knows the big players: Lipton, Tetley, etc. He's apparently done quite a bit of work on specialty/gourmet teas — testing, developing, etc. Right now he's working on new methods of creating tea concentrates for iced tea — a lemon mint flavor.

He's going to send us some background materials on himself and his company. He sounds like a nice older guy — who's more interested in kibbitzing about tea than making a lot of money at it.
He could conceivably be retained to develop a couple of products with us. He's the complete opposite profile of a person I would have originally imagined. (I see a hipp-ish chemist/Oriental expert from Berkeley who lives in Big Sur . . .) but this was enlightening.

— Progress

← TROT Logo on top

WRAP — I CHING coin with raffia

ancient mythical animal printed on tin or wrap around label

White Peony Tea

white space to stamp name of tea

GIFT TEA in specially wrapped cannister

PACKAGING

Tins for Special Vintage Teas

LOGO

SILK TASSEL

The Republic of Tea

print old imprints from Chinese paintings

OTHER CANNISTERS

ENHANCE TINS WITH SILK TASSELS or WRAP w/ RAFFIA & COINS or SEALS

Philoso-Tea Shirts

THE MINISTER OF LEAVES

17 April 1990

To: The Minister of Progress

Re: I need a cup of tea

Tell Mr. McMellville that the big tea boys don't even know what they're selling, and on top of that they're selling it mostly to old ladies. Maybe I'll be made to drink my words someday, but as far as I'm concerned, the tea business has been dormant for about a couple thousand years, and TRoT has now appeared to revive it.

— Leaves

THE MINISTER OF PROGRESS

18 April 1990

To   Leaves

Re   Two steps forward and one step back

Leaves,

Last night was restless — full of mid-night brainstorming. Many random thoughts anxious to be recorded. Some thoughts focused on the matter at hand and others aimed at the big picture. I lay them out here for your review. Forgive, dear Leaves, the Joycean organization of these scattered thoughts.

1. Based on some reading, the tea business in the US is between $1–1.25 billion per year. The herbal market is between $75–150 million per year as of 1988. (I have conflicting accounts of this.) 75% of all tea in the US is used for house-brand iced tea — the kind primarily served in restaurants. CS has 52% of this herbal market (according to a *WSJ* article in 1988) and Lipton has 30% of the herbal tea market.

2. Restaurants are a big market in themselves. CS has not attacked this market really, because their packaging does not individually

wrap and seal the bags. Stash tea has gone after restaurants with success — their bags are individually sealed in foil.

3. We're talking about being in the *specialty* tea business. If we can grab 10% market share from CS and 10% from Lipton and 5% from the other specialties, we're talking about having a $25–40 million tea business. That's not that big of a business — but that's not really the whole business of TRoT either.

4. The black tea market is humungo. Herbal tea isn't considered tea by many tea experts or by other parts of the world. Tea is at a crossroads between what was and what could be. . . .

5. McMellville said green tea used to be popular where the water was hard: Great Lakes area, Upstate New York. That's interesting.

6. Iced tea is something that manufacturers are just starting to address: larger tea bags, different packaging, etc. Kids' teas are a natural extension.

Bigger picture for TRoT. (Submitted to the Minister of Leaves in the spirit of this tennis match of ideas.)

> Mission: The purpose of this business is to make the world a healthier and safer place for our kids and their peers.
> Strategy: We will accomplish this by educating people about how to make the world a healthier and safer place — one person at a time — through direct experience. We will educate by engaging our customers' imaginations and by entertaining people with information.

The Republic of Tea is a place where people feel both content and inspired. It is a place both tangible and imaginary. It is through The Republic's products and the messages they convey that the aforementioned strategy is accomplished.

TRoT produces a range of proprietary products. Agriculturally, the principal crop is a variety of incredible teas. Integral to the experience of TRoT tea is the ceremony that accompanies it. TRoT also has a community of skilled artisans that craft beautiful tools for the enjoyment of tea and life. The Republic has a highly refined sense of the aesthetic of nature and this is represented in the products — including clothing, furniture, and tools that the land exports. TRoT also places an extraordinary importance on education of the young, so there is a preponderance of fine books, inspiring tales, and healthful foods.

1. The world will continue to be a tense place to live.
2. Change (particularly technological change) will continue to overwhelm more and more people.
3. Growing numbers of people will seek a formal respite from the tensions of daily life.
4. Eastern philosophies, new age thinking, and new paradigms for spirituality will continue to get attention as we move toward the Millennium.
5. More Asians than ever live in the United States and will continue immigrating to this country, bringing their own customs with them.
6. People will continue to become conscious of their personal health and make choices in the marketplace that reflect this consciousness.
7. People will achieve an unprecedented level of global awareness in the next decade.
8. As computers provide bridges for relationships, many people will appreciate the value of face-to-face interaction even more than they do today.
9. People like to escape from the stress of day-to-day living.

RANDOM QUESTIONS?
1. Is anybody trying to market green tea to the Asian population of this country in a creative way?
2. Is it possible to sell green tea to the masses the way Mexican food became popular in the western US?

THOUGHTS ON BUSINESS MODELS
1. We're in the change-the-world business.
2. Tea is our entree into that business.
3. Tea is a vehicle of communication.

4. Other TRoT proprietary products and licenses will account for far more revenue than tea in the long run.
5. We're looking at the possibility of entering several businesses concurrently: tea via catalogue and retail, manufacture and sale of other proprietary products, licensing of our concept, potential franchising of our stores and concept.

FINALLY,

A friend is visiting me here in Sedona. We worked a good bit yesterday and then went for an absolutely amazing hike down the canyon to the creek. We hiked along the creek for a couple of miles, relishing the freshness of the air and water and the rustling of the wind. It was a cleansing and invigorating experience. On the walk it occurred to me that an important part of TRoT is serenity (tea). Our land must be designed to provide easy access to this state of mind. . . .

Minister, a question of a personal nature for you: Am I sending you too much stuff? Is this process infringing on our vision of the type of role you want to play? I can send you more or less or keep it as it is. Let me know. I want you to be as comfortable with the process as I am. Needless to say, I'm enjoying this process of discovery and immersion and particularly our dialogue. I look forward to your forthcoming responses.

P.S.   We are on to something.
        I like the way you think.
        Our plan to enter this business will be masterful.

As much as I loved volleying with Bill over the fax machine, it was not in my then Tea Mind to actively involve myself getting another business started. I had stashed enough money in the bank to buy myself the time to smell the flowers for a few years, to reflect and read and write and raise my child. As much as I liked Bill and loved the idea of being in the tea business, I could see no reason to torture myself by going round and round in the mind-thick unreality maze necessitated by lawyers, accountants, and investors, who not only tend to see business in the most boring and narrow terms, but who usually also lack the humility to see how tiny a pinprick is their view on the world.

I knew where I stood, but I was a little worried for Bill. If he truly wanted to see The Republic of Tea exist, in addition to refining the idea he would need to talk to lawyers, accountants, investors, and take whatever concrete steps were necessary to get things under way. But for the moment I chose to not say a thing about this, confident that in time he would find out for himself.

I was in no hurry. When I started BR I hurried, and I found out afterward that it would have been a lot more entertaining, and probably no less profitable in the long run, had I not hurried. At that point in my life hurrying made me feel I was getting more done, but the fact is I was more likely just making more work for myself. What is it about business that makes one forget that no matter how fast or slow one goes, no matter how straight or meandering the path, all business people end up in the same place, even if one gravestone happens to be bigger than another? There is only the journey to savor. The end is the same end for all of us.

The opportunities in tea were screaming at anyone who could be quiet enough to sip and listen. It was a perfect example of the fact that, although entrepreneurs might like to think otherwise, one does not create a business. A business creates itself when the circumstances are ready for it. And if the people it needs to create it are not yet ready, or up to the task, it will wait. For the moment, I was happy to wait along with it. — **MZ**

THE MINISTER OF LEAVES

Date: April 18, 1990

To: Progress

Fr: Leaves

Re: The Tao of Business

Thank you for your sensitivity regarding the nature of my involvement. For now, don't worry about it. Send me everything and anything. Call me anytime. I love this jazz.

Meantime, listen to what found its way into my Tea Mind today: How about an arranged marriage?

We've got the ideas; Celestial Seasonings has the machine.

Right now, and probably forevermore, they are stuck in the herbal teas. (They're also stuck in the sixties, but that's another story.) They have failed to develop any new products (other than more herbal teas) of consequence; worse yet, they have failed to leverage themselves at all in the tea business. They have the largest specialty distribution system in the country, and all they use it for is *one brand*!

They can either contribute cash or services to TRoT, and what they get in return is a piece of the company that's going to give them the biggest run for the money they've ever had. (Let's not concern ourselves at this point with the fact that they haven't even heard of us yet.) Through us, they get a way to enter the green and black tea markets, and also get to leverage their facilities, their expertise, their distribution system.

What we get is instant expertise and instant distribution. We quick-start. We find the neatest undiscovered, unappreciated teas that can be found. They pack the tea into tins and boxes and get them into the store.

We do our own promotion and marketing. We let the world know sip-by-sip, not gulp-by-gulp.

Will CS go for it?

What do you think, Minister? Have I accidentally sipped a cup of insani-TEA?

— Leaves

P+L:
These antique Chinese "chops" could provide inspiration for labels, cookies, giftwrap paper, etc.
— E

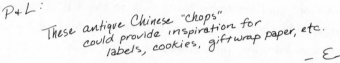

THE MINISTER OF PROGRESS

18 April 1990

To   Leaves

Fr   Progress

Re   Response to the Tao of Business

You're a persuasive Minister, Leaves. But the big question is **Do they need US?** Sure, they've been a failure in extending — but we don't bring anything to them, YET. The CS alliance might be an expansion move, but it looks scary to me in the startup. Confidentialitea agreements don't stand up too well in this type of situation — particularly when you're dealing with a market leader.

I want to compete and take them on. They are not the big boys that McMellville referred to. He was talking about Lipton and Tetley. I think we could take CS on as an investor once we've got something for them to invest in. In a way, Leaves, I want to really see how difficult it will be for us to get distribution on our own. I think we have the smarts to put together something that will beg to be put on the shelf. . . . It's hard to say how much we would have to give up for the quick-start opportunity.

Here's my goal for tomorrow: Talk to the VP of sales and VP of marketing for CS under the guise of being a recruiter looking for someone in the business. I'd rather pick these guys off then join up with CS. . . . We could get the expertise and the distribution connections this way too.

I'm on a cold call streak, so I'm feeling like it's well worth the shot. I'll let you know how it goes.

— Progress

. . . .

I wished I had had a tape recorder running when Leaves and I talked on the phone. Mel had a very vivid picture of The Republic — in its fullest sense — and talked as if the whole thing already existed. I yearned to be able to describe The Republic as fluidly and confidently as he could. I wanted to listen to what he said over and over again. I knew I wouldn't be able to really take the idea and run with it until I saw the business as completely as he did.

Through our conversations and correspondence our relationship was developing quickly and unclearly with three different voices. One moment we interacted like "partners" working together "equally" toward the same goal. (But I certainly didn't feel like an equal, neither in wit or experience.) At other times I felt like the front man for The Wizard of Oz. *Still other times, Mel was clearly the mentor, and I, the "mentee."*

I enjoyed these multifaceted roles, yet now I realize their intermingling created confusion for me. Mel and I both floated spontaneously and unconsciously between these roles. One moment he reveled in the idea of being behind an exciting new company; the next he retreated to the more passive role of guiding me, like a detached teacher. Occasionally Mel expressed an intent to be the majority owner of the business, and at other times was clearly ambivalent about getting committed to anything in business again. We didn't talk about this dynamic in our letters, but I know we both sensed it was there. It was fun (and easy) sharing an idea on a plane, and now expanding it in our letters, but it wasn't clear how we would share it in an actual business.

A successful partnership in business still seems to be one of those mysterious, rare occurrences. I'd heard about so many collaborations that ended in ugly disagreement. That's certainly not what I wanted. I didn't want to push to define this business relationship; I felt comfortable following it where it took me, even if it created some confusion and frustration (mutual, I'm sure) along the way. For now it was enthusiastic brainstorming all the way. — **Bill**

. . . .

THE MINISTER OF LEAVES

18 apr 90

Progress:

My thoughts last night were around the nature of the TRoT organization. Here's what I say: Let's think of ourselves as a *federal* entrepreneurial republic. By this I mean we should create a structure that invites participation from other entrepreneurs who endorse our basic premise — i.e., putting forth, in their own unique expression through product or services the larger metaphor of tea as an opportunity for their own "right liveli-hood." Perhaps what we create will be a holding company with a core business out of which all the offshoots will spring from a single creative source. Therefore, instead of structuring conventionally into divisions, we will go into a series of businesses, with each one run by its own entrepreneur who operates in association with us. The entrepreneur would have an equity stake in his division. This would be fun to think about — it's a hybrid between classical entrepreneuring and intrapre-neuring, and it strikes me as an inventive way to launch a business for the next millennium. The key will be to find the right-talented like-minded people to *own* the offshoot business, and to lure them into helping The Republic of Tea create itself.

— Leaves

THE MINISTER OF PROGRESS

18 April 1990

To   Leaves

Fr   Progress

Re   We're rolling now

Spent a half hour on the phone with Jim Reynolds, GM of Peet's (The Bay Area's Leading Specialty Tea and Coffee Retailer). He's been there since '84. Nice guy. Really open. He's a part owner too. Peet's has been around for twenty-four years. Mr. Peet lives in Berkeley. He sold the company a number of years ago. I called up the general offices for Peet's and asked to talk to the person in charge of tea. I got on the phone with Jim and told him that I was interested in going into the tea business. I was straightforward about wanting to learn as much as I could, and Jim obliged with some helpful information:

He said tea was a tiny part of their business, but he really enjoyed the buying process. He buys a year's worth of tea at a time in a chest. Black teas from India really outsell green teas in their business. We talked about the increasing Asian population, his catalogue, their business, SF coffee, etc. We established a good rapport. He likes Sedona — and I kidded him about opening a store here. . . .

He ended up giving me the name of the guy he buys Chinese tea from in SF. Said he was extremely knowledgeable and that his family has been in the business for three generations. His name is Mike Spillane.

I followed up and called him right away. Mike was extremely helpful and knowledgeable. His company has been importing tea for over 100 years. They import/broker teas from all over the world. They stock 120 different types and deal in over 500 varieties. They bring in the very best (top of the line) green teas from China. They import tea in their original containers (chests) of 66 to 100 lbs. each. The minimum they sell is a chest. Peet's is one of their good customers.

I asked him about what his view of the potential of the tea business was. He said, "If you listen to A.C. Nielsen, they say to get out before the ship sinks. But they're talking about supermarkets." He also said: (Here's the good news) "Specialty teas (as opposed to the mass-market "Lipton" type) are going through the roof. We're importing more specialty tea than ever before. Our business has doubled every year during the past ten years."

He was friendly and open and very willing to share his expertise. I set up a tentative meeting with him on May 3.

— Progress!

GREEN TEA PKG IDEA

CLOSURE:
ENVELOPE
OR
SEALING
WAX

RICE
PAPER
BAGS

REPUBLIC OF TEA

SUMI BRUSH TEA POT
DARK GREEN LOGO

How we insult the water! There is nothing that water cannot overtake, and yet its nature is to yield. Were it not for water's grace in yielding to the leaves, allowing them to realize their grandest potential, we might never have had the chance to taste a true cup of tea.

— The Minister of Leaves

THE MINISTER OF LEAVES

April 19, 1990

To: Progress

Fr: Leaves

Re: Let's talk product

PRODUCT IDEA #1:

Water! The leaves are only half the beverage. Quality of water has everything to do with quality of tea. Certain kinds of tea leaves need certain kinds of water. I spoke to a Chinese gentleman who said he will brew his tea only with rainwater collected at particular locations at particular times of year. (Can there be such a thing as too much sip-by-sipping?)

From *Food in History* by Reay Tannahill: In ancient China ". . . the ideal tea water came from a spot near the mouth of Yangtze." Let's bottle the stuff.

From the same book: "None of the new tea-drinking nations . . . quite appreciated how much difference the quality of the water made to the final infusion. China, which had always known it, seems to have passed on the knowledge to Japan. There is even a permanent reminder of the fact in Tokyo, in the form of an underground station, Ochanomisu, which takes its name from the once-pure stream flowing nearby — a name that means "the emperor's tea water."

Water could be a key to the connoisseur market. Wouldn't you like to taste the same tea that Lao Tzu sipped?

PRODUCT IDEA #2:

Cultural food products from tea leaves. In Tibet there's a concoction of tea leaves and yak butter that is used as a convenience food for mountain journeys. For that matter, how about a whole line of tea snacks? These could be great-tasting herbal lifts.

PRODUCT IDEA #3:

Here's our standard for every product The Republic of Tea offers: *If we don't love it, we don't sell it.*

— Leaves

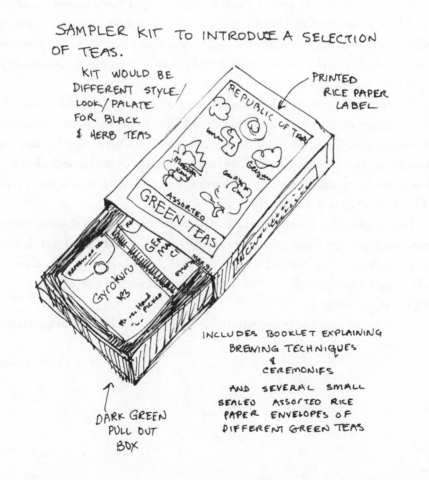

SAMPLER KIT TO INTRODUCE A SELECTION OF TEAS.

KIT WOULD BE DIFFERENT STYLE/ LOOK/PALATE FOR BLACK & HERB TEAS

PRINTED RICE PAPER LABEL

DARK GREEN PULL OUT BOX

INCLUDES BOOKLET EXPLAINING BREWING TECHNIQUES & CEREMONIES

AND SEVERAL SMALL SEALED ASSORTED RICE PAPER ENVELOPES OF DIFFERENT GREEN TEAS

THE MINISTER OF PROGRESS

20 apr 90

To   The Minister of Leaves and The Minister of Enchantment

Fr   Progress

Re   Art beyond expectation

The sealing wax idea is great. Each ministry could have its own seal or it could be a personal seal of the person who packages the tea . . . like a quality control stamp . . . it should bear some true purpose in the process of getting the tea to the customer. It could provide personal accountability for product reliability and quality. . . .

The sampler box brings to mind the idea or concept of the *invitation*. The invitation could be an integral part of The Republic — both tangible and conceptual. The bottom of the sample box is an invitation (or maybe its inside) to The Republic, which includes the ideas of tea tasting, slowing down to sip-by-sipping, etc . . . in essence it's an invitation into the world of TRoT and what it stands for. . . .

This could also carry forward in our marketing. What some companies send out are direct-mail marketing pieces. What TRoT sends out are "invitations." We really like the colored inner box idea too. Green, black, rose? (for herbal) . . . the color identity within the product line will give it meaning. . . .

Your latest graphic transmittals have provided a leap of inspiration. Thank you.

— Progress

THE MINISTER OF PROGRESS

20 apr 1990

To   Leaves

Fr   Progress

Re   TRoT Progress Report

• Had a nice conversation with a VP of sales at CS. He was friendly (said "Glad you called back, messages like yours I usually throw away"). Told him we were looking to hire someone with beverage/specialty/gourmet food sales experience. Said he'd have to think about it. Said he'll talk to a guy who's VP of marketing (came from Schweppes/Cadbury) and will talk to me in a week after he returns from his trip. Said he'd keep his eyes open while traveling during the next week. It wasn't a home run, but it's a little foot in the door. . . .

• The average specialty tea bag retails for $.087 each (CS) on the low end to $.18 (Yogi) on the high end. Celestial Seasonings and Lipton are very competitive at between 9 and 10 cents per bag in the supermarket. The health food stores are 10 to 12% higher.

• Bigelow is taking both CS and Lipton on in the supermarket herbals department and has basically kicked them out here in Sedona. There are over 30 flavors of Bigelow at this market to 6 of CS. The weird merchandising thing is that CS shares the tea section with Lipton (reducing each of their individual shelf space) while Bigelow runs rampant with lots of product on the "healthy" aisle. Interesting positioning and merchandising.

•   I wonder if we could go into some ranch type of markets and do tea tastings as an evening program as a promotion (à la wine tastings). They could be a very entertaining social/seminar. Our representatives from TRoT would be well trained and dressed for the occasion and make a spectacular presentation. Participants could learn about tea and ceremony . . . walk off buying our product and then be inspired to share it with their friends. I think this type of marketing might make it possible to push a much higher ticket item, which might be a ceremony starter kit (or a tea party kit for children?) . . . or something that is like $100 . . . that has teas, tea set, candles, music, etc.

— Progress

THE MINISTER OF PROGRESS

23 apr 1990

Good Morning Leaves:

I've been spending time thinking about how to differentiate our product and make it superior to the competition. I've been studying our competition (Celestial Seasonings, Stash, Traditional Medicinals, Bigelow) more closely. I'm trying to summarize the positioning of these companies' products and the focus of what they are selling: (This is more of a clarity-of-thought exercise than anything that breaks new ground. . . .)

CELESTIAL SEASONINGS:
1.   herbal teas an an alternative to caffeinated teas
2.   lots of flavors (variety) and clever combinations of flavors
3.   a nice package with an established character

STASH TEA
1. quality tea and herbal beverages
2. convenient packaging (both individually wrapped and iced tea packs)
3. a good variety of flavors and names

TRADITIONAL MEDICINALS (price varies — as high as $.36 a cup)
1. medicinal/curative effects of teas
2. specific applications of herbs to symptoms
3. tamper-resistant packaging (to more closely align themselves with medicine)
4. a "creamy carob" line that is fragmented — the packaging is so different you wouldn't even know they come from the same company. Seems to be a specialty coffee alternative.

Yogi is selling a change of state that results from the tea — but they're a little out there. ($.18 per cup)

Suma is selling an adaptagen beverage. A nutritional supplement to the body. ($.29 per cup)

Good Earth teas are selling off the Good Earth name and awareness, "naturalness" and low calories. They also emphasize caffeine free and freshness. ($.14 per cup)

In general, all the herbal teas are playing up the "caffeine free" message. Bigelow herbals appear to be a complete "me-too" to CS.

So, here's how I say we differentiate ourselves:

Conceptual: Our product represents the tea culture/experience. a path to an enhanced quality of life (and access to some of the products and experience of that life).

Tangible: A better blend of ingredients resulting in a fuller taste and richer benefit of the experience. More entertainment in the form of information.

On another subject, I spent a couple a hours delving into the mysterious world of on-line information over the weekend. I confirmed via DB that Celestial Seasonings was a $40M company in 1988. More recent info is not available. I did however pick up two articles of interest. (They confirm the tainted tea situation, the tough financing of the LBO, and the growth of the specialty tea area. . . .)

Here are a few other interesting catches from my database fishing expedition:

From *CFO: The Magazine of Chief Financial Officers*, Oct 1989: Celestial Seasonings Inc. has experienced difficulties since a bad batch of a new tea blend caused it to abort an initial public offering in 1983. The firm has been a subsidiary of major food conglomerate Kraft. Now it is independent, following a management-led leveraged buyout (LBO). President Barney Feinblum's most critical task is to integrate the free-spirited culture of the organization with the sophistication and discipline required to handle the debt load created by the LBO. Vestar Capital Partners Inc. acquired the majority of Celestial's common stock in the 1988 LBO from Kraft. With virtually all of the company's profits going toward paying down some $45 million in debt, Feinblum has adopted more sophisticated cash management and marketing techniques. He is also promising staff to institute an employee stock ownership plan.

From *Working Woman*, April 1989: According to a spokesperson for Celestial Seasonings Inc. while overall tea consumption has stagnated over the past several years, the specialty-tea category has shown an average annual growth rate above 20% since 1983. Like others in the food and beverage industries, tea manufacturers have had to respond to consumers' increasingly health-conscious demands and particular tastes. Herbal teas make up 60% of this specialty tea market.

— Progress

THE MINISTER OF PROGRESS

23 April 1990

Leaves:

Thinking about your comment that tea could be the new wine. . . . we can instill a sense of value in a great beverage. . . . The leaves for a truly great cup of tea can't cost a customer more than $.50 at retail; combined with the right water you've got a tremendous beverage and experience . . . and a nice value compared to a great glass of wine at $4 to $5.00.

    Further on this note: Did you know that coffee yields about 50 cups per pound, while tea produces more than 200 cups per pound? Therefore a specialty coffee selling at $7.00 per pound is comparable to a tea selling at about $28.00 per pound.

— Progress

THE MINISTER OF LEAVES

April 24, 1990

Good Morning Progress:

Thought I'd give my early Tea Mind the chance to pause and take a look at where we are. As wholesalers and retailers, I think we have seven tea product lines:

1. Herbal teas
2. Green teas
3. Black teas
4. Medicinals
5. Children's teas (powdered)
6. Bottled iced teas
7. Gift packs (tea as the new wine)

Each line has its own unique packaging, but there's a unity to them all evident at a quick glance.

As retailers (catalogue), we also have an accessory line. This includes not only the accoutrements of tea, but TRoT tea-shirts, exotic bottled waters for tea preparation, and a whole host of other items that fit into "tea culture."

The question we've got to ask ourselves is: Should we come out of the box with all of the above, thereby making a profound statement about who we are, or do we start with a few lines and introduce new lines gradually?

Five Thoughts about this, in favor of the splash:

1. The catalogue would not be complete unless we had the full line, so if we introduced lines gradually, the catalogue should be delayed.
2. If we go all-out, it seems inevitable that we'll have to bring in outside investors, and therefore we will have the money to do it right and do it big.
3. Good story. Media attention could help frame TRoT as a phenomenon. Much excitement.
4. We stand the chance of making TRoT a household word in two years.
5. Much easier to sell to stores; with a high-profile introduction, we'll do great in the shelf-space wars.

Five Thoughts about this, in favor of a slower buildup:

1. We'll need less money, and therefore we'll own more of the company.
2. Learning curve. We get to make our mistakes quietly.
3. People factor. It's *always* hard to find good people.

FROM THE
MINISTRY
of
ENCHANTMENT

PHILOSO·TEA SHIRTS

I WANT
WHAT
I
HAVE

The REPUBLIC of TEA

HAPPINESS
NEEDS
NO
CAUSE

The REPUBLIC of Tea

SIP by SIP...
GULP NOT BY GULP

CONTENTMENT
IS
LOVE
OF
CONTENT

4. Timing. We're still a few years ahead of our time from the perspective of the world coming around our way.
5. What's the hurry?

I'd be interested in seeing what you had to add to both lists. A key factor in this decision is your own sense of how it ought to be, since you will be the one who has to implement whatever plan we decide on.

FURTHER REFLECTIONS ON TRoT:

Wouldn't it be wonderful if through our mischief tea could come to represent a big new idea about living in gratitude and appreciation *for what we already have.* If people would only pause to want *what they have,* they would be so much happier. It's that idea that we will sell with a simple cup of tea, and it's that idea that could change a lot of lives in this crazy can't-get-enough country of ours. I'll say it again: I'm as excited about selling Tea Mind as I am about selling tea.

One final thought. This morning's SF *Chronicle* has the results of a poll. In the Bay Area, an astounding 44% of the population is drawn to mysticism and "New Age" practices, as opposed to the traditional religions. "New Age," although well-intentioned, is full of a lot of charlatans, and therefore I can't say it's my cup of tea. But the reason people are interested in things "New Age," let's not forget, is because of a primordial *thirst.*

We are talking tea-drinkers, my dear Progress.

— Leaves

THE MINISTER OF PROGRESS

24 April 1990

To   The Minister of Leaves

Fr   The Minister of Progress

Re   Surmountable questions and other ramblings

Dear Leaves:

I just concluded a quick poll in Sedona and found that an astonishing 98% of the nonretired population is drawn to mysticism and New Age practices. 76% of these people drink 2 cups of tea a day. . . .

Your morning Tea Mind is impressively coherent. I enjoyed your thoughts and offer these rebounds and returns:

1. HOW DO YOU FEEL ABOUT THE PRODUCT LINE DEFINITION? Your tea product line makes sense, although I still have questions about blends of black and green and herbs . . . anything that has tea in it cannot be sold as an herbal beverage (certainly not caffeine free), but it could say a blend of the finest green tea and herbs from The Republic of Tea. I guess the product should be categorized by whatever the lead ingredient is. The FDA labeling requirements basically say that the tea has to contain 51% of a specific tea if it is labeled as such.

    I'm also not sure about separating the medicinal category. I think that teas within each of the main categories could have medicinal qualities and ingredients. The packaging could support this: "particularly good for colds and stuffy noses . . ." but not exclusive to that application. I think this is one of the limiting flaws with Traditional Medicinals. Too narrow a focus.

To simplify: In the tea business we have four categories:
A. Black (and black blends)
B. Green (and green blends)
C. Herbals
D. Children's (powdered)

2. HOW MANY TEAS DO WE HAVE IN EACH CATEGORY? The depth of each category in the line is one of the next areas of exploration. What is the optimum selection to offer initially? Three kinds, five kinds? This is a question which I will present to a tea buyer or two. In many ways we need to build trust in our customers so they'll try some of the new things we bring out. You don't enter the market as a new company with customers that trust you. We have to earn it.

3. HOW BIG A PRODUCT LINE DO WE NEED?

3a. WHAT'S MY FEAR ABOUT INITIAL STORE DISTRIBUTION? Shelf space. I think we're going to be fighting like crazy for shelf space. We have to come in with a reasonable program that a retailer can buy into and build into a success. How much shelf space do we want initially? How big a commitment do we want from a retailer to get started? We want to make a big enough impression to get noticed but small enough so that the retailer doesn't say "I don't have the room." We can have a palatable intro and then a very aggressive intro of new products. (That's what retailers generally can't count on from a startup.) This is where we can really differentiate ourselves . . . it will require more capital . . . but I would like to think in terms of phased rollouts of product . . . perhaps three rounds that are all planned for within the first eighteen months . . . very aggressive to build momentum.

3b.   WHAT ABOUT THE CHILDREN'S TEAS? The children's teas really represent a breakthrough in the marketplace. I'm not sure where they would be merchandised in the store: with tea or with children's foods? In either case, we need to create the shelf talkers and promotional tools to cross-sell and motivate sales. The children's teas could really lend themselves to couponing and advertising in very specific magazines. It should be easy because the target audience is well defined. Initially we can build a good direct business until they catch on in some special markets.

4.   HOW EXTENSIVE IS OUR CATALOGUE? The catalogue is the likely core of the business initially. We have the opportunity to establish a direct relationship with our customers. I think we could economically start up a full and exciting line of teas (twenty maybe) if we private-label our product. This would mean that we find an existing product that we could buy at the right price, make it distinct in some way, and add value to it through better marketing, packaging, and communication. We wouldn't have to commit the time or resources to original product development; we would just have to find the right product. The down side to this is that most private-labeled products fall into the commodity category (napkins, canned vegetables) so it may be difficult to find something of premium quality. In this scenario, we're not really selling better tea, which doesn't feel right.

The first catalogue is critical in defining who we are to all of our customers. It's also a wonderfully nonthreatening way to show retailers that we're going to build the market for them and lead the way. We have to show them that we're interested in creating a new context for tea, not just another brand to take up shelf space. It reduces some of the anxiety they might have about venturing into unproven territory (particularly with loose tea).

5.   DO BOTTLED TEAS REPRESENT A DIFFERENT BUSINESS? Bottled teas represent an enormous opportunity, but they are a completely different business. Different packaging, bottling process, different shelf

space (sometimes refrigerated) and different marketing. In fact, it's a different trade and business. It's the bottled beverage business. Going into this business at the same time as the tea will definitely require additional capital. It needs its own product development resource, its own manufacturing resource, and it also (in most cases) will have a different distribution channel. It brings us to a fundamental question: Are we in the tea business or the bottled beverage business or both? We may want to explore the opportunities of small scale private labeling/bottling of tea waters for the catalog initially and then see if we can get them into the store. Any product that would require refrigeration will be doubly competitive for space. I understand that these days many supermarkets require the manufacturer to subsidize the shelf space in the store. We obviously need to talk about this more.

My feeling right now is that the bottled teas, distributed on a mass scale, are a spinoff product or license to a bottling company that is already in the water business. If we can really concentrate on the identity, quality, and culture of TRoT, we'll have a slam-dunk joint venture or license with a Crystal Geyser or someone else. My hunch, too, is that the bottling commitments (breakage, packaging, etc.) are more complicated than the tea products that we will sell.

Seems to me that the carbonated teas could be very big business, but we don't really bring anything unique to the table (except the idea) at the onset. Any other water company could wipe us out if they thought it was a viable idea. It's important for TRoT to exist and have a value in the marketplace, then perhaps a licensing or distribution deal makes sense. Distribution will be key.

6. WHAT ARE MY THOUGHTS ABOUT PRODUCT LAUNCH? I would like to see a commitment from a major retailer like Williams-Sonoma or Macy's Cellar to do a whole island devoted to The Republic of Tea. This could be a special exhibit/display that we create and could be the center for the launch of the product and the culture. We would work exclusively with this retailer at the launch to create a sensation

around the product and the big picture of TRoT. This is also where some of the special tastings and gift packages would be launched. These exhibits could highlight tea and products from the catalogue. The launch site needs to be a retailer that works in both gourmet foods and housewares/gifts. . . . The crossover should already exist.

7. SO HOW BIG A DEAL IS THIS? I think we need to go in perceived as a company bigger than Stash (in terms of tea and catalogue) and more imaginative than CS. That may tell us how much capital we need. We need to be in a position to garner national attention.

BIG QUESTIONS TO BE ANSWERED:

A. What business(es) do we want to be in initially?
Right now I see us in two businesses: The TRoT Mail Order Business and the Proprietary Product Tea Business. The PPT Business has a Children's Tea Group that will concentrate on the special needs of that product.

In terms of launch, the children's teas could lead us into the market, followed by the mainstage teas and catalogue . . . at this point I think the children's teas might generate the most attention because it's so novel. . . . It might give us a head start in terms of entry into the crowded supermarket distribution. . . . Then a year later we come back with another big story — carbonated teas. . . .

B. What resources will these business(es) require in terms of capital and people?

C. What are the key market factors for each of these businesses?

NOTE TO THE MINISTER OF ENCHANTMENT
Your sketches are wonderful! I see a business materializing before my very eyes! Thank you.

Dear Progress & Leaves,

I love the idea of bottled carbonated teas — both herbal & caffeinated.

Some sweetened w/ honey?

CreativiTea, Sportea, ClariTea etc.

—E

THE MINISTER OF PROGRESS

---

25 April 1990 Already

Dear Leaves,

I put on my morning Tea Mind this morning and came up with a list of expectations and guidelines for myself and this new venture. It's kind of an expression of my personal ideal, but I think it is relevant for you to read in light of us embarking on a venture together.

 Commitment is an underlying component to all of this. Commitment implies mutual trust and attention — from person to person, or person to company, and vice versa. It is clear to me that I am ready to commit to a major venture in my business life. The past two years have been spent doing some very worthwhile (and educational) *projects,* but they have lacked the longer-term potential and rewards of a *business.*

Each day I am feeling more confident about the business potential of our idea and also more confident about the type of choices I have to make in the near future.

It is clear to me that partners in life and business must share a similar sense of ethics and integrity. I have an intuitive sense from our conversations that you and I share many of the same values. As I focus on this, it is becoming clearer to me how imbalanced and absurd another endeavor (to which I have been invited) would be. As I have stepped back from it, the vast differences in my values and the values of my potential partner in that business make the venture unworkable for me.

What follows is a statement of my own *personal goals and vision* for building TRoT:

I WANT TO BUILD A COMPANY THAT
- has at its core a long-standing, open, and trustworthy relationship with my partners
- provides a valuable, meaningful, and fun product
- communicates a positive message through its products and way of doing business
- is respected as a model of a successful socially responsible venture
- nurtures employees and takes care of customers
- develops its own creative spirit, culture, and way of doing business
- has an infrastructure that promotes individual ownership, responsibility, and risk-taking
- generates a healthy and ample return on investment
- works as a team and makes decisions as a team
- is aggressive, yet realistic in its goals and expectations
- doesn't use up its people
- provides for innovative benefits and rewards such as child care and sabbaticals
- knows that it's special

AS THE LEADER OF THIS COMPANY I WANT TO:

- earn the trust, respect, and confidence of my employees, suppliers, and shareholders
- build a team that shares responsibility for key decisions
- set the tone for open and effective communication at all levels
- act, think, and make decisions creatively
- attract and motivate the very best people to be involved in this venture
- recognize my own limitations and provide for a team that is successful and well rounded
- grow personally with the business and its employees
- operate the business in a healthy environment (physical and mental)
- develop good ideas into viable products and ventures
- head up some remarkable and groundbreaking projects
- be able to succeed
- be able to make mistakes

AS AN INDIVIDUAL I WANT TO:

- maintain a healthy and stable balance between my work and my family
- live in the best environment for my family
- continue to contribute to my community
- integrate my personal interests with my work where they make sense
- travel to exotic places on business and pleasure
- avoid lengthy trips without my family
- pursue an opportunity that has at least a ten-year possibility
- make enough money to live comfortably and provide a secure future for my family
- take on new challenges
- build long-term equity in an idea that I believe in
- be able to have the option of working or not working ten years from now

— Progress

All things have their own inner truth, no matter how "imper-fect" they might seem. If a sip of tea causes me, no matter how briefly, to be transported outside myself, I arrive into perfection itself. And I have known a cup of tea to do just the thing. The best of many good praises that can be sung for tea is that it inspires Tea Mind.

— The Minister of Leaves

25 April 90

Dear Progress,

Your Tea Mind is impressive. Reading over your personal goals and vision, I find myself moved. I was not nearly so clear-thinking when I set out to establish BR, and a lot of the problems I endured in the last decade could have been avoided had I then been able to see life in the full spectrum that you now do.

Your goals nearly mirror mine. In fact, with one notable exception. In starting a business, mine would be a different expression of priorities.

To explain why, I need to back into it:

In my view, all things are born to thrive. You cannot go wrong when you create something, be it a life or a business, if you take responsibility to see to it that it thrives.

What makes a thing thrive?

People thrive on happiness. There is nothing elusive about happiness. It's *here* always; the only problem is that sometimes we're not *here* for it. One sure way of not being here is to resist the uninvited, which is sadly what most people do most of the time. But happiness is the primal birthright of the man or woman who does not resist it. The common fallacy about happiness is that you have to *do* something to attain it. Not so. Happiness is built into the DNA; it's not an add-on option. Happiness needs *no* cause. It is an unspeakable great tragedy of our times that so many people are desperately looking *outside* themselves for the source of happiness when it's already inside them, waiting to be tapped.

To make a business thrive, however, takes a bit of effort. Business is about another kind of relationship, the one between *you* and *me*. When we conduct business together, we create a *third* entity, the business relationship. Unlike you and me, the business itself is not endowed with a natural, innate happiness. It's our responsibility to make it happy, and that means making it thrive. What causes a business to thrive is the mutual agreement we make between us that we will both *benefit* from our business relationship. Fortunately, business guides us with an absolute way to measure its success: Business always thrives on *profit*. So when everyone who has an association with a business, its investors, its employees, its vendors, and its customers *all* realize a profit from the association, the business is happy.

This is why if you start a business, you assume the responsibility to make it thrive. You will hire others, who will join you in your cause, and whose families as well as they will depend on you to captain their ship through the choppy waters of reality. In other words: The first order of a business is to be successful. And a business is successful because it is profitable.

Because for so long business has measured itself *only* in terms of profits, there is a tendency now on the part of young entrepreneurs like you to overcompensate and think more in terms of saving the world than making a profit. For all its virtue, there is a fundamental flaw in this thinking. There won't be a business to save the world with if the business does not make a profit.

— Leaves

THE MINISTER OF PROGRESS

25 apr 1990 about 9:00am

Leaves,

Your latest message makes perfect sense. I agree wholeheartedly with your reprioritizing of priorities: The purpose of a business is to thrive — and it needs at its foundation the goal to thrive financially.

Some people say that profits result from a job well done, but I think your message is stronger. I also agree with you that the "do-gooder" companies run the risk of double failure if they are not first and foremost financially successful.

What we have to prove and re-prove is that a business can thrive and its people can flourish on its own *and not at someone else's expense.*

Leaves, not to sound overly emotional about this, but I'm learning a tremendous amount from you and I appreciate it.

— Progress

THE MINISTER OF LEAVES

Tea Time
April 25, 1990
Mill Valley, Ca.

My dear Progress,

I can't remember the last time I had this much fun. Between Progress chattering away on my fax machine and Enchantment sketching away in her study, this is getting to be like heaven.

I must also confess that what truly appeals to me about this business is its naughtiness. Here we are, three fairly peculiar tea-headed know-nothings, going about like we know which tea leaf will sprout where on which tea bush in Tanzania. By golly, I think I've convinced myself. By the time you perform your full mischief and get these leaves on the shelves, we may actually have found a megaphone loud enough to shout, "Hey, everybody: Smile! Have a cup of tea on us."

— Leaves

THE MINISTER OF PROGRESS

25 April 1990 at 4:30pm or so

Leaves,

Glad you're having so much fun. I want to make some more PROGRESS!

I set up another meeting for us (it's open now) next week with an herb maven from the East Bay. He owns the SF Herb Company and private-labels "40 or 50 different tea company products." He has been involved in blending and manufacturing . . . has his own plant, bagging facilities, etc. He knows the business — seems extremely laid back and is open to meeting with us.

Sound ok? Let's start penciling a rough agenda/schedule for the visit next week so we can firm up some of these appointments.

I canceled my trip to LA tomorrow. (Just the beginning of making choices.) I'll be here making progress.

P.S. My last question of the day:

What are a couple of extremely driven guys like us doing in the slow-down business?

Yours,
Progress.

THE MINISTER OF LEAVES

HiBEARnating Tea Time
25 April 90

Progress,

In response to your last question of the day: Can you think of a better way to break the caffeine habit?

— Leaves

P.S. The Minister of Enchantment has departed for a yoga farm, leaving Leaves the sole gofer for the little Prime Minister. I say this in the event you find my communications over the next four days less frequent and ornamented with scribbled trucks.

THE MINISTER OF PROGRESS

April 25, 1990
11:30 p.m.

Leaves,

Re: Lingering questions about our idea to sell unique products like children's and bottled teas:

1. If we bring out bottled teas as the lead (positioned as an alternative to soft drinks in the bottled water category) do we build support for our conventional tea line? This product line (bottled) has perhaps the largest and quickest potential — so does its success generate interest in the boxed line or vice versa?

2. The whole discussion of bottled beverages brings up the question of whether we're going after CS or Crystal Geyser/Koala or both?

3. Seems to me that the bottled tea market has yet to be born . . . do we create in consort with our packaged line (including children's powdered)? Sounds like a pretty powerful concept and an exciting, ambitious launch . . .

4. There's got to be synergy at the market in terms of a cross-product introduction, don't you think? (i.e., Is a retailer more likely to take the whole line and build promotion around it as opposed to a single product category . . . ?) Who can we talk to that might have experience with this in the food industry?

— Progress

THE MINISTER OF LEAVES

26 apr 90 1 a.m.

Progress:

You've hit the central question, and it needs full reflection.

My fear is that if we focus first on the bottled, and, to a lesser degree, children's concepts first, we will not have established our credibility as *tea merchants*. It's important that customers understand first and foremost that we sell great tea, and then we'll have earned the right to extend our line in any and every direction.

On the other hand, I recoil at the idea of not launching with our strongest ideas, which are bottled and children's. Since the Practicality Department is yours, Leaves leaves the decision with you.

— Leaves

THE MINISTER OF PROGRESS

25 April 1990

Leaves,

I feel like buying a company today. I'm talking to a couple of companies in the herbal side of the tea business. Just had an interesting chat with the folks at Wildcraft Herbs — they do the Good Earth brand of teas. They are in Santa Cruz . . . 17-year-old company, 60 employees . . . how would you feel about jogging down there next week if it made sense? I'm going to be talking to their products manager later and will try to get a feel if it's a worthwhile investment of our time.

Today I'm determined also to demystify the distribution channels in the business and figure out how we can end up selling five million dollars worth of the stuff a year by the third year. I want to start getting into the sales side . . . how much tea can we sell in a year? I want to understand more thoroughly the distribution through food brokers, chains, etc. . . . (I've started on a proforma, but when all you can show is expense, it doesn't look too good.)

Next week I want to concretely and succinctly answer the question

Why does the world need another tea company? I'm also putting together questions for our herbal and tea specialists whom we will meet with on Wednesday. I'll send these to you so you can amend and extend them when you have time. More conversation later in the day . . .

— Progress

· ·

I guess even though I was talking "big" at this time and really batting it around with Leaves, deep inside I was still unsure about this whole thing. The "game" had been progressing rapidly for a little more than two weeks now, and it was moving beyond the passive research stage (inquiring conversations, reading articles, and dreaming) into the active "acquisition" stage. Even though I could dream the big dream with Mel, I didn't have the confidence that I could actually pull off buying an existing company. It was beyond my own sense of capability.

Although I didn't reveal it in my letters, I was definitely lacking confidence moving this quickly from researching businesses to buying real companies. But if I revealed my hesitancy, I was afraid Mel and Patricia would think I wasn't capable of the challenge. I kept analyzing the business (just as I did as a consultant) instead of doing anything about it. The analysis had an unexpected result: I started questioning my commitment to this project. I began to sense the potential for failure. My inability to move forward confidently probably had to do with the fear of discovering my own limitations. I still didn't have a clear enough sense about the business to know if it would succeed or fail (in sharp contrast to Mel and Patricia's confident assertions that it would be a success). I was starting to feel uneasy about changing my life in order to go into the tea business — the great unknown. — **Bill**

· ·

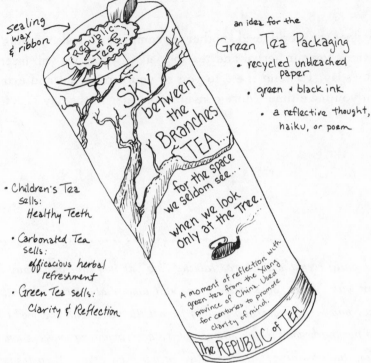

sealing wax & ribbon

Republic of Tea

an idea for the

Green Tea Packaging

• recycled unbleached paper

• green & black ink

• a reflective thought, haiku, or poem

Sky between the Branches TEA...

for the space we seldom see...

when we look only at the Tree...

A moment of reflection with green tea from the Xiang province of China. Used for centuries to promote clarity of mind.

The REPUBLIC of TEA

• Children's Tea sells:
  Healthy Teeth

• Carbonated Tea sells:
  efficacious herbal refreshment

• Green Tea sells:
  Clarity & Reflection

THE MINISTER OF PROGRESS

April 26, 1990

To   Leaves

Fr   Progress

Re   Logical deductions and wild ideas

RANDOM THOUGHTS IN FAVOR OF AN ACQUISITION:

1.   If we start from a base of distribution and quality control of our product, our catalogue will be a much quicker success.

2. If we buy into an existing distribution, the extension into Children's and Bottled Beverages categories will be much stronger and likely to succeed. Otherwise, the cost of entry for a new product to get on the shelves and gain substantial distribution is prohibitive.

3. Money that would be needed just to establish initial distribution (working capital) could be applied to the promotion of the bigger message. This fits with our desire to go out and find our customer.

4. If we handled the positioning of the acquisition correctly, we could establish TRoT as a sizable, stable entity from the onset . . . in other words, rather than being perceived as a startup, we are perceived as the acquirer. "Traditional Medicinals announced today that it has become part of The Republic of Tea, a specialty tea and beverage company based in Sedona. . . ." In a way, we build an instant story and avoid the small-timer syndrome.

5. The logic in #4 supports the big-splash thinking that our marketing plan will require.

6. If we jump-start with an acquisition, then we can build the TRoT brand a little more slowly and cautiously. We won't be under the tremendous pressure of hitting home runs if other parts of the company are already successful in the marketplace. Also, I feel strongly that the catalogue will have a more immediate impact and can be launched simultaneously with the product.

7. We will probably have to enter into two contract packing relationships (one herbal and one tea) at the onset. But to avoid the competition with the packer/manufacturer and gain their distribution, we buy them. On the tea side, we're leveraging the relationship in the stores to get additional shelf space. It seems that by being a full-line tea/beverage company, we are offering the retailer a more complete line, a bigger, more exciting story, and a drink "for every time."

8. Judging by the number of private label brands on the market, it may require a business plan in itself to get off the starting blocks if we were to start from scratch.

9. It may be easier to raise capital if we are buying into an established asset. In a way, we're looking for equity capital to buy off a share of the company, and then working capital to launch a new brand

(and message/experience). Investors may be more comfortable buying into tangible financials rather than the "concept" of what we're selling. (Although you and I understand it and articulate it — it can be a difficult sale. It takes the ability to demonstrate what we're talking about and that takes time and money (of course you know that better than I).

LEAVES, THIS IS GETTING TO BE FUN NOW.
THE KEY QUESTIONS:

1. Could we pick up TM at an undervalued price? (If we tell them too much, they might get too cocky and want to compete . . . putting us at a disadvantage. We should be careful not to be too optimistic about our views of the forthcoming market . . . they've been in it for a long time . . . they may be too close to see it.

2. Could we generate profitable distribution quickly by coming on board with them and then eventually buy them out?

3. If we proceed, what will be the obstacles to purchasing a management-owned company, or do they participate in a stock swap so that their asset automatically becomes worth more in the transaction too. In a way, a management-owned buyout would be more attractive, because it would provide stability in the transaction and already provide a base of motivated, committed employees.

I'm excited to be coming up to see you next week. I feel like we're really making some progress in our thinking now.

I'm awaiting Doug Green's (he's a maven of the natural food industry, publisher of its leading trade magazine) phone call so that I can find out more about TM and Wildcraft Herb as well as the whole distribution system out there. He's supposed to call me back anytime.

— Progress

THE MINISTER OF PROGRESS

4/26 at 4:30p

Leaves:

I would call today a bit of an illumination. (The result of days of saturation) . . .

Good call with Doug Green. Confirmed a couple of hunches I had . . .

1.   Said that the whole-foods industry was very receptive to new products. "It's all new products . . . as long as you're not me-too . . . and offer something better, you're in." This is in contrast to Drake Sadler's remark that the whole-foods stores are as difficult to crack as the supermarkets. Doug's retort: maybe that's just Traditional Medicinals' experience. (Doug doesn't care for the TM tea bag line although he likes the company and has known the Sadlers for years.) Doug said the company has been real successful.

2.   Doug had lunch with Barney Feinblum the other day. Doug says CS is trying to kiss and make up with the whole-foods industry. Doug says they burned people when the Kraft deal made them turn their backs on the natural foods market in lieu of the bigger, more lucrative supermarket trade. "They're vulnerable. They don't have a conscience that appeals to the whole-foods industry. They are big business." ($50 million) We talked about the fact that they don't participate in Earth Day, green causes, etc. I asked if it was debt burden that makes them slow in the marketplace, but he thinks it's lack of marketing expertise. CS has had a tremendous turnover lately too. They've lost five top managers in a short time.

Doug mentioned to Barney that he had a friend [us] who was

interested in going into some private label tea . . . and Barney said "have him call me, we'll pack for them." That's interesting — They've got quite a bit of excess manufacturing capacity with their new plant.

3. I asked Doug where he thought the real innovations in the whole tea area would be and he said organically grown is probably the hottest area. CS is trying to get into this now. He made an analogy that the herb tea business is like the publishing business. . . . CS has some old-time best sellers, but there's always room for a new hit on the list. . . .

4. I asked him if he thought that mainstream markets would respond to the trends that are happening in whole foods . . . he said absolutely. He cited the whole tuna thing about dolphin-free tuna. Originally, whole-food stores provided the alternative — people sought that out — then the manufacturers had to change their way of doing things. It's response to pressure in the market.

He had to run . . . but we promised to talk again soon.

CONCLUSIONS AND REFLECTIONS:
1. I need to find out more about "organic herbs."
2. The whole-foods market is the place to aim initially. I can begin to build a proforma based on that market. Then we can expand into mainstream distribution.
3. My earlier Tea with a Purpose could really be a hot idea. It would give us that current "best seller" that is timely and topical. In a way, it is parallel with the Body Shop approach to informational campaigns.
4. We might work with TM. They have sophisticated packing machines and an edge in the medicinal area. Sounds like a marketing vision could really enhance their business. They have a mixed reaction from consumers in the marketplace. Their packaging with its old-time apothecary-style topography is a little weak in an industry where packaging is critical . . . still, they are successful. That says something.

Also, TM is on the right track in terms of participating in "1% for Peace."

5. The tea business is really full and booming. Stash is both a tea and herbal company already. They are big on packaging — I'm trying their new iced tea–size orange spice stuff now. It's gotta be really profitable. All you get is two big tea bags. I don't like the taste — the flavor separates from the tea. Bigelow is really enhancing their packaging — especially their sampler: It's flooded with info about how many cups the bags make, the ingredients, and the historical value of the company. I like the idea of providing information that helps the customer understand value — particularly how many cups the package provides. This will be important when selling loose tea because we will be able to provide a much higher quality loose leaf product at a price comparable to bagged tea. Lipton is big, but has been unable to knock off CS — and I think it's cultural, not taste . . . it's perception of the big guy/little guy. Or the establishment vs. the underdog.

6. I don't think an existing herbal company (who's entrenched from the onset in caffeine free) has a good shot at being a "tea" company with a well-rounded brand. That's a key distinction for TRoT and one that we will have to handle carefully for full impact.

7. This is feeling better and better. Let's go for it. We're on to something.

I might call later because I feel the need to talk about some of this.

— Progress

THE MINISTER OF PROGRESS

April 26, 1990

Leaves:

Here's something interesting: (or meaningless) —

Both the product manager at Wildcraft and the production manager at TM are "gone for the day" at 4:30. . . .

Is this indicative of anything? (I guess it depends on what time they start their day. They're either really together and are done with their work, or it's a hang-out company.

At TRoT we could stop working at 4:30 too, but the last half hour or hour of the day could be spent as a group a couple of times a week talking about how to make the company THRIVE even more. . . .

What's interesting to me is that neither of these managers returned my call (although I did talk to the president). . . . It's indicative of middle management not being receptive or aggressive about new business. The thinking at this level is usually — "don't complicate my life, I'm doing enough already, I don't want to take on any more."

We will endeavor to build an organization where everyone feels he or she is part of the big picture and understands the importance and priority of the *customer*. Every call is a *potential* customer . . . and is worth a minimum investment of time. . . .

— Progress

THE MINISTER OF PROGRESS

26 April 1990

To: Leaves

Fr: Progress

Re: Beverage Bottling

Had a very interesting talk with a guy who started up a sparkling water business which he sold a couple of years later at a nice profit.

He was intrigued with our idea. Said he hadn't heard anything like it before. Healthy water (herbal additives) is what I described.

He said the business gets very tough in the distribution end. Grocery stores and supermarkets are virtually impossible to crack unless you have a very very strong brand identity. Said supermarkets want you to pay for space and the competition makes it very difficult to squeeze in.

He said that in a commodity business like tea, marketing and packaging and story were paramount. Said people are really intrigued with the source of the water. They want **legend and mystery,** he said. It seems that people want to have an "experience" with their purchase. They want to enjoy the vicarious thrill of participating in something exotic, unique. He said we have to be prepared to really promote the product at the customer and store levels.

He said that even though the bottled water business is expected to grow a lot — don't expect the big guys to be giving up market share.

He concurred with me that licensing of the concept and the concentrate formula is probably the way to go. Said it was very very expensive to actually be a bottler. Said we had to decide how we were going to get it made and get it to market.

Overall he was very positive. Didn't advise me not to do it.

— Progress

THE MINISTER OF LEAVES

April 26 90

Dear Progress:

Before joining The Minister of Enchantment today for a stroll up The Mountain, I brewed a pot of a tea I call *PEACEPOWDER*, comprised of four parts Gyokuru Asahi, an ethereal leaf that promotes clarity, and one part Gunpowder, whose smoky pellets are opened by boiling water to release a calm energy.

Under the influence of *PEACEPOWDER*, I found my thoughts drifting to our bottled line. I see our bottled teas as herbal spritzers, and perhaps we should not even call them teas. I am particularly anxious to brew a cup of *GRAPEFRUIT MINT* for its tangy properties of energized refreshment. I can see this, and other flavors, replacing Perrier and generic iced tea in restaurants.

As *PEACEPOWDER* peaked, my thoughts drifted to our Little People's Teas. I see *INFANT WELL-BEING* as an infusion that provides all the necessary minerals for a newborn, such as iron. For the same child a little later on I see *NIPPLE TO NIPPLE*, a weaning tea.

When we came home I filled the kettle and brought some water to a boil, pouring it over half a teaspoon of black tea flavored with peach to make half a pot. I quickly added room-temperature bottled water to fill the pot, then poured the greenish golden elixir over ice some sixty seconds later, allowing the tea leaves and dried peach leaves to float to the bottom of the glass. This beverage, my dear Progress, has the possibility of making humankind a most happy species from lunch through early evening on hot summer afternoons.

I am now most curious to read the long white ribbon flowing on to the floor from the fax machine. I like how our enterprise is unfolding. TRoT is a splendid teacher.

— Leaves

The Minister of Progress

27 April 1990 morning

Dear Leaves,

Today I took *that* walk you suggested up the side of our mountain and pondered the commitment that lies ahead — either to make TRoT the work I devote myself to — or to take a job that's just been offered to me with a firm in SF. I am invigorated with the super-clean morning air and the sight of bright wildflowers popping up in all directions. I share with you some of my personal reflections:

I *thrive* on being very busy, working hard, and making things happen.

I am at my very best when I am fully immersed.

I enjoy the process and the goal.

I am prepared to focus my full energy on this vision. I know I need to realize my own goals and potential. My wife is fully supportive of this path. There will be certain sacrifices made initially in search of a larger goal and opportunity that the future offers.

It has been five years since I operated a company of any magnitude. Since that time I have grown up and had many valuable experiences that have prepared me for this next step.

I want to build this business in a supportive community because I believe that a successful business and a supportive community can be a very dynamic combination. I feel that I can be successful on several fronts simultaneously.

The time I spend with my family is of paramount importance to me. I want to set the example that proves that an extremely successful executive or business person can also be extremely successful at home.

I am going to build a business that knows how to thrive and go all-out—but also knows when to cool down and step back. I am going to manage people (not goals). I am going to build an organization that is balanced—yet willing to commit and go for the extremes. We will work very very hard and play hard. We will build in rewards for hard, long hours in the form of retreats, and sabbaticals.

I am going to build an organization that is responsible for itself. I am going to cultivate a team that plays like a team and picks up when a player is out. This organization is always going to be as lean and tight as possible.

We will use technology to work smart. We will build systems to streamline repetitive tasks and to provide superior customer service.

I will be effective at all levels of the business.

I refuse to spend unnecessary time commuting to work each day. I want to work within five–ten minutes of where I live. I want to live and work in a community and physical environment that offers a retreat from the natural stress that is generated through hard work.

I am willing to travel regularly to oversee the various components of our business. The plant, the shareholders, suppliers, etc.

I recognize that I will be a very busy man. I am up for that. I want to set aggressive yet realistic goals for myself and my team.

I want the business to be sufficiently capitalized but always a little hungry. (But not so hungry that our minds are taken off the tasks to move forward.)

I am going to build a company that is resourceful.

I am going to set an example within the company of balance and health. I am going to build an organization where the team can be very successful at work and in their personal lives. We do not want to achieve business success at the expense of personal relationships. We will do things as a company that involve the extended family. We want to provide for a special TRoT way of life . . . that sets an example of what we are selling.

TRoT *is* a fine teacher, Leaves.

— Progress

PS. I guess I am more at home in the vaporous possibilities of The Republic than the definitive job descriptions of San Francisco.

THE MINISTER OF LEAVES

27 April 90

Dear Progress,

I am continually amazed that you have so many true flashes of wisdom at such a young age.

As you set out on your expedition, I want you to think of Patricia and me as wells available to you when you need us. Should you need a drink, we will be here.

It is becoming clear that destiny is taking us all for a ride. I am willing to do whatever I can to help you materialize the TRoT vision. We need it. It needs us.

"I'm going into the tea business." I like the sound of that.

— Leaves

THE MINISTER OF LEAVES

27 April 90, 9 p.m.

TO: PROGRESS

FROM: LEAVES

I've got a hunch that we should take in only one investor so as not to waste a lot of time and energy on having, or feeling, the obligation to explain ourselves. The investor must bring more than money. He should ideally bring a particular talent that we, individually and together, do not have. What's our weakness? Who's our man/woman? Or is my hunch correct? Would it be better if we put together a group? This discussion is an important part of our agenda next week.

— Leaves

THE MINISTER OF PROGRESS

28 April 1990 at 6 am

Dear Leaves,

I like your thinking about the single investor. . . . What are our weaknesses? Well, the one strength that would really aid our team might be someone who owns or influences some significant distribution relative to our plan. My first thought is, of course, in stores, but it could also be in the catalogue/retail area as well. Who owns big store chains or distribution companies? If we think about complementary products (where there is some assumed overlap in customer profile) I imagine companies like Nature Company, Smith & Hawken, Body Shop? Is there a company out there that would take a big interest in our product that is owned by an entrepreneur?

Or how about a tea packer? Most tea packers sit around waiting for somebody to come to them with a private label assignment. As part of the deal where they invest in us, we would agree to help them brainstorm private label opportunities for prospective companies.

Other areas where we could be complemented? On the actual source/supply end? If we had contacts to the front line of the raw products end, we might find breakthroughs more quickly.

Another complement would be someone with a medical/physiology background who could better help us understand the healthy component of what we're doing.

And, of course, another complement to our weakness would be someone who has actually been making and selling tea for some time (although this could get tricky).

Another asset might be someone in a business that we expect to spin off to . . . i.e. retail . . . clothing . . . bottling. I think we're looking for another perspective and someone that has a lot of keys on their key chain into doors of opportunity.

I think a single investor would be brilliant in terms of operations — it would simplify things — (on the other hand, it could complicate things) and I like the idea of someone who would bring more than money. Of course this will all depend on the capital requirements. . . . The down side of course has to do with control issues — if a large sum of money is spread out among a group, there is less individual control the investor side. This is definitely an important topic for discussion. I'll absolutely come down to a specific person(ality) if we do go the single investor route.

Up till this point I've been thinking "group of passive investors" . . . but you're wise to turn the tables and explore another active or semiactive (or semipassive?) partner. . . .

Leaves, one thing is clear: We've got to own this market. . . .

I'M THINKING INITIALLY OF TEN PRODUCTS.

1. Four herbal teas (each with a special ingredient having a special property)
   a. one fruity that makes great iced tea
   b. one minty that's a great digestive, soothing, head-clearer
   c. one fresh and zingy for the morning
   d. one that is calming for slowing down
2. Two green teas
   a. Sky Between the Branches
   b. Find Your Way
3. Two black teas (or blends)
   a. One for balanced energy
   b. One prestigious that is all taste
4. Two powdered herbal children's teas
   a. Monkeying around
   b. Hibearnating

And perhaps one Tea with a Purpose at some point near the start of the company — maybe four months later. We want the social component of our business to be integral but not dominant. In other words, we don't want to create our company around the social conscience, we just want to have one. I think that we should plan a media/promotional strategy that creates news every couple of months . . . this will affect the launch so that we don't dilute our own excitement by having too much at once . . . our product development intro schedule will be well thought out and full of strategy.

I've been studying the packaging of different companies. TM and Good Earth and Bigelow are the very high end with sealed individual pouches. These are great for the pocket packs and for sampling — something Drake said they make extensive use of. He also said the individual tea bags work well in gift sampler baskets when combined with other products. They are tamper resistant and keep the tea fresher too. Of course they create more waste and paper. . . . I think one of our long-term educational goals for the consumer will be to get them to see the value in buying in bulk (not just tea . . . everything). At this point, 80% or so of all US tea is sold in bags (not counting restaurant iced tea). . . . This isn't something we'll attack up front, but makes sense as a long-term business goal. . . . Perhaps a campaign or a tea with the purpose of eliminating unnecessary packaging is something that makes sense in the future. The box or tin of loose tea could come with a free tea ball or TRoT infuser.

I've really been enjoying our dialogue the past weeks. We've made substantial progress toward defining some directions. It's fun to reflect on the fact that three weeks ago tomorrow we were just meeting in a hotel lobby.

We're all looking forward to our visit in a couple of days. I'm excited for Sam and Zio to get together. It might sound silly, but I'm excited because it would be great if they had as much fun as we do. . . .

Well, this next stab at a rough plan is calling me (and so is Sammy), so I'm off to "color" and then to see what this next little flow chart of progress might look like.

— Progress

. . . .

"Brainstorming by fax" was exhilarating, but if we were really going to start this tea business we were all going to have to get together and define our business relationship. Sometime during the second week of our conversations, Mel invited my family and me to Mill Valley to spend some time together. Concurrently, a lot of my research ended up being centered in the San Francisco Bay Area. We planned to visit for a couple of days in early May at the Ziegler home, and I scheduled a number of appointments with tea brokers, packers, and competitors at the same time.

I was excited and nervous about the trip. Although we'd developed a wonderful and instant rapport in the creative department, we really hadn't spent any time together other than the airline ride. Major questions (that went far beyond this "dream" stage) loomed in the background. Questions like: "Will we all want to be business partners?" "How will we actually define our responsibilities in a business?" "Who will own the business?" "Who will finance the business?" We had talked plenty about business scenarios, but never about business structures. Beyond these sorts of questions lurked an even stranger and unsettling concern for me.

The Republic of Tea had swept me off my feet. I had become an obsessed researchaholic, spending hours and hours a day and my passionate energy to figure out how to do this tea business. My wife, although always wonderfully supportive, was also a little bewildered by what was happening to me and how fast it was happening. (Husband goes away to conference. Comes back with new idea and new acquaintance. Becomes obsessed with new idea. Spends most of time writing letters to California. Buys every type of tea imaginable and serves it at every meal. Says he's thinking about not doing the job in San Francisco, but starting a tea company instead.) Try that one on your spouse sometime.

My single biggest concern about this upcoming visit was my hope that my wife would become comfortable with the possibility and opportunity of The Republic of Tea. I had hoped that perhaps Mel could explain it better than I could so that Faye would find some assurance that all this time I was spending was worthwhile. I wanted her to like the Zieglers and the Zieglers to like her, and I wanted Zio Ziegler (then three years old and six months my son's senior) and Sam Rosenzweig to be best buddies. I'd always heard that becoming business partners was similar to marriage, so I had that funny anxiety related to getting to know better those to whom I had been "engaged" these last several weeks. — **Bill**

THE MINISTER OF PROGRESS

The 29th day of April, 1990 about daybreak

Good Morning Leaves,

Been thinking a great deal the past two days about *plans* and I've roughed out this thinking. Please help me clarify it.

Plan A: Acquisition and New Brand Launch

OBJECTIVES AND STRATEGY:
1. Acquire the distribution, product development, and manufacturing of a desirable herb/tea packer.
2. Launch TRoT immediately as a separate brand. Use existing distribution as leverage into a broader market.
3. Launch and build TRoT mail order catalogue business.
4. Consolidate or re-tune the entire company line for maximum profitability and efficiency.
5. Maximize the profitability of the manufacturing facilities through aggressive private label marketing.

ADVANTAGES
1. Quick-start sales opportunity into existing distribution.
2. Best pricing and margins as a result of owning manufacturing facility.
3. Competitive issues with respect to private labeling relationship are not relevant. We will benefit from the in-house experience and expertise in blending and production.
4. More latitude (potentially less cost) with product testing and development as owner of the company rather than an outside client. We have more control over manufacturing schedules and inventory requirements.

5. Opportunity to bring marketing savvy to existing brands of acquired company to boost asset value.

DISADVANTAGES

1. May require substantial capital investment to acquire company and distribution.
2. It may take longer to consummate this kind of deal (although much of our product development can continue at the same time).

Plan B: Launch New Brand Using Contract Packaging Resources

OBJECTIVES AND STRATEGY:

1. Create new TRoT brand of tea, encompassing black, green, herbal, and powdered beverages.
2. Develop our own product development capability. Use contract packaging resources for manufacturing.
3. Build initial distribution through whole foods and specialty markets.
4. Launch and build catalogue business.

ADVANTAGES

1. We can fully concentrate on our own product and distribution strategy.
2. We can shop the packaging contract to our own specifications and are not confined to the equipment facilities of one packer.
3. We have less operations to manage initially.

DISADVANTAGES

1. We have to establish our own initial distribution. This could be very time-consuming and costly.
2. We will pay more for our products.
3. We will have to meet minimum order requirements which could burden inventory as we explore the success of our line.
4. We will inevitably end up competing with the tea packer if they have

a proprietary line. It will be difficult to develop innovations in that environment.

Well, Leaves, as you can see, I need a lot more help with Plan B. Plan A has kind of crystallized in my mind, but it's putting me at a disadvantage to write Plan B right now. Plan A at this moment is a much stronger plan.

— Progress

THE MINISTER OF LEAVES

29 April 90

Dear Progress,

I was in the living room, watching the sunrise, savoring the Keemun — Oolong's magic as its calm energy began to flow through my creaky morning body, when I heard the fax chattering in my study. I found myself breaking into a broad smile.

When you come up here I want you to sit outside on the front porch in a rocking chair alongside me and watch the freighters come and go on San Francisco Bay. There is something about the way they move that tells everything there is to know about the movement of life. Unless you look very closely and do not turn away, you cannot see them move at all. If they are coming from the east, heading to the Golden Gate, they first appear on the horizon between the Bay Bridge and a ridge of Mt. Tamalpais. Then they crawl, passing Alcatraz and San Francisco, until they finally disappear behind the Sausalito hills. Watching these freighters, you can see the movement of time in space.

I had an almost simultaneous dual response to the ten-product intro idea. On the one hand, disappointment ("Can ten items be enough to make the point?), and on the other delight ("What a great selection; what a smart, pragmatic, *do-able* plan"). Like you, I love to dream, but when it gets time to do, I recognize the wisdom of doing in such a way that gets the dream done. The operative word here is to proceed *skillfully*. The truly gargantuan task we have before us is *editing* ourselves.

Regarding Plan A, Plan B, these thoughts: Plan A will write itself, depending on what we acquire and how we acquire it. Your scenario is ideal. But the moment Drake or whoever hands over the keys, the world is going to look entirely different to us. An acquisition requires us to be even more supple than a startup. We have to take charge and not spook the troops. We must be even more yielding, willing at first to go with what we've got (even though it might not be what we expected to get). So I would put as the overriding modus for Plan A to be flexible and pragmatic about maximizing the asset we have just acquired. And because we will be inclined to put together a lean-mean financial plan (so that we can own as much of TRoT as possible), any such plan will call on you to be ready to move in and camp out.

It's Plan B where we need to do the work. I will give it some thought in the next few days. My first hunch is that the catalogue is the best chance we have for putting ourselves on the map overnight. We may not make any money at it, but we won't be ignored. (In the early years at BR the catalogue was a financial drain, but it greatly stimulated store sales.) With the catalogue leading the attack on the tea market, we simultaneously end-run around the retailers and win the hearts and minds of the customers themselves. Once we have the customers, selling this stuff to the stores will be a cinch. But the one assumption that must be fully investigated is that starting a catalogue in 1991 is as viable as starting one in 1979. I know that two things have certainly changed: It's much more expensive (mailing, etc.), and American mailboxes are a lot more crowded.

All of these strategies are in flux, like the freighters on the bay, moving but not appearing to move unless you watch them closely. Plan B has a course. It's for us to see it.

— Leaves

A man is rich in proportion to the number of things he can afford to let alone, wrote a tea-drinker named Thoreau, who discovered what we have known from the time before time in our little land: Tea is wealth itself, because there is nothing that cannot be lost, no problem that will not disappear, no burden that will not float away, between the first sip and the last.

— **The Minister of Leaves**

THE MINISTER OF PROGRESS

30 apr 1990

Dear Leaves,

Leaves, will you forgive a little personal reflection on this Monday morning?

I find myself running to and with this new idea of yours. Excited, inspired, and mostly confident. When I catch my breath, I marvel at the turn of events in life. When things are meant to happen, they happen. You can't force things to happen that aren't going to happen. I see this scenario spelled out before my eyes time and time again.

I have tried to start several business concepts with other people at times in my life. Generally they were me taking an idea to someone else who I thought I'd like to work with. In these instances the projects proceeded, but they required a tremendous amount of coaxing most of the time. They didn't flow naturally. They needed to be pushed . . . they didn't sprout and grow the way ours is. The energy of the participants didn't catalyze the development of the ideas . . . there was an imbalance in the contribution of spirit and energy that hindered the flow of progress.

When things are meant to happen, the laws that confine everyday life seem to make way for them. Faye and I had to overcome major obstacles to be together, but we were meant to be together and so we are. Faye and I spent several months apart (before we were "together") writing to each other every day. In a way we were describing our ideas of the life we wanted to share together. A couple of years ago Faye transcribed all the letters and poems and printed them in a book which she gave to me on Valentine's Day. It's a treasure of mine.

I've learned that if we're open to it, one's course in life can change dramatically, instantly, serendipitously. Perhaps these unforseen possibilities have been vaguely visualized somewhere in our imaginations, and then they suddenly tangibly appear and make themselves available to us. They're not really goals, but wishes. One of my wishes has always been to work with amazing people — and you're such a person. You are an inspiration, Leaves.

I arrive at these thoughts because when I look around my office I see the remnants of paths less traveled: projects I thought I would be working on at this point. A path that never felt right but nonetheless seemed to be the path of least resistance or the best path at the time. I tend to think more intuitively (than logically) about business decisions — this seems to go against much of the current "business strategy" that I sense in the world. In Carlos Castañeda's first book, his mentor Don Juan tells him: "Your decision to keep on the path or to leave it must be free of fear or ambition. I warn you. Look at every path closely and deliberately. Try it as many times as you think necessary. Does this path have a heart? All paths are the same: they lead nowhere." Our path has heart, which accounts for the certain vulnerability I feel on occasion as I walk (and run) with our idea.

I'm looking forward to talking TRoT with you the next couple of days. I'm also looking forward to getting to know you better. I appreciate your extending the invitation for our visit to my family because they are a big part of me. I know we share this value. Needless to say, we're looking forward to the time together. I'm eager for Faye to meet you and Patricia (because all she knows is what she reads in the [fax] papers).

NOW, TO PLAN B. HERE ARE SOME OF MY TROUBLES
WITH PLAN B:

1. Contract packers seems to have fairly tough minimums for a startup to hit. Drake told me that their minimum is 100,000 bags per blend. That's about 5000 boxes — not a lot if we've got some wholesale distribution — but it is a lot if we're going primarily mail order. Imagine ten teas (or more) 5000 boxes each in our startup inventory.

   Also, he mentioned that you generally should print 10,000 boxes and corresponding bag envelopes to have it make sense financially —

so that's another substantial investment in an unproven product to move through a catalogue. . . .

Solutions: Negotiate agreements that are flexible and tough on price. Work it out so we don't have to take the full lot of 100,000 bags at once. Try to do smaller runs on more flavors.

2. We lack control of the manufacturing process. I'm more concerned about timing and scheduling—in a startup mode it will be difficult to forecast sales and timing on product needs. We'll end up having to take more than we really need if we can't count on getting an order turned around quickly. This is something to explore with the packers at our meetings.

3. Slower turnaround time in terms of bringing new products to market. We'll be waiting in line behind the needs of established customers and their own proprietary product.

4. If we want to be an innovator and develop a product that has proprietary qualities, it's risky to work with a co-packer who is also our competitor. We would be wide open to people blatantly taking our ideas and running with them faster and with more resources than we have as a startup.

These concerns will be the basis of many of my questions at our meetings this week. Once we get comfortable with some of the answers, Plan B will make a bit more sense. . . .

During the past three weeks we've received lots of information. But it's interesting to note that neither of the tea organizations in the US have responded to our phone calls or letters. They are both uptight, closed groups that say that you have to be in the tea business to be a part of their group. We wrote letters saying we were in the tea business . . . yet we haven't received a thing from them. That says something about that industry. The tea industry and the herbal beverage industry are in two different worlds. It will be interesting for us to bring them together in our undertaking.

The reason I bring this up is that I've been thinking about a national campaign to get people to drink tea again. We need to create the Everybody Needs Tea or the Walking Campaign for Tea (at some point in the future) that will really put tea on the map again.

One of my personal challenges is going to be to change the entire restaurant iced tea market so that customers come to expect a selection of premium iced teas at fine restaurants instead of just the house brand. Imagine a little menu on the table (like wines by the glass) that describes the teas available. I also really like Enchantment's idea about TRoT iced tea glasses. . . .

Just one of the many challenges ahead. Enough for now. Gotta go get Sam's breakfast . . .

— Progress

THE MINISTER OF LEAVES

April 30, 1990

Dear Progress:

Thanks for sharing your personal reflection. I've been around a few years longer than you and, if it's worth anything to know, nothing like this has ever happened to me before. You are the only person (outside of Patricia) I have ever worked with who not only instantly absorbs what I'm trying to say but has the unique ability to make it his own and in so doing take it further and *make it better*. That's why we've done a year's work in three weeks, partner.

— Leaves

Notes from my journal on the trip to Mill Valley. May 1, 1990.

The two-and-a-half-hour drive from Sedona to the Phoenix airport was a little hard on Sam, who was confined to a car seat. Plane trip went fine. MZ picked us up at SFO and we drove through San Francisco, over the Golden Gate Bridge on our way to charming Mill Valley. We wound our way to the top of a steep hill, where I gazed a breathtaking panoramic view of the San Francisco Bay and the shimmering city with its unmistakable skyline. With an extra tug at a particularly sheer driveway, we reached the summit and the home of Mel, Patricia, and Zio Ziegler. (Their home is amazing. It is majestic yet homey and warm, built with a myriad natural materials and textures. A sense of quality and rare craftsmanship is evident in every detail.)

Much fun and warmth. I'm at ease. We had tea (of course) and were shown around the grounds and the neighboring mountain (Tamalpais) with its dense redwoods and madrones. I quickly learned that a morning or afternoon hike was almost ritual in the Ziegler household.

First night we were treated to a wonderful dinner that Patricia cooked of completely fresh vegetables, whole grains, and just-baked bread. Followed it up with tea (of course). I was impressed with the healthiness of the meal without any self-consciousness that it was "healthy."

Morning. Fog in the Bay. The big Adirondack porch with its tree-limb rocking chairs beckons. I had been trying to imagine this from MZ's letter. Peaceful. Slower. Fantasized about being able to retire to a place like this someday.

Now "the walk." Actually, it was a hike. Mel is in great shape. I was short of breath. I basically listened. He talked for a good two hours as we trekked the backcountry trails that weave through the Marin headlands. Mel was mesmerizing. His enthusiasm and insights, his dreams and metaphors, had me engulfed. His philosophy was heavily Eastern influenced, but he was entirely conversant in capitalism. This guy was a "zentrepreneur."

A couple of the quick memories of this walk and leave it at that (my mind is too full to do otherwise): MZ took Republic of Tea to the limits (and he seemed entirely serious): TRoT, the Movie; TRoT the Retail Chain; TRoT a new model company with new forms of ownership, governance, and collaboration (don't understand entirely). Lots of vision. I wondered if it was past success that enabled someone to think so big.

Still, I didn't feel entirely comfortable about bringing up those lingering questions about structure. I didn't know what I wanted or what he wanted. Does he want to run this thing? Or does he want me to? Is he willing to put up the money, or does he expect me to raise it.

Next Day.

Bruce Katz (who I had met at the April SVN meeting; he's the founder of Rockport shoes, and, like Mel, sold his company and left it for the new owners to run) came over to the Zs' house. Mel and Bruce are good friends and like to bat it around in the idea department. We talked tea with Bruce and he returned the favor with a barrage of great suggestions (network marketing tea parties, wholesale distribution strategies, product ideas) and we quickly appointed him Minister of Big Ideas. BK seemed to like the tea idea. We even showed him some of our letters. Spent the better part of the afternoon in the kitchen working on product development and experimenting with some of the samples I had brought along. Hit of the day was the creation of Passion Fruit Peppermint iced tea, one of our first inventions.

Sam and Zio are enjoying themselves. Zio was into trucks (Minister of Distribution) and Sam was into eating (Minister of Peas). Patricia has been sketching ideas and has an amazing ability to translate the complex philosophical charm of this idea into a warm and enticing graphic. I'm awestruck by her ability to communicate ideas in her work. Faye is becoming a brewmaster too.

Third Day. Digging through the closet in MZ's study to look through the archives of Banana Republic. Sat for hours reading catalogue after catalogue. Chuckling a lot, but really serving as a sponge to soak up the art of this business. Learning from the masters. (Couldn't help but notice all the awards hanging under the stairwell in a storage room for "Best Catalogue" etc. from the Direct Marketing Association.)

Still in the research mode. How are we going to make this thing more than a dream? Whose move is it? — **Bill**

THE MINISTER OF LEAVES

5 May 1990

Dear Progress & Family,

The Prime Minister and The Minister of Enchantment join me in wishing you a hearty farewell. Your visit has brought a new lightness to all of us. The teas we shared will long be remembered. My only regret is that we neglected to serve you Ginger Peach Longevity tea on one of our late afternoons together. Nonetheless, the afternoon of Passion Fruit Peppermint will itself live a long life as a treasured moment we all shared.

As you settle back into the red hills of your faraway province, it pleases me to think that you have found your true calling: working to show the citizens of a gulping nation the peace and happiness that awaits when they begin to sip the tasty teas of our most serene Republic.

Reviewing our visit, here are the matters and issues that first come to mind:

Our enchanting wives have rendered us the greatest service of all. They have told us what the business is really about. It is about caffeine.

The world does not need another herbal tea. What the world needs is a sensible alternative to coffee. An alternative that reduces caffeine by 75% and at the same time provides a new flavorful taste in a hot beverage. The undervalued commodities in the tea market are the flavored teas. Black Currant, Passion Fruit, Peach — these are surprisingly little known. Look at your own experience and you will see what I mean. How many of these teas did you know about three weeks ago? And yet, as you have very quickly learned, they are smashing, delicious, uplifting. Our focus *should be* flavored teas. These are: healthier (than coffee), tastier (than any other teas popularly available), and have a whimsy about them (as they should, coming from our mirthful little Republic).

Patricia and Faye are not only correct, they *embody* the customer. It will be women who drink the most of our product. With breast cancer reaching epidemic proportions, coffee is a special demon to women.

By staying focused on flavored, *lightly* caffeinated teas, we are espousing the ethic of "Everything in Moderation." We are about balance and harmony, about looking at ourselves and liking what we find. Coffee is slimy overkill. Tea is sweet union with life.

Peach Pekoe, Passion Fruit Peppermint, Blackberry Nut — these are among the first twelve treasures we will make from the obscure, vastly underappreciated asset of flavored black teas. We will be welcome on the shelves of natural food stores *and* (even if only for our novelty value) on gourmet supermarket shelves as well.

We could test the concept inexpensively in one major market, then use the results of the market test to raise a national treasury to blitz the country.

As you know, this idea is entirely inconsistent with my previous utterings. Consistency can offer only safety and certainty. There is no such thing as safety and certainty — it's human folly to think there is. So in a world where nothing is certain (except you-know-what) and nothing is safe, what I'd like to do is offer the customer the next best thing, a great cup of tea.

— Leaves

THE MINISTER OF PROGRESS

6 May

Dear Leaves:

It's about tea...

Brightest of mornings to you, Leaves, and that friendly household of yours. Although I'm still groggy at this pre-six A.M. hour, I'm full of ideas and an idea of where to start.

In response to your memo of last evening and your focus on the *caffeine* issue:

It sounds like caffeine could become a major issue of product positioning, but I'd like to think about this long and hard. I still find it a dangerous point of front-line definition for our company (in light of your sense-making thinking). . . .

I agree that it is a major issue. We must offer, promote, and focus on the specialty flavored black teas that offer that light caffeine feeling and effect. We have to meet the caffeine issue head-on—the need for caffeine and the distaste for caffeine. It would be very dangerous to promote tea as an alternative to coffee. It's one of those things people must *discover*. We have to lead them to discover it—but not tell them it. Therefore you can't position the product solely around the caffeine issue.

We also have to offer a **balance** of noncaffeinated beverages. Health food stores are going to be a big market for us potentially. (CS has made that very clear.) Also, I don't think we should be known as the company that just specializes in a particular niche. (CS has also made that clear. Did you know that they have twenty-five herbal products and thirteen black tea "gourmet" products?)

This is what hit me last night stronger than anything after I read your thoughts:

THE REPUBLIC OF TEA . . . THE MOST BALANCED
TEA COMPANY.

Balance is at the **heart** of what we're selling, and our product line should reflect that. Therefore I remain convinced that five black teas—five herb teas—two green teas is the right way to launch. This way there's something for every citizen in The Republic at any time of the day. Also we don't hinge the success of the company on such a controversial issue. If light caffeine tea emerges as a powerful idea in our balanced line—we run like hell with it. The line can grow in proportion to the success and needs of the people, but it begins in balance and hopefully grows in balance.

There's a tremendous amount of progress to distill and interpret from our intensive meetings. I'm going to take a little time out today to outline the paths we have traveled these past few days. Before I forget, I want to just document some of your thoughts in our discussion as a reminder for future topics that I would like to explore more fully in letter with you:

- casting a company
- inviting citizens to find their calling in The Republic
- If it can be done, it can be done in two weeks.

It goes without saying that we had a magical time with you during our stay. It exceeded my every expectation in every way. It just *was*. It flowed. It worked! We're high from the warmth and camaraderie we found. You made us truly feel at *home*. That's a special gift. Thank you.

More later as the thoughts abound. Now to greet The Minister of Peas with his morning potion . . .

— Progress

THE MINISTER OF PROGRESS

6 May

Dear Leaves,

I've really been drinking herbal tea only the last year or so. You've taught me that there is a "tea for every time." Now I consider a black tea in the morning or a fruit tea in the afternoon. I came at this from the herbal tea side, not the coffee side. I think our initial market is people who like to drink tea—any tea. We have to broaden the palette of those people first. Some coffee drinkers also like tea occasionally. They're the ones we grab next.

I like all your ideas about going after coffee drinkers with humor. A campaign. I think that if we imagine The Republic of Tea as a government, then each Ministry has a mission. One Ministry's mission is to convert coffee drinkers, while another's is to promote tea ceremony, while another's is to explore and promote sensual smelling and tasting products. It is this breadth and diversity that is The Republic of Tea—and a key to its place in the world. The Republic of Tea cherishes its respect for the individual. We don't preach, we don't sell. We only make the tastiest, healthiest, tea in the world *available* to every man (woman and child).

— Progress

. . . .

A vaguely uncomfortable feeling began to set in, and then I suddenly realized: The discomfort was Bill's, not mine. He was obsessively thinking the business through (quite brilliantly, I might add), but other than typing words on a computer, he wasn't yet doing anything to get the business started. Did he find the doing of starting the business less compelling than the idea of it? If he represented the Apple generation of young business mavens, and indeed he bought every new Macintosh computer as soon as it was released, it made me wonder if a generation of great thinker-typers was not about to inherit the world. I started to worry about who might be able to spare a moment away from the keyboard in the 21st century to grow my fruit and vegetables.

The whole idea of our exchange was that Bill was going to start the tea company. He wrote about it. He talked about it. He came to visit about it.

But no tea company.

Now, I am not unaware that the reader could easily view me as quixotic, if *not demented, for expecting a young gentleman he converses with about starting a tea business on an airplane at the beginning of the month to have the actual tea on the supermarket shelves by the end of the month. Perhaps a more reasonable assessment of me would be to recognize that I am a man who himself once started a business on $1500 in three weeks and got lucky. Therefore, I tend to place a greater value on ideas in the form of action than action in the form of ideas.*

That experience of founding my own undercapitalized, highly impractical business taught me an indelible lesson, not the sort one might hear in the hallowed halls of business schools: Life is not an idea. Starting a business is not an idea. It is getting things done.

This was the most valuable thing I had to say.

But Bill was not ready to hear it yet. And I decided a better messenger to tell him was the business itself, not me. Meantime, as The Minister of Leaves waited for the tea business to snatch Bill away from the computer to get itself started, he himself thought it best to serve The Republic by taking the opportunity to further explore the philosophical underpinnings that made him so excited about tea as an agent to change the world — **MZ**

I say you can trace the whole mess on this planet to the fact that we lose ourselves in ideas for living while life awaits us to inhabit it. Tea is not an idea, but the end of all ideas. With a single sip the cloud of busy mind is made to pass and the effulgent light of life breaks through to show us what we have kept concealed from ourselves all along.

— The Minister of Leaves

THE MINISTER OF LEAVES

6 May 90

Dear Progress,

Let's get things in the biggest perspective. There's you, there's me, there's Patricia, and there's TRoT. We are *not* TRoT. TRoT is not us. TRoT has come to life, and it is its own entity, a living energy separate from us. It speaks for itself. It knows what it needs to realize itself. Our job here is to get out of the way and allow "it" to be. If we can learn to listen to it, it will make perfectly clear what we are to do.

Here are some of the things I hear it telling me:

The Big Front Is: Life as Tea

Life is a teaching; tea is the teacher. The universe is in a teacup. By paying close attention, everything is revealed in tea. I myself have just finished a cup of Mango Ceylon. It has transported me into a metabolic frolic. What it reveals to me is this: Tea energizes life. Tea revives us. No person who feels as I do right now could hide any longer from peace and happiness.

The True Front Is: Tea as Community

Tea has the power to bring us together. It can make us whole within, and whole with others. It can bring us to the understanding that a community (of two or two hundred million) is a living thing composed of each one of us, and that as we change, it changes.

The Behind-the-Front: The Tea of Real Life

The sip-by-sip approach opens up a powerful insight: As a society, we are compulsive mentalizers of all things, allowing our minds to run amok over our feelings, our senses, our intuitions. Failing to accept the limitations of our minds and allowing them to go out of control, what we sigh and call "real life" is often quite the opposite: the unreality we've made of it. Sipping the nectar of the leaves frees us from nightmares of our own making and sends us off to dreams waiting to have us.

— Leaves

THE MINISTER OF PROGRESS

Dear Leaves:

How are Leaves and The Minister of Enchantment feeling about the product mix at this moment? I'd like to receive your latest votes.

Had a nice talk with The Minister of Big Ideas about direct selling, etc. He told me that he was really touched by our including him the other night. He's off to the East Coast to look after one of his new acquisitions tomorrow.

Did you know that our tiny little Sedona health food market carries eleven different brands of tea? I made a remark to that effect out loud and the saleswoman said, "Ridiculous, isn't it." And I responded, "And we're starting one more."

— Progress

The Minister of Big Ideas (Bruce Katz) brought an entirely different energy and talent to the possibility of The Republic of Tea. Like Mel, he mesmerized me with his intelligence and confidence, but he talked in very grounded, nuts-and-bolts terms. Bruce had built a truly amazing success story by sticking to some very sound and basic business principles. ("Buy shoes, sell shoes.") He could quickly cut through the B.S. of a shiny marketing plan to scrutinize the underlying foundation of a business. If Mel's vision represented "Heaven," then Bruce's was surely "Earth." I hadn't really realized how much sheer dreaming we had been doing until BK began to ask tough questions about distribution, pricing, and product. I quietly wished I could get him more involved because he offered a wonderfully complementary (and sometimes contradictory) voice to this collaboration. I knew he would push me and the business in directions that Mel wouldn't, but that also scared me a little bit because I knew I would discover more of my own weaknesses in the process. I was having growing pains as it was. Was I prepared for more? — **Bill**

THE MINISTER OF LEAVES

6 May 90

Dear Progress,

The Minister of Enchantment wanted me to be sure to tell you that she favors your balanced, moderate approach to the product line. Indeed, so do I. You're beginning to develop some sound instincts about the product line. I hope we can get the teas to taste as good as they are starting to sound.

I'm curious to see what you turn up on the direct selling idea. In the end, this may be only another tributary, or we may have come upon the *most appropriate* way to distribute our product. The more agile we are in exploring the possibilities at this juncture, the more assured our success when we launch.

— Leaves

· ·

I had that peculiar feeling one sometimes has in love-at-first-sight relationships: that things were moving so fast that I needed to keep "under control" so I didn't lose myself. On the other hand, I just wanted to go with it. I often felt that "I thought too much" and I can see the continual self-consciousness that accompanied me through much of this early exploration. I was constantly reflecting on my own search for the "right thing." I badly wanted this to be "it." Although I yearned for tea to be right for me — to be my true calling, I knew this was beyond my control. But I kept on pushing. In retrospect, I might have been trying too hard. — **Bill**

· ·

THE MINISTER OF PROGRESS

7 May 1990

Dear Minster of Leaves & Minister of Enchantment:

A couple of things to do and think about:

1.)   Please take a long, hard look at what CS is doing now. On the
       boxes and on the shelves. They are struggling to articulate and

communicate some of the things that TRoT is up to. Not entirely successfully, but we will have to work hard to make sure that the public doesn't perceive us as a copycat me-too. For instance: Much of their copy reads "for children and adults." "Try our complete line of specialty teas, including our gourmet black teas, and naturally caffeine-free herbal teas. . . ." I would appreciate it if you would both go to a couple of supermarkets and really study the merchandising and content of the competition's packaging. By the way, I think our competition initially is: Stash, CS, Bigelow, Lipton Specialty, Twinings.

2.)   Think about incorporating wine terms in with our names: Darjeeling Select Reserve, Brewmaster's Choice, Estate Blended, etc. Take a look at a couple of the typographic ideas I'm experimenting with and let me know what you think.

— Progress

THE MINISTER OF LEAVES

7 may 90

Dear Progress:

You've got our full support. Plunge in. It's a massive undertaking, but don't worry. When you undertake to follow your True Calling with the level of awareness you naturally bring to things, what can go wrong? Let's all enjoy the ride, and see where it takes us.

On another subject, allow me a thought from the Siberia of my Ginseng mind. As you begin to think about structure keep in mind: *Money cannot own this business.* Think of TRoT as a work of art accomplished by several friends who share values and a way of being in the world. This is the way it must be. TRoT is an expression of their relationship, a manifestation of their collective wisdom, and therefore it is greater than any one individual. Although a single investor might own a share of the company that is disproportionate to the friends (the investor, in fact, could, *should* even be one of the friends), he or she can own only the financial benefit of those shares, not a proportionately greater voice in establishing policy. For an investor, it would be like owning a work of art. You own it, hang it on the wall, give it to the museum, show it to your friends, take great pleasure in it. But *you don't doodle on it.*

So we must invent a cabinet-style structure, where The Prime Minister serves at the pleasure of the other Ministers. It is important that we forge new territory in the realm of structure. The existing business models do not constitutionally pay sufficient heed to the one inalienable fact of our existence: Nothing, nobody, exists except in relationship to something, somebody. I'm saying: *We exist only in relationship to one another.* The Republic of Tea must be an ongoing exploration of our interconnectedness to each other, to customers, to employees, to everyone with whom we deal, through tea and business. Any other way is business-as-usual, a perpetuation of the selfish model in which the businessman fattens himself at the banquet that belongs to all. The energy of business is money, to be sure, but the soul of business is love. A business needs both to thrive.

— Leaves

THE MINISTER OF PROGRESS

7 May 90

Dear Leaves,

It has already been a full morning and the clock has yet to strike 11:00.

My mind is full of my last conversation: about 30 minutes with Drake Sadler. It was the most discouraging conversation to date and the one it seems you always come to when you want to start something *new*.

This was the conversation where you hear these kind of things (coming from a person who is there and who has tried):

1. The market is controlled by several big players
2. There is little opportunity left
3. The field is not as hot as it once was
4. There's a lot of people already doing it
5. Who needs another one
6. Difficult if not impossible to move within the market
7. Difficult if not impossible to enter mass market
8. Very risky to get involved
9. Nothing new to be done

In a bigger context, these are the types of things you always run into when you start a new business. I guess it means you are starting to be successful with your research — discovering the down side and risks as well as the potential.

But this is the moment that separates entrepreneurs from weenies. We have to plug ahead to find the opening.

The conversation with Drake was very cordial. Said they have a lot of people approaching them about making tea and most of them aren't serious, so they try and tell you that it's not as easy as it might seem or look. Drake is a neat guy. He's modest and centered. Happy where he is. I approached him with the purchase/co-venture idea:

He has no intention of selling the company. He wants to turn it over to the employees. He says he's made a seven-year commitment to the business. Thinks he'll be out of the driver's seat well before that.

Says he's spent half his time fending off offers, friendly and unfriendly. Says that Crabtree and Evelyn people wanted to buy them last year. Lots of offers, capital, etc.

He said (kind of out of the blue) "to be frank: Mel and Patricia and you really don't bring anything more to the table for us. You don't bring more money, more marketing, or more creative resources than we already have or have had available to us."

I pressed him a little about the marketing side. He thinks that the best talent is readily available. I stopped before I asked him why he didn't use it.

So, it's frustrating. But everyone I've talked to has said a similar thing: You've got to know your niche! And a niche begins small. **We have to concentrate on our niche in a very tangible, practical, and real way!**

(Aside: I don't think our niche is flavors or philosophy.)

Drake was very friendly about working together. Said they are exploring niches too. I said we were interested in exploring flavors. He said there is nothing that you could do that hasn't already been done or tried. He said a good formulator could dissect a blend down to percents of ingredients. There's nothing proprietary about the blends or flavors. I think this is true. This is why we have to be careful not to believe that we have the secret recipe or can get it. . . . We can't fool ourselves into thinking that we are going to deliver an incredible new flavor when we're using stuff that's basically out there. Sure we can make passion fruit taste better by adding mint, but anyone can do that. **We have to be able to market it better.**

I also had a good conversation with your friend Terry Dalton *(he runs the largest natural food market in South Florida — Bill)* this morning. He said the tea area is very full, that we have to find our niche. He had an idea for teas that specifically aid in digestion. Also had an idea about naturally sweetened tea.

He was very helpful and suggested some other names of people to talk to. We talked about distribution, access. He's a wealth of info. We should get him involved in some way, perhaps on an advisory board.

Oh, he mentioned that Bigelow does a good job, but that they have a stuffy, kind of corporate approach. Is there an opportunity there?

Great guy to talk with, most helpful.

So, to summarize some of my thoughts (this is going to lead to a plan):

Niche: We've got to find a niche that is based on product differentiation if we're going to sell wholesale. (In a retail setting we may have an opportunity to create a fuller presentation of tea as lifestyle. Wholesale does not afford us that opportunity as well.) This niche and position needs to be easy to communicate and generate enthusiasm and customer need.

Distribution: We are not going to enter this business through the supermarkets. We **will** be able to enter the whole foods market by:

a. having a product that fills a niche
b. having a more imaginative product
c. your personal credibility and relationships

Direct selling is also a real possibility, but we've got to learn more about it.

Products: Our products need to be balanced. We need to be the complete tea company from the outset.

Thought: I wonder if we worked with TM and Drake if there is a way for us to make use of their FDA status with a couple of our products?

Catalogue: We must have a catalogue from the onset that sets forth TRoT to the world. It is key to our differentiation.

CONFIDENTIAL TO LEAVES:
Personal reflections on what's tough about this.

Leaves,

I share this in the spirit of our friendship and in the interest of thinking out loud in search of your voice.

At the moment I am being pulled. And unfortunately for me, I guess, and for many, its root is monetary.

I am pulled by opportunities that exist today for me that provide an income. These opportunities are real and tangible, although they lack many of the qualities that are important to me.

I am pulled by the excitement and potential of our new endeavor. I believe in it. Yet it is unproven. It offers unknown potential and unknown failure.

I like to take risks. How much risk can I afford?

I need to provide an income for my family. My challenge is to transition from my present income to my new income as smoothly as possible.

TRoT needs me full-time right now. I want to spend all my energy and concentration on this. It's tough when your head and heart have to be at odds.

This clarifies my goal: I want to develop the plan for TRoT to make it a viable, income-producing entity soon. I want to be working full-time for what I believe in. I want to end the frustration of working with my head (for income) while my heart lies elsewhere.

(I guess it's a little like going out on a date with someone when you know you're in love with someone else.)

— Progress

THE MINISTER OF LEAVES

7 May 90

Dear Progress:

The flip side of every opportunity is a problem. You may think it a remarkable thing that you've come face-to-face with the problem *within hours* of expressing your commitment to taking on the challenge, but I am not surprised at all. Among your many talents is a clearheadedness *(attributable, of course, to the tea you drink)* combined with a willingness to see. This is probably so much a part of you that you may not even be aware of it. Problems drive most people to distraction. Distraction is a way to avoid looking at what wants to be looked at. So after your sobering day, let me offer you a few hopeful words from J. Krishnamurti: "The answer is *in* the problem." I take him to mean that if you want the right answer, you better be careful you're having the true problem.

A suggestion. When you define the problem—i.e., "This is a niche business, and we need a 'tangible, practical' niche to succeed"—I understand your frustration. And I agree, we do need a niche. But is this really *the* problem? I hope you can find the time this afternoon to take a walk and look at this.

You may not want to hear this, but no matter how good yours is, the world *never* finds it easy to welcome a new idea. And that's all the more true in business. And it will be even more true in a sleepy business like tea. Who has time for yet another product, especially one that's already 5000 years old? In a society charged on replacing yesterday's gadget with today's latest, greatest technological breakthrough, not a lot of people are going to be eager at first to use up their MasterCard limit on an item that they might think was already obsolete before Rome was built.

Here's another thing to think about, Progress: Where would the computer industry be today if it focused on selling computers only to people who already had computers? I think you'll readily agree — *it wouldn't be.*

Oh, and as long as I'm rambling, allow me to comment on this thing called *shelf space.* Let's not forget whose shelves they really are. The shopkeeper may pay the rent, but those shelves belong to the customers.

So I say: Sell the customer, not the shopkeeper. It's not our job to make the business, Progress. It's our job to deliver the tea. The tea will do the rest. The time is right.

— Leaves

THE MINISTER OF PROGRESS

7 May 90

Dear Leaves,

I love this process.

We are on a path filled with fun and opportunity.

I love it when people give me conflicting advice because it spells opportunity.

I cherish your words of wisdom.

I'm going for a walk.

— Progress.

THE MINISTER OF PROGRESS

8 May 90

Dear Leaves and Enchantment,

Feel very strongly that The Minister of Enchantment is really on to something with *Sky Between the Branches*. This name *is* The Republic of Tea.

Here's an idea of how we could organize the line:

4 Black Flavored Teas
Vanilla Assam Peach
Ceylon Passion Fruit
Mango Pekoe
Orange Oolong Spice

1 Green Tea Blend
Sky Between the Branches

5 Herbal Teas
Finest Mint Herb Tea
Papaya Herb Tea or Papaya Mint Herb Tea
Cranberry Herb Tea or Cranberry Blush Herb Tea
Grapefruit Herb Tea or Grapefruit Light Herb Tea
Cinnamon Plum Herb Tea

Logic is based on:
1. Several best-selling flavors (orange spice, peach, mint, cranberry)
2. NEW flavors (cinnamon plum, grapefruit, papaya)
3. Tastier, healthier

I think in terms of naming we can differentiate between black and herbs by using a TEA PLACE for the black, and the word HERB for herb. Clear enough?

— Progress

THE MINISTER OF PROGRESS

---

7 May 90

To: Leaves and Enchantment
Fr: Progress

Some other names to ponder for TRoT:

> *In the World Tea*
> *Without a Care Tea*
> *Each Time It Is New Tea*
> *Little Bamboo Hut Tea*
> *Reach the Source Tea*
> *Upward and Onward Tea*
> *Vortex Energy Tea*
> *The Minister of Leaves Special Breakfast Tea*
> *Path of Virtue Tea*
> *Singing in Silence Tea*
> *All My Stars Tea*
> *Earth Sky Trees Tea*
> *Houdini Tea (for a quick escape)*

. . . and yet another twist on the business just phoned in by The Minister of Sibling Support (my sister).

She wants to do afternoon teas for companies on a "subscription basis." Once a month, once a week, our local distributor stages an afternoon tea at a company's offices (this may lend itself to smaller creative companies or departments (ad agencies, PR firms). He/she brings in everything, brews and prepares the tea, tea cakes. All the beautiful cups, pots, etc. are from our catalogue. The teas and goodies are served in the conference room — nicely done. Presented as a time for people to share. Could be the basis for a formal meeting or just a social event. Might be interesting to test.

— Progress

P.S. Let's keep thinking about the retail possibilities. That would be something that would make us completely different. Perhaps a catalogue and one store really works to differentiate us?

THE MINISTER OF LEAVES

8 may 90

My dear Progress,

It's always a pleasure to see your white-hot thoughts streaming from the fax machine.

I agree with you we have one winner name so far: *Sky Between the Branches*. The name works, quite simply, because it breaks form. The wondrous thing about form is that often nobody even knows it's there until they see it broken. It's like finding yourself saying "five" to the Tai Chi master who, asking how many, shows you the fingers on one hand.

And then you realize, *of course,* NINE! The things would not be things without the space between them. Just because it doesn't have a form it fills doesn't mean it isn't there. So this name does double duty. It shows us the sky between the branches and it shows us that it is our habit (form) to focus on the branches as if that's all that's there. The space between things is an exquisite thing to see. Once you start to see it, perception widens. TRoT not only gives the customer a good cup of tea, but it *shows* her how much by herself she can *see.*

So break form . . . wherever you find it. I just saw a bumper sticker that read: "Why be normal?" I'm saying the same thing. Business that's not original is busy-ness. But there's an important caveat here. Breaking form for the sake of breaking form is only an empty gesture unless the *content, the stuff inside the form,* is intrinsically special and unique. Advertising is indiscriminate in this regard. Advertising will break form if it finds that breaking form is useful to get attention, whether the product has any value or not. The advertising industry thrives on the proposition that it's not *what* you sell but how it's sold that counts. Fortunately the customer is growing up. In all human history consumers have never been as sophisticated as they are now. (I temper my optimism, however, with the thought that *materialism* is the true religion in this country, and "enlightenment" has become the cultivated savvyness to pick a product with intrinsic value. Perhaps I should take solace in Alan Watts's observation: The problem is not that we're materialists, it's that we *hate* the material. "If the materialist is one who loves concrete materials, what modern city looks as if it were made by people who love material?") Shall we, in any event, be hopeful and say that in the coming era, intrinsic value (meaning *content*) will lead us out of the darkness? Give the customer *substance.* The TRoT idea is for us to sell the tea so that the tea can sell the Tea Mind. It's important that we never forget this. If we sell tea from our own Tea Minds, we'll be happy doing it, and the customers will join the party.

Another subject: There need be no hard-and-fast rules about names, except one: Every name must describe a true experience of the product.

Here's an idea: Let's try giving all the teas, as their primary title, a fanciful name (as above), but also designing the boxes so that there is an exotic-generic description of the tea as a prominent subname. For instance, bear with me,

Space Between the Thoughts **Mango Ceylon Tea?**
Be Friendly to Your Mind **Orange Oolong Tea?**
Humility Is Energy **Oregon Mint Tea?**
Back in the Body **Assam Breakfast Tea?**
Names in another genre:
The Cup of Poetry
The Tea of Three Virtues (sensitivity, spontaneity, creativity)

Another subject revisited: When I suggested to you yesterday that the answer lies within the problem, I had an instant flash about how to "position" TRoT. Here's what I see: Why even bother to create yet another niche in a niche market? The tea market is overniched, but no company occupies it front and center. Therefore, the problem as you define it is the *opportunity.* Let's go for owning the market, not shunting ourselves into another esoteric corner of it. Let's shoot for the long-range goal of making TRoT synonymous with Tea, all tea, whether black, herbal, or green. We have the chance to do this because we are entering the business with fresh eyes, and so we seem to understand the one essential fact no other tea company has yet to grasp: that tea itself is a vastly undervalued commodity! Who today looks at the tea shelf in the market and thinks: This is a three-dollar product that's 5000 years old! So, as I see it, the only way tea can rise to its true value is for a company like TRoT to (1) find very special teas, and give people a chance to sample them, even if the quantities are limited (so it is with vintages); and (2) by charming prospective tea drinkers (the coffee slugs) into an awareness of the pleasant effects, tastes, and properties of tea, the rituals of sipping it, and the history behind it. You've been saying tea is about slowing down, and I agree. Slowing down and taking a look. You know what coffee is about? Speeding up and losing sight. If we can get coffee drinkers one-one hundredth as mesmerized by tea as we are, then we're going to have started *some* business, let me tell you.

— Leaves

P.S. The Minister of Enchantment just returned from a walk with a friend who is a target customer in phase one. The Minister mentioned she might be getting into the tea business. The friend replied, "Oh, that's great. I'm so sick of Red Zinger!"

There's a world in that remark. I think if we really probed, lots of people are sick and tired of CS teas, and there have been no viable alternatives for twenty-five years.

THE MINISTER OF PROGRESS

8 May 1990

To: Leaves
Fr: Progress

Very good to talk to you today. I consider it another breakthrough kind of day in the definition department. My next task is to set this all down.

Our trademark search came back cleared. The name and mark are available. I suggest we go ahead and file for the trademark. In order to do that, someone or some entity has to own the trademark. I suggest for the time being we form a general partnership with a handshake and file for the application under that name. What do you want to call our partnership? Any suggestions?

I've got to run now, but have much more to write.

On a personal note, I just wanted to tell you that it is amazing to me that I've known you for a month but I think of you as one of my closest friends.

— Progress

THE MINISTER OF LEAVES

8 May 90

Dear Progress:

We've got to offer loose teas from day one. If our plan is to hook new tea drinkers and take them through the same conversion we experienced, they, too, will soon realize the taste limitations of a tea bag. Everything we do must signal the customer that as lighthearted as we are about our marketing, we are *serious* about tea.

— Leaves

THE MINISTER OF PROGRESS

8 May 1990

evening time, Suma mint time, Mac portable on the kitchen table time

Dear Leaves,

I wanted to recount for you what happened this afternoon. We went to a community planning meeting at the home of a friend. As we were walking toward the house, Faye muttered (out of nowhere), "I feel like a cup of tea." We went inside, and there on the table, beautifully set, was an Oriental tea service. The woman of the house was brewing her own recipe which she discovered at a bed and breakfast in Santa Cruz. It was called Well Within.

There were five of us and our conversation revolved around tea for about forty-five minutes. Everyone had something personal to recount about an experience with tea. One woman described the special energy tea she had tasted in Sri Lanka. Another talked about Mint Tea in Africa and tea shops in Paris. Another told about a friend from Europe who brought her medicinal teas.

Our hostess today created her tea blend with tea from four different companies: Stash Peppermint, CS Lemon Zinger, Select Camomile, and Bigelow Licorice. Interesting.

• Only one person had a problem with caffeine.

· I like your new names. Perhaps we should use *The Cup of Humanity* since it is where we started. I still vividly remember you giving me that old (1906) book (*The Book of Tea* by Kakuzo Okakura) last month.

My evening tea mind is a blur. I may just go Joycean on you now . . . a bit of stream of consciousness. . . .

coffee coffee coffee people want less coffee they know it's not good for them so they don't want it so they want tea tea tea tea people need to know more about tea that not all tea is herbal that there is a generation out there that thinks tea is herbs and not tea at all. We've got to bring that little plant back into the lives of everyone and really educate the world about that evil caffeine which isn't really evil at all everything in moderation.

Tea *is* undervalued right you are. There is more tea to be had and more tea to be made. There is tea for taste and tea for spirit and tea for friends. There is a tea for every time. Why do I keep coming back to that?

— Progress

Chalk one up for the strange-but-true department: One afternoon during a visit to Mill Valley, Mel, Bruce (and a couple of Bruce's friends), and I went for a mountain bike ride along the infamous Mt. Tamalpais Railroad Grade — a challenging trail that climbs from the damp redwoods at the base of the mountain up to the sunny chaparral near its peak. Bruce set the pace and Mel and I rode alongside, chattering nonstop about tea. (We must have been pretty sickening by now, we were obsessive with the topic.) Bruce tried to change the subject numerous times, but to little avail. (I could sense that we may have exhausted his interest in TRoT for the time being.) Mel and I kept at it, insisting that tea was going to be the next big thing. Bruce had his doubts (the world runs on coffee and for those few who drink tea there's so much tea already). I'd heard these kinds of discouraging words before, but I had a lot of respect for Bruce's ability to spot a business opportunity and I was bothered a little that he didn't think much of this one.

After an hour of nonstop, sweat-provoking cycling we reached West Point Inn, a historic cabin hidden in the rustic backcountry that now serves as a rest stop for hikers and cyclists. We almost fell off our bikes from exhaustion and made our way up the steep walkway that leads to the old wooden porch and entry. I was dizzy from the ride when we hobbled in. The inn was empty and quiet. Soon a man appeared, wearing an apron. He approached us and kindly offered us not a glass of water, not a Coke, but a CUP of TEA! He brewed it from scratch, boiling the water, and serving us in china cups and saucers. Mel and I went for the tea. The others for a lemonade. Then he offered us a "Peanut Tea Cake." (I don't think I've ever been offered tea and a tea cake before, anywhere.) Here we were, overheated and exhausted, drinking a hot cup of peppermint tea in the middle of nowhere. I was stunned. I can't explain much more except to say that I took this mini tea ceremony on the mountaintop as some kind of confirmation that we were on the right track. I remember Bruce smiling at us, shaking his head. While sitting on the porch, listening to the silence of the wind and staring at the vast canyon below, I experienced "Tea Mind" for the first time — a feeling of tranquil aliveness. . . . I remember that I finally stopped "thinking" about tea for a short time and just lived it — enjoying the cup for what it was. — **Bill**

THE REPUBLIC OF TEA

FIRST DRAFT BUSINESS PLAN SUMMARY

PREPARED BY THE MINISTRY OF PROGRESS

May 1990

Executive Summary

This business is about tea. The Republic of Tea (TRoT) is dedicated to selling tea to a market that does not fully appreciate or understand the value of tea. A full-line tea nation, TRoT sells specialty black, herbal, and green teas as well as a full line of tea-related accessories. TRoT's mission is to offer a healthier, tastier product than anyone else in the market.

The Republic of Tea's message is both whimsical and philosophical and appeals to the millions of people who know (somewhere in their consciousness) that they are moving too quickly. The TRoT message is about slowing down and enjoying the moment. In The Republic of Tea, tea is a medium of communication, urging individuals to be in touch with themselves and their world. It is a medium of community, too, where the tea *ceremony* serves as a vehicle that encourages sharing of time and spirit among friends. The Republic of Tea is a place where individuals thrive because they are enjoying a life in balance.

THE PRODUCT

Initially, TRoT will offer a balanced line of distinguished black teas and flavorful herb teas. TRoT will also offer two teas specifically blended for children's tastes. All products will be available in tea bags, packaged in beautiful and colorful boxes of sixteen bags each. Some teas (including some special edition offerings) will be available in bulk, packaged in tins and boxes. The teas are named in three ways: philosophically, whimsically, and practically.

All teas are of the utmost quality and taste. Some represent "classic teas," others new tastes and flavors. Above all, TRoT teas are known for their fine quality, distinctive character, and for their health benefits for both mind and body.

The message of The Republic of Tea is as important as its product. That's why an impressive catalogue of the land's thinking and products is offered quarterly. The catalogue contains valuable information from The Ministers of the Republic as well as an in-depth presentation of all the teas and related products that TRoT manufactures and imports.

The Republic of Tea emphasizes "Tea Process" in its communication — that is, the enjoyment of tea individually and in groups and the wonderful ceremony that surrounds the enjoyment of the beverage.

DISTRIBUTION

The Republic of Tea makes its products available through an exclusive distribution network that includes mail order and selected retail locations. TRoT tea is also presented in homes and business offices via a unique method of direct selling and catalogue merchandising.

THE MINISTER OF LEAVES

9 May 90

Dear Progress.

Needs work. Try it again in the morning with Tea Mind.
Get out of the way and let this business tell you what it is.

— Leaves

THE MINISTER OF LEAVES

10 May 90

Dear Progress:

    MORE NAMES
        Rainy Season Tea   *The Tea of Inquiry*
        Dry Season Tea   *Metabolic Frolic Tea.*

                      — Leaves

THE MINISTER OF PROGRESS

10 May

Dear Leaves,

My morning Tea Mind is more of a blur today, but The Minister of Detail and I so much enjoyed your last stab at naming our products.

    We love Metabolic Frolic! It's a sure thing. I think we have three winners right now:

        Sky Between the Branches
        Back in the Body
        Metabolic Frolic

    I would very much like to name one of our teas

        My Romance

We also came up with

Mountain in the Sky

today in honor of where each of us lives.

I'm a big hazy this morning after the trek into Phoenix on other business which amounts to four hours of driving in an eight-hour trip. The drive is wonderful, except in the dark of night it's a bit of a strain. I did have many redeeming thoughts that seem to come only when you float into that right-brain driving rhythm where the world seems to whiz by and stand still at the same time.

The Disease of Familiarity: The beginning is always the most magical time for anything. It is when everything can go right. It is the time of unlimited potential and newness. It's the time for *Fresh Eyes* (another tea perhaps) and rapid discovery.

Once we've been doing something for a while, it becomes familiar. We begin to focus on what exists rather than what *could exist*. We fail to see opportunities because we know too much and suffer from the disease of familiarity. It's a killer. It not only stunts growth, in can kill a business.

In The Republic we have a special tea that cures the disease of familiarity. It's a special tea that makes the world anew. It's like seeing for the first time. But I can't think of what it's called. Any ideas, bright Minister?

I appreciated your "needs work" memo yesterday regarding the summary, but I need to study it awhile before I really understand what I'm doing. I'm going to let this one incubate a bit longer and then give it another try.

THOUGHTS ON DRINKING TEA ON A REGULAR BASIS
Regular tea drinkers — say the kind who drink a cup in the morning, afternoon, and evening — drink a lot of tea. They crave variety. We need lots of quality choices. We have fifteen kinds of tea in our kitchen and today I found them all boring. I want something new. This world needs another tea company.

Thoughts on Tastier, Healthier, Sillier

1. Most people have never tasted good tea. Lipton is to tea what early Gallo was to wine. It's a standard of a beverage that doesn't do it justice. People think black tea is bitter because that's what they get hot or iced in a restaurant. TRoT is going to tell the world about tastier teas — what makes them tastier, how to brew them tastier, and how to appreciate and enjoy the taste. Even the experienced tea drinker will turn to TRoT because we are more imaginative, and in a subconscious way this will translate into tastier. Not only will our product *taste* tasty, it will be a tasty product. Capish?

2. TRoT tea is healthier because it offers balance. A tea for every time. More subtle than coffee, less corrosive than cola, more beneficial than water.

3. This world of ours takes itself too seriously to begin with. It is through humor that true insight is achieved. It's fun, moving, and memorable. The world needs TRoT to help it lighten up through Tea.

On Asking Questions

We need a tea that encourages questions, not answers. Why is it that we go through life looking for the right answers when the secret of life is being able to ask the good question. Perhaps a tea that brings forth "Good Questions" would be a winner. This needs to be another mission of TRoT: To get the world to better appreciate the value of a good question. Perhaps TRoT could get involved with schools and offer scholarships for Good Questions at some time in the future.

On Ego

When I first got your brief note in response to my summary, I thought it was a little terse. As I was writing the summary, I didn't really like it too much, but when I finished it I thought it was pretty good. I made a mistake: I started to think that I owned the words, that they were mine. Then, if *you* didn't like the words, or didn't think they were right — you didn't like *my* words. I learned a lesson from this. We don't own anything:

words, ideas. They belong to The Republic. We are just the vessels for communication. Therefore our feelings need not get in the way of growth or understanding. (In The Republic, criticism is offered in the spirit of trust, friendship, and the desire to make things the best they can be. Not to take something away from anyone.)

In the traditional model of business, ownership is everything: ownership of equity, product concepts, ideas, etc. People are driven to *own* and *possess*. This model creates unnecessary competition and mistrust.

—Progress

THE MINISTER OF LEAVES

10 May 90

Dear Progress:

Please send the tea you had this morning. I don't care what you call it, I'd love to have some of that blurry Tea Mind. By all means, please be more blurry. I think we're getting somewhere.
Let me address some of the specifics you raised:

1. Name for Fresh Eyes tea: *Beginner's Mind Tea*
2. You have created the greatest argument yet for the reason the world needs another tea company: The widely distributed existing product lines are uninspired.
3. You can be sure that we will not only not be uninspired, we will be tastier, healthier, and more whimsical.
4. It is a splendid idea to promote Questions rather than Answers. You have really hit something here, and I can see having fun with this one. A contest perhaps. We could create some serious mischief in

the educational system. There's too many people with self-important answers out there these days, and not enough people using Tea Mind to find the right questions. I can't think of a better cause to promote than teaching kids to forget about looking for the right answers — it's finding the true question that's important.

5. Ego. Now I know how amazing you really are. The fact is I sent you a "terse" note because it said everything I wanted it to. (Have you heard the saying, "Sorry for the long letter; didn't have time to make it short"?) I can't begin to tell you how delighted I was at your response. You not only got the point, but you got the point around the point, and then as usual you launched off that point into yet another universe. Yes! Yes! Yes!

I could not agree with you more. *This business is not about us. It's about tea, and an ongoing dialogue between us and our customers.*

Drink tea and you don't need answers. But you just might get a clue as to what the questions are.

— Leaves

THE MINISTER OF PROGRESS

10 May

Dear Leaves,

I sent out a preliminary proposal for contract tea bag packing today to three possible companies. I created a worksheet for them to work with to get an idea of who supplies what and how much they charge. It will give me a starting point of real data to begin negotiating when we get closer to having our product definition stage done.

A personal aside: I talked to a colleague and friend on the phone this morning. Said she was dragging a little. I suggested a cup of tea. (She knows nothing of what we're up to.) She said she doesn't usually drink tea, but she'd try it. I told her it would make her feel more balanced. When I called her back late this afternoon and asked her how it worked, she said, "It was great!" It was a small triumph, but the simple power of suggestion can shift a person from coffee to tea in a cinch when they're not feeling quite right.

Imagine what we could do if we could just get everyone to drink one cup a day.

We need a tea called: *Get Up and Go!* A no-nonsense stimulant aimed right at coffee drinkers, but much tastier, healthier, more balanced (and a bit sillier). I think this could be a best seller.

Written later, after dinner:

I'm sipping on the peppermint leaf tea of Traditional Medicinals now. I noticed that their new packaging is really spiffed up. So spiffed up it looks just like CS. From a distance, they look like the same company. TM cost $2.20 for 16 bags, CS $2.00 for 24. Wow! Which is better?

I'll tell you one thing. Our names and packaging are going to have to blow these guys away. We have to try some really new things with packages. This is going to be exciting.

— Progress

THE MINISTER OF PROGRESS

11 May 1990

Dear Leaves,

When the moon is full it shines so brightly in our glass house that it is hard to sleep. I had a restless night — in and out of sleep — mostly out — thinking, breathing.

I'm in my pre–Tea Mind this morning, out in the studio. I wanted to discuss a few things even without the benefit of the brew this morning.

I kept thinking last night *people, process, product* like a mantra. I realized that my little experience with my friend yesterday (when I suggested a cup of tea) was an insight into the **people** part of this.

"Changing the world, one person at a time."

This is something I thought you said on one of our walks.

So then, in the middle of the night, I walk into the bathroom, turn on the light, and pick up a 1988 report from the Body Shop. Now I'm starting to understand process: "Who we are" the report begins. "What we do," it continues; and "Why we do it." People Process Product.

So, the business is about tea, but it's more about Tea Mind. It's about Good Questions. It's about products with a purpose that articulate a point of view that is enlightening in some way. It's about EXPERI-ENCE. This tea business is about *experience for people*.

How do we create the experience for people? You did it in stores. Anita does it in stores.

How do we make our product jump from the shelves, beckoning and communicating to our customer?

TEA with A PURPOSE

The message is as old as the world: Enjoy the unique specialness of *this* moment. We're saying: Do it through our tea.

Rambling onto another subject:

I have a new model of how to design our tea line: Draw a circle on a piece of paper: and make a tea clock.

The purpose of this exercise is not to assign the "appropriate" tea to the "appropriate time," but to think Tea Mind or tea day. It also might be a useful exercise to create balance in our line in terms of highs, lows, caffeine, and no caffeine, coffee drinkers, and tea drinkers.

We clearly need a high tea for tea time at 4 P.M. What do you suggest?

I'd be interested (if you are so inclined) to see what you and The Minister of Enchantment might do on such a model.

Something else I want to talk about is the dichotomy between *making* things happen and *letting* things happen.

The entrepreneur *makes things happen.* He or she initiates, takes charge, creates. I'm not sure what I'm on to here, but I am struggling with a new business model that makes things happen and lets things happen at the same time.

It's fascinating. In your letters to me you encourage me to move forward and to **make** things happen. At the same time, you tell me to slow down and **let** things happen. So, how is it possible to do both?

First: You have to love what you're doing. You have to love what you're doing without being in love with the *idea* of what you're doing.

Second: You have to be secure enough in yourself and in your position to focus your energy and trust your instinct. This tells me that the best of all possible incubator environments for an entrepreneur is a situation where his or her most basic needs are taken care of in one way or another (like mine are, very comfortably, as a matter of fact. If I had to worry about paying my house payment right now, I wouldn't be free enough to pursue the new opportunity). An entrepreneur in the startup stage has to be free enough to trust his or her own instinct.

Third: You have to be patient. You have to know how to push things along without *forcing* them. You have to be willing and able to back off when things don't go according to your preconception of the way they

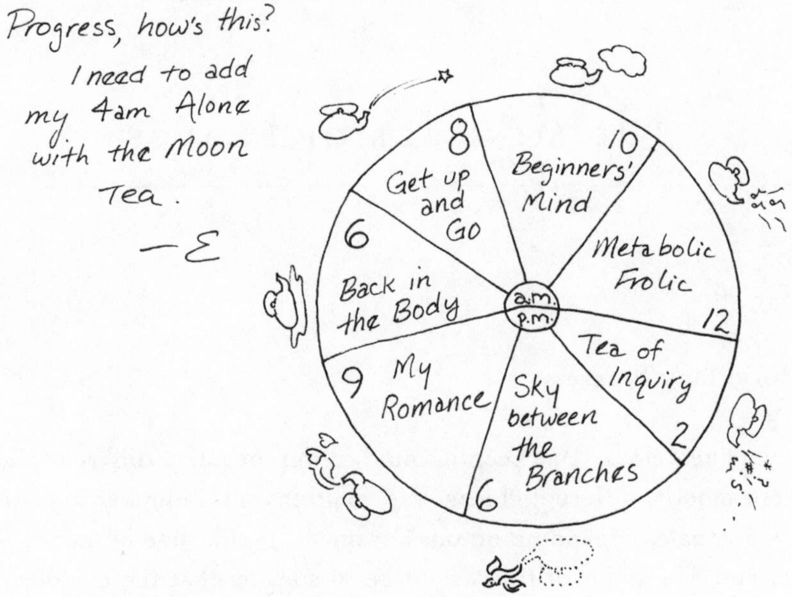

Progress, how's this?

I need to add my 4am Alone with the Moon Tea.

—E

Wheel diagram labels (clockwise):

8 — Get up and Go
10 — Beginners' Mind
Metabolic Frolic
12
Tea of Inquiry
2
6 — Sky between the Branches
9 — My Romance
6 — Back in the Body
(center: a.m. / p.m.)

should go. You have to be willing and able to wait it out — either for the next burst of inspiration or for the appearance of another path.

Fourth: You have to be willing to fail, but know that you won't.

Fifth: You have to be facile in being able to move between the practical world and the world of bigger perspective. You have to be able to dig in and then step back. You have to listen twice as much as you talk.

_____

This notion of what qualities a person needs to take an idea and turn it into a business fascinates me. Leaves, can you offer any insights to help bring this more into focus for me?

— Progress

PS. A challenge for you and The Minister of Enchantment: Perhaps you might want to take one of our winning names and start on an entire box design for it. Copy and artwork. I've got some ideas about using the WHOLE box to COMMUNICATE the TRoT vision. I'm intrigued to see what you masters might come up with.

THE MINISTER OF LEAVES

11 May 90

Good Morning Progress:

I *love* your tea clock. But keep in mind, different folks, different clocks; different moods, different clocks. We could invent a number of *suggested* daily tea rituals, depending on one's frame of mind, time of month, time of life, etc. The point of this would be to suggest that the customer try our ritual (clock) for a while as a way of finding her own. The customer can't know her own tea routine until she knows herself. For instance, if we had a tea for agitated minds (stress), the customer would first have to recognize that she was in a state of agitation, and the very act of *noticing* would begin to serve as a salve. This is the great thing about this business. By selling tea, we have the privilege of indirectly peddling awareness. Can you think of a better thing to sell than awareness? Of course, in truth we only get to sell the tea; it's the tea that sells the Tea Mind.

When I said, *"change the world, one person at a time,"* I meant that I can't change you and you can't change me, that no person can truly change another. By our actions we can only be a model for others. What I have to say to you is in itself meaningless. But if you know me and see that I have truly changed, see that I live what I say, see that I am happier and more at peace, then the change I have undergone carries with it the possibility of having an effect on you. If you want to *change the world, one person at a time*, it follows, of course, that you must start by changing *yourself*. My interest in this business is that maybe we can get a few people to do just that — simply by bringing them to tea, or tea to them. What stopping to sip tea has the power to do is make us realize that every conflict that appears to be outside us in fact has its roots *inside* us. And when we see it, it tends to vanish before our very eyes. That's the magic in awareness, that's the magic in tea. That's Tea Mind.

Finally, you ask how can I talk about *making* things happen and *letting* things happen in the same breath. I can imagine that this must be terribly confusing to you. Business is about making things happen, finding needs and filling them, making plans and following them, *arranging and controlling* things as best as they can be arranged and controlled to achieve a given end. If you look at it in this light, business is the antithesis of life. Business thrives on order. Life is chaos. Business is invented. Life happens. The fact is that, for all our hubris as business people, there is no such thing as *making* things happen. *Life happens.* And it happens without re-gard for our best-laid plans. What I mean, then, by *letting* things happen is listening. Yielding. Changing course, as need be. The ancients watched nature and they came to understand the ultimate dynamic of life very clearly in the element of water. There is no element more yielding than water, yet nothing that water cannot overcome. Try to glimpse the move-ment of our tea business mirrored in the movement of water. It twists and it turns, it yields and it gives way, always flowing. *Making* things happen is directing the course of the flow. That's what you do, Progress. But while it can be directed, water cannot be stopped. So *letting* things happen is recognizing the inborn nature of water (the tea business) to do what it wants to do anyway, allowing it to flow through, under, and around what stands in the way of its own natural expression.

— Leaves

To: The MINISTER OF PROGRESS,
FROM: The MINISTER OF ENCHANTMENT

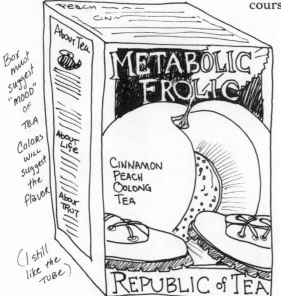

Box must suggest "MOOD" OF TEA Colors will suggest the flavor

(I still like the TUBE)

PEACH CIN

About Tea

About Life

About TROT

METABOLIC FROLIC

CINNAMON PEACH OOLONG TEA

REPUBLIC of TEA

THE MINISTER OF PROGRESS

---

11 May 90

Dear Leaves,

Do you think everyone is internally **motivated** to search out and find a path? Or are we more inclined to stand around and wait for one to appear?

Is the process of the search *making* things happen, or *letting* things happen?

— Progress

THE MINISTER OF LEAVES

---

11 May 90

Dear Progress,

The path finds the person, but not the one who stands around waiting for it.

The search *is* the happening.

— Leaves

The leaves take the water, and the tea takes me. I put up no resistance, surrendering myself to what has entered. Soon I am the tea, and the tea is me.

— The Minister of Leaves

THE MINISTER OF LEAVES

11 May 90

Dear Progress,

Try brewing some **Metabolic Frolic Cinnamon Peach Oolong. . . .** It's a happy tea. The peach drenches the cinnamon and out comes the surprise of a coconut nose. I have it on late afternoons when the sun is bursting on my symphony of cinnereria, and the cat is on my lap. We sit drinking it on the lawn in the white iron chair under the cluster of birch. It makes my light days grow lighter and my dark days disappear. I take it with milk.

— Leaves

THE MINISTER OF LEAVES

11 May 90

dear progress:

Here's the Big Key:
    The Republic of Tea is Business as Art.

— Leaves

FROM THE
MINISTRY
of
ENCHANTMENT

Matte color TOP — Green for the Green Teas
with color   Black for Black Teas
LOGO   Vermillion for Herbals

MANGO
CEYLON
TEA

TEA
NAME
?

FULL
COLOR

The REPUBLIC of TEA

METABOLIC
FROLIC

Illustration
for
each tea
that
invokes
a sense
of
PLACE,
Exploration,
Humor
Mystery
History

Caffeine Content: 3%

REPUBLIC

Caffeine
content for
ea. Tea

(should be
relative to
coffee, cola,
chocolate?)

5 OZ.
LOOSE
TEA

MANGO ASSAM TEA

MANGO CEYLON
TEA

BREWING

MANGO LEAVES

Description
of Tea &
Brewing
Instructions
on BACK

THE MINISTER OF PROGRESS

12 May 1990

Good Morning Ministers of Leaves and Enchantment,

Yesterday represented a breakthrough in product definition. The idea came together with a name, taste, words, and graphics. Now we have something that we can sell!

I've been trying to add to (y)our wonderful names list, but feel that I'm just a little off target. I submit these to you in hopes that they might inspire the *right name* which is somehow related to these thoughts.

Poetry of the Leaves
Mingling of the Senses
Make a Little Mischief
Break with Tradition (has some good marketing potential
     with the competition)
True Calling
Present Tense Excluded
Sweet Cup of Youth

Your thoughts and comments would be most appreciated.

More thoughts: We have to stress and communicate a couple of things on the package: All natural (that's a given. People expect it); finest quality (to justify a higher price); and somehow address the caffeine issue. Also, by law we have to give the net weight. We need to discuss the 16 bags (makes 32 cups, etc.) issue. A number of companies are starting to advertise the number of cups on the package. It's going to be a challenge to integrate these components in with the beautiful art.

The questions I'm addressing now concern how many different directions of distribution should we go for (at the launch, or when to enter them). In that context, Leaves, I would appreciate your current thinking regarding the media making the message visible. We need to be able to time the media exposure with the ability to get the product out. In any case, it is a given that we will have direct mail fulfillment available from day one.

— Progress

THE MINISTER OF LEAVES

12 May 90

Dear Progress

We are really getting into it up here in the Northern Province. The Lady Minister just handed me a cup of Darjeeling steeped with fresh orange peel, dried cardamom and ginger. This may be the start of
The Tea of Teas
(The world's best Darjeeling blended with the world's best Oolong, we sell it no matter what the price, and we also find a way to get it into tea bags. Even if it cost the customer a dollar a tea bag, you can be sure that she never tasted a tea like this before in her life.)
In addition to the Tea of Teas, how about if we offer at least three more super premium vintage teas in our initial offering? This part of our line is distinguished in that it offers vintage teas that change year to year. Only a fool would believe that teas taste the same from year to year. So that: Tea of Teas is a different tea every year. Limited supply. Hand-sewn cotton tea bags. On the box we identify the year, the specific camellia plant, the plantation where it was grown.
The remainder of our line are great reasonably priced teas. Since we will be known for our top-of-the-line super premium teas, the customer

will correctly assume that our popular teas have that something extra special in them.

Our superior margins and higher unit prices will permit us the opportunity to sell directly to the customer, through a catalogue.

We offer at least one Tea with a Purpose in our high end, and another in our low end. We have no middle in our pricing structure.

Something else different about TRoT. All other companies have two names on a box (brand and item name). We have three: brand name (TRoT), experience name (Metabolic Frolic) and item name (Cinnamon Peach Tea).

Finally, here's seven words more useful than a million dollars worth of market research:

If we'd buy it, it will sell.

— Leaves

The Minister of Leaves

12 may 90

dear progress:

more tea names, these from The Minister of Enchantment —
　　SECOND WIND SPORT TEA
　　EGO EVAPORATION TEA
　　CAMPFIRE CAMARADERIE TEA
　　INVISIBILITEA (one of your earlier offerings, as i recall)
　　ALONE-WITH-THE-MOON TEA
I also came up with the idea of a work tea to be called
　　CHOPWOOD CARRYWATER TEA

— leaves

THE MINISTER OF PROGRESS

12 may 90

Leaves and Enchantment:

More good names this morning!

I particularly like Second Wind (will we be infringing on Sport Tea? I really like (Second Wind) Activi-Tea, but that takes us into another genre. Maybe just Second Wind works and the graphics can say "Sports" somehow). Also, I think Alone-with-the-Moon is a winner.

I'm in complete agreement about herbal tea/tea labeling. Let's go with that.

We should be receiving some more flavor samples/ideas this week from a domestic jobber. Also, another twenty or so samples from a European company.

I think all the Ministers need to convene for as much tasting as possible. We will assemble the database so that our names are accessible to us. We've made so much progress here that our line is now beckoning to be born. Can't wait till we get together again.

What's The Prime Minister liking to drink these days?

— Progress

. . . .

If tea is the juice of patience, at this point I must not have been drinking enough
of it. The brainstorming for names before we had even decided on the teas we
would sell (that is, if we were going to sell tea at all) began to unsettle me. I
found myself yearning for Bill to stop typing faxes and start starting the company.
While starting a company is a different exercise for every company, and there is
no prescribed way to do it, writing about starting a company does not get a company

started. Taking action, not talk about taking action, is the one absolute requirement to start a business. You check your instincts, you check your information, you check the known risks against the anticipated rewards as best you can in an uncertain world, and you plunge. You take action.

By this point it was clear to me that whatever names we ultimately chose for the teas, and how we packaged them, the most important thing Bill and I and Patricia shared was our own unique style that would translate into our own unique tea business. In contemplating a new business, what more could an entrepreneur ask for than uniqueness in product and style? Whether that business will be a success or not is ultimately an unknown, and unknowns, no matter how unsettling they are to business people, cannot by their very nature be known. The recognition of that fact separates the business leaders from the business tykes. Ultimate success in business will depend on whether the business person is yielding and flexible and responsive enough to go with the unknowns as they present themselves, day by day. A willingness to see all the factors at play in the gestalt of a new business idea will reduce the risk of failure, but it won't assure success. It's that simple. Whether it was the right time to go into the tea business, what forces were at play in the market, the up side and the down side, the five-year plan, the best- and worst-case scenarios — these are inventions of those who approach business as a science, but the science of business, like all science, is slow. Business is fast. Successful business is an ongoing dialogue with change. Nothing remains the same from one day to the next. Therefore, if a business is to keep pace with reality and thrive, sooner or later the science of business must be left to chug behind at its own pace while instinct is summoned to navigate and drive the business in an uncertain world. Certainly, Bill had exhibited superb instincts. This is what puzzled me. In his heart he felt he was on to something. But his mind was playing tricks on him. Bill was suffering a self-inflicted case of analysis paralysis. He clearly wanted to start the company, but as the days went by he seemed to me less and less inclined to do so.

What was holding him back? Had his years in the consulting business, where *the actions is in* the explaining, *not in* the doing, *led him to think he could start his own business by consulting to it? Did he expect me to spontaneously pull out my checkbook and write a check? Did he expect me to assure him that I would sit at the other side of a big partner's desk and help him make all the important decisions? I could not be sure what, but there was something . . . had to be something . . . he expected to happen that did not as yet happen, or else he would have already been out climbing up cloud-shrouded mountainsides in Darjeeling to find tea gardens whose leaves had never touched a Western cup. All he had to do to get started was come up with a deal proposal, negotiate it with me and Patricia, propose how he wanted to finance it, put the lawyers to work drafting documents, and find a few investors willing to to throw a little money at him and the idea. I could have spelled all this out, but then, if I had to spell it out . . .*

If anybody shows you a list of the attributes that make up the entrepreneurial spirit, don't even bother to read to the second item if the first is not nerve. *It takes nerve to start a business. Lots of it. I started to wonder: Where was Bill's nerve?*

Or perhaps it wasn't nerve at all that he was lacking. Maybe he was just at a loss for how to turn our wackier, highly impractical schemes into reality. Often ideas that seem so wonderful in the dream phase tend to flake apart when one gets down to the nitty-gritty of starting a business. But then, if nerve is the first attribute of the entrepreneur, then practicality *is number two. It was time to probe a little, to find out if this whole affair was never going to be anything more than the clever finger exercises of two guys tapping on computer keyboards?*

I decided to give Bill the benefit of the doubt in the nerve department. Where I would make my push was in the practicality department. If I could at least get him to think practically, he could decide one way or the other about going forward.

—**MZ**

PLEASE POST

PROCLAMATION
THE REPUBLIC OF TEA

By the authority invested in me by The Honorable Prime Minister, I hereby declare that the week of May 13–19, 1990, will be observed in our Republic as "Practical Week."

Signed with full authority,
— The Minister of Leaves

· ·

Having made my edict, and before I was to lay the bomb on him in the fax that follows the next one, I felt it was necessary to let Bill know it would be okay with me if he did not create Amalgamated Gigantic Tea Company, that it would be fine with me if he created something more within his grasp, as long as it made sense. I also wanted him to fully understand and experience his own relationship to risk, and to know that both Patricia and I thought highly of him, and saw ourselves as supportive if he could bring himself to make the big leap. — **MZ**

· ·

THE MINISTER OF LEAVES

12 may 90

Dear Progress,

A few random thoughts and reflections to wrap up yet one more re-markable week:

• The Minister of Enchantment calls you a "fearless generalist," and I concur. It's even given me the idea to brew up a cup of
Fearless Tea

• I am feeling increasingly comfortable with the idea that we launch this business *modestly* for a few reasons: (1) We are inventing something that cannot easily be explained in terms of something else that already exists, and it's a waste of our time and energy to try to explain ourselves; (2) Our best shot is to find a way to take this product directly to the customers. They will become our sales force; (3) I want us all to own as much of this business as we possibly can, because this is a winner; (4) We have between us all the talent and skill it takes to get this under way, and what we don't have we know where to get, and can get it reasonably or free; (5) You need to learn four businesses, at least: tea, direct marketing, manufacturing, food wholesaling; (6) What's the rush? (7) Your list of reasons why we should start modestly, which might even be longer than mine.

• On Risk. It is becoming evident that this is an important issue for you. Things like this can be very tricky on the psyche, and I think it's vital that you tune in until you get a clear signal from this station. You'll probably find, as we all do, that the voices you're hearing are not necessarily your own. I'd be happy to listen to your thoughts and concerns on this subject, if you'd like.

• As you put together the puzzle on how all this is going to work, I thought it would be helpful for you to know how The Minister of Enchantment and I see our roles. We see ourselves as here when you need us.

— Leaves

· ·

The best perk of being The Minister of Leaves is that you have the privilege of making unannounced leaves. I decided to take off for a week at a meditation retreat to clear my mind, and give Bill some time to noodle things over so he could find his own level of comfort with starting, or not starting, TRoT. — **MZ**

· ·

THE MINISTER OF LEAVES

12 may 90

progress:

I'm observing a week of silence starting Monday. You won't be able to get hold of me by phone, fax, computer, or hook. If you have any questions, let's be sure to talk today.

— leaves

My self-defined job description for Minister of Progress had involved a lot of digging around but no decision making. I wanted to become the leader and driving force of this business, but I was still looking to Mel for the big answers like "When is it time to start the business?" After all, he was far more experienced than me. I figured that if I kept bringing in new information and plans that he'd pick one and say "let's go."

Mel saw TRoT's potential more clearly than I did. I continued to work away, trying to fill in the blanks of the company vision with logical stepping stones of facts. Then I'd try to sort them into plans. I wanted to create a plan that would please Mel. What I didn't realize was he was waiting for me to create a plan that I myself was sold on.

At this point I lacked the confidence and understanding to do the business on my own (and didn't want to), so Mel's departure was that much more unsettling. But I also didn't want Mel to lose confidence in me, so I kept trying to make a plan. I wrote several "Progress Reports." Yet, left on my own, I wondered if I could make it happen — or would I fail? I'm sure Mel was wondering the same thing. — **Bill**

The whole problem with Western civilization is that ever since the Greeks we've been trying to squeeze the mind into the brain—and it won't fit. The great Gift of the Leaf is that it relaxes the brain, freeing it to float to its true home in the boundless and the inexhaustible—the sublime state we call Tea Mind.

— The Minister of Leaves

THE MINISTER OF LEAVES

18 May 90

Hello Again, Progress:

Just getting my voice back. Have been up in Sonoma County at a Buddhist meditation retreat, leading the monastic life this week. Up at 4 a.m. to sit and watch my breath. Enchantment heads up here tomorrow to take my place on the cushion as I resume her duties here in the Northern Province in service of The Prime Minister.

A quick glance at your Federal Express package tells me that there has been a busy mind at work down there in the Southern Province this week.

I'll call as soon as I get a chance to read through it . . . in between The Prime Minister's diaper changes and fleet inspections.

— Leaves

. . . .

Awaiting me from Federal Express when I returned was a 25-page "Progress Report" from Bill that was a rehash of everything we had brainstormed to date. As it contained nothing new in the Practical Department, I was not heartened. I had the impression that he had lost himself in the minutia when what he really needed to do was grasp the big picture. I can't remember what I said when I called him, but as I sifted through all the pages, it left me with a sinking feeling that he was growing more and more lost and groping for what to do next. If he was waiting for me to do something, he was in trouble.

At this point, the reader may be wondering how I could manage to stay detached from the unfolding events. There are people who do business even when they don't have to, do it compulsively for the game of it, do it because it offers a clear measure of success in an otherwise chaotic world, but I am not one of them. To me, business is something you don't bother with if you don't have to, and fortunately I didn't have to when Bill came along. (I have come a long, meandering path to agree with the Indian philosopher who said, "Nothing profits the world so much as the abandoning of profits.") On the other hand, I firmly believe that if you do have to do business, then you should do it without complaint, without ambivalence, with full mind and heart, as best you can — never allowing yourself to forget why you are doing it. That way the "how," not the "what," drives the business, and you don't get lost.

I "did" a business, was lucky enough to succeed, and left it gladly because the reason I went into business in the first place was to free myself of ever having to work for anyone — including myself. I was glad to leave because it had become increasingly clear to me that the true (subtle, tricky) path to personal growth for me would be to "do nothing," not to "do more something." At its worst, business is so much busy-ness, and I'd had enough of that for three lifetimes. Because business demands it, there was much knowledge I had accumulated, things I had to know to be successful in business, to make my way through the complexities of earning a living and surviving in the so-called "real world" (which we all know in our hearts is the "unreal world"). But I hadn't really ever dedicated any time in my life to know the knower. The point of business for me was to become financially independent so that I did not have to spend my life acting out anybody else's construct of what life is all about. Having sold my business and having left it, I had the unique opportunity to no longer live life as if it were an idea (marketing a business demands that life be seen as an idea). Instead, I wanted a direct experience of life. I wanted to make things with my own hands; I wanted to be with my child, have more children. I wanted to enjoy my friends, not for what they could do for me, but for the pleasure of who they were. I wanted to read and write and garden and learn masonry and carpentry and photography and yoga and any esoteric art that caught my fancy — all the things that cannot be measured on balance sheets. I was simply not looking for any more entres to preneur. What I was looking for I had found ("I want what I have") in a couple hundred ancient books that I loved digging into, a two-and-a-half-year-old son I loved getting down in the mud with, a mountain at my gate that held every secret from the beginning of time in the folds of its slopes that I loved exploring. To my unexpected delight, before I knew it I wasn't even "Mel Ziegler, Founder of Banana Republic" at all anymore. I was nobody, doing no business, having a wonderful time. I had made it my practice not to resist that which comes uninvited, and that is why I was so open to Bill's energy about starting the business.

However, in looking to me to fashion the "what" of the tea business, Bill was clutching at vapor. I knew I wasn't going to run the business day to day and I knew the business could never have any staying power unless Bill felt in his bones that it was his. I truly wanted to help him, but it was beginning to seem to me that the help he needed was not the help he wanted. He needed to figure for himself "what" to do. To succeed he would have to stake his all on The Republic of Tea. He had to get over the compulsion of turning to someone outside himself to tell him "what" that business should be. Nobody invents the business for the entrepreneur. That's his job. — **MZ**

· ·

· ·

Starting any business, no matter how modest or exploratory, requires capital. Like many startup ideas, this one was beginning as a "bootstrap" where cash expenditures are kept minimal and time is "managed" away from a regular job. I was doing this research on my own nickel and time, but was still in the position of having to work for a living. I needed to buy more time to follow this idea — not only to learn more, but to also discover if it was right for me.

I hoped that Mel might just "hire" me to get the business started. That would have relieved my insecurity about making a transition from my job as a communications consultant to a paid Minister of Progress. When he didn't, I had to find a way to continue funding my exploration. — **Bill**

· ·

THE MINISTER OF PROGRESS

20th of May Already 1990

Dear Leaves,

Good to speak with you yesterday afternoon. It's somehow funnily uplifting when we get to talk. I consistently seem to get a strange sense that we're on to something.

So much to do, yet we've come so far, so fast. In the interest of further progress this week, I suggest work in the following areas:

1. Tea Names/Types. Yesterday you asked me to outline the type of teas that should be within our line. I mentioned that we needed some names that were clever yet grounded. Too many *Beginners' Minds* or *Teas of Inquiry* will lead us off into the land of esoterica. As far as I can surmise, we really need only a couple of favorites (flavorwise). They would be:

a. A sleepytime, sandman, sweet dreams herbal type that says a good night's sleep, before bedtime, etc.

b. A Constant Comment, Orange Spice, Mandarin Orange Spice type of tea — this being the absolute standard now in flavored teas. This is really how Bigelow made it big-elow. They took crummy black tea and flavored it a little.

c. An herbal mint tea. Very popular on all brand fronts (mind medley, mostly mint, etc.).

d. A Morning Thunder — clearly a get-up-and-go type of morning. Breakfast tea is perhaps too English, Morning is too limiting?

e. Something lemony and zingy. Lemon is a very popular flavor too. The Zinger part of this really seems to turn people on — maybe this is the second wind, wind in your sails, etc.?

So, meditate on this for a while and see what comes up.

2. I mentioned to you yesterday that I have made peace with my consulting relationship, upping the monthly ante (on their part), thus resolving some of my frustration and conflict about working in two places. Now that I see the light of TRoT and am firmly committed to her adventurous path, I see no harm in continuing my consulting relationship month to month to pay the way for our newer endeavors. This accomplishes a couple of great things:

1.) I continue my source of income on a monthly basis; and 2.) I get to make expense-paid trips to SF on a regular basis.

In light of this development I would like to talk with you good Ministers about our Republic in its legal entity embodiment. When you are here in a week and a half I'd like to discuss these ideas:

a.) Agreeing on an organization plan which will take us through the day we are ready to SELL product. (This first stage would encompass all the design, product definition, catalogue development, inventory location, etc.)

b.) Form the company as a partnership or corporation and discuss the formal details of ownership and capital contribution. I would like to talk about the concept for me of contributing a combination of money and "sweat" equity. I think the longer I can "run" the business without drawing money OUT, the better, but I would like somehow to earn into the future potential with this type of plan. It will also be useful to form it now so that we can build a mini–track record of existence prior to our quest for credit from vendor and

cooperation from banks for things like merchant Visa accounts. . . .
When we form the company, we can prepare a cash flow proforma
that coincides with our plan and fund that plan (the out of pocket
costs) in a very modest way.

I would like to officially exit the "research" stage (per my first project
plan), clean up the books and any remaining major questions, and
move onto the organization stage.

c.) Work toward refining the TRoT logo a little so that I can have
the lettering done. I have a very talented friend who I think can do
a masterful job for little or no charge. I might offer him a little now,
more later, to conserve cash.

d.) Since we are all feeling more certain and committed to this idea,
and are beginning to share more and more of it (but in a small way)
with the outside world, I want to trademark the logo and name to
protect us. I also want to trademark names that are winners. I plan
to do this myself (file the forms) to conserve cash.

I would very much like to see some outlining, sketching, playing around
in the catalogue editorial department. With our desktop publishing capabilities we could arrive at some comped-up books very easily. We could
review many "works in progress" as we go. This would be beneficial in
a couple of ways:

1. I'm sure we'll discover new things about the catalogue by doing it
   rather than thinking about it.
2. We can use the comps as promotional tools/feedback tools to get
   opinions from valued counsel. Who knows, they might help us pre-
   sell some product. . . .
3. The feel and style of the catalogue will influence the selection of
   mailing lists — so the more focused and tangible our catalogue/mag-
   azine is, the more likely we are to be successful in selecting good
   lists.

So, when inspiration hits — feel free to let those keys rip. We can turn
that stuff into pages quite easily.

Days Ahead. I will be exploring SALES and how to make them. I'm outlining (actually refining) a distribution pyramid. I'm into this idea of direct engagement. I want to figure out how to get TRoT to be the tea of choice at the country's best bed and breakfasts very quickly. There's something magical and timeless at a good B + B. It's the perfect environment for creating a new tea experience. I want to figure out the distribution path into wholesale and explore the world of lists and which might make sense to us.

I will also be looking into the wonderful world of PRICE, and will be putting together some facts for us to ponder.

I will also be trying to crack the barrier of co-packing. I sense that a line as big as ours is getting (10) is a bit threatening. This may eventually limit us to whom we can work with.

With all this in mind, I humbly ask that Practical Week be extended by another week.

— Progress

. . . .

I was all over the place with my thinking at this point. I was trying to wrap up this self-funded research stage and was trying to establish a formal partnership with Mel and Patricia. I was encouraging them to get practical too, to move from brainstorming to producing a tangible catalogue or package. I didn't see it as my responsibility alone to get us into business and was probing to see what their level of commitment might be.

Although I was becoming facile in my letters at marketing an imaginary product, I didn't know what being in the tea business meant. The simplicity of this notion (and the enormity of this hole) became much clearer months later when Bruce Katz related a key to his success at Rockport: "We buy shoes, we sell shoes," he told me.

Inside, I was struggling to get comfortable with Mel's big vision of The Republic of Tea. I wasn't entirely convinced how much people wanted or needed

tea, and I had absolutely no experience selling tea. Although I was floundering in
the get-the-business-started department, something was driving me to keep going.
I didn't want to let myself or Mel down, so I kept trying. — **Bill**

. . . .

THE MINISTER OF PROGRESS

May 1990

Dear Ministers of Leaves and Enchantment,

Faye and I have just returned from a wonderful 24-hour getaway up the
canyon near Oak Creek. We stayed at Garland's Lodge, a magical little
place. The highlight of our getaway was a spectacular hike we took
yesterday afternoon, trekking for four hours up a trail, climbing 1700 +
feet to the rim of the Oak Creek Canyon. We traveled through varied
geologic zones from canyon, to sandy desert, to dense pine forest. The
wildflowers are in full bloom, fragrant and colorful.

As we reached the rim, tired and out of breath, we leaned against
a beautiful tree and at that moment a new Republic of Tea product was
born:

Vanilla Through the Pines

It felt like a breakthrough as the name, flavor, and package concept
melded in our minds. We're busily preparing a package to share this with
you. Hope you like it. It has a certain similarity in tempo with *Sky Between
the Branches*, but has a flavor and fragrance all its own.

After we sat in silence on top of a lookout rock high above the cliffs
of the canyon, we ran all the way down the trail to the lodge. It was
quite a day.

— Progress

THE MINISTER OF PROGRESS

22 May 90

Good morning Leaves,

The sun is so low and so bright this morning that it burst in my bedroom window unannounced and with a surprise said "this is the best time of the day."

I've been thinking a lot about SALES and CUSTOMERS and have been working toward defining our customer. (I know first off that WE are our Customers, but who are WE? I also know that a lot of people are not WE, THE CUSTOMER.) I remember you telling me that at BR you never thought about this, but indulge me for a few minutes and perhaps jump into this game. It is a practical exercise leading up to a marketing plan.

Do our customers like to read? and if so, what do they read? What books, what magazines?

Do our customers like to travel? if so, where and how?

Do our customers like to cook?

Do our customers seek enlightenment or insight? or a retreat from life? Do they seek wisdom and understanding? Do they want to have a good time socially with friends? Do they have a sense of humor?

What does our customer value?

Which leads us to some important questions which we've asked once or twice before:

What business are we in?

The tea business
The beverage business
The entertainment business
The human potential business

I guess the answer depends on who's asking the question.

The reason I bring all this up is that I've been thinking about how to target our customers directly. **Direct Engagement.** How can I reach potential customers in a very personal way? What I'm getting at is that we have many customers. But we must reach out to each one of them in their own language. PERSONALLY. The Republic of Tea is a personal place. The challenge: HOW do we do this in an economically viable way?

It's clear that we need to break form in direct mail. (This is why a list broker probably won't be able to figure this out for us.) In our immediate target market (the United States for now) where are the tea drinkers and would-be tea drinkers and how do we reach them? Not just how do we get their names and addresses, but HOW do we REACH them. HOW DO WE ENGAGE them directly. HOW DO WE GET THEM TO BUY FROM US OVER AND OVER AGAIN?

Enough shouting. This world of marketing is about building bridges to people. Identifying a need, creating a solution, and then building a bridge to deliver the solution. In a very practical way, I am now going to concentrate on answering this question:

Who needs us?

— Progress

THE MINISTER OF LEAVES

---

22 May 90

Dear Progress:

Maria is entertaining The Prime Minister at this very moment, and I will take the opportunity to send on some reflections.

You have fallen into a treacherous booby trap when you say "I also know that a lot of people are not *"WE, the customer."*

This is the trap into which many businesses fall. By definition, it creates a *boundary* between the business and its customers. It signals the possibility that the business has something to sell that the customers may not have any use for. Since *need* is today so infrequently the criterion for whether a product is sold or purchased, it's no wonder that this booby trap has become so prevalent. The entire "marketing" profession has grown up to fill the trap. We are in the fortunate position of actually liking what we sell, and this makes us feel that the customer *ought* to have a use for it, but even that doesn't matter. Whether we like what we sell or not, whether the customer truly needs it or not, the formulation that *We-are-not-the-customer* obligates a business to cajole, charm, scare, trick, hype, or fool the customer any way we can into buying what it sells. So I say: Be the customer, not the seller. Approach business from the standpoint of the customer's needs, not yours. And all else will follow.

What I mean is this: We are every person who drinks tea, or would drink tea if he only knew what tea held in store for him. We are even the customers we don't particularly relate to.

It's true that the customer I relate to will most likely understand my product better than the customer that I don't relate to, but if I *try* relating to the latter, I'll do just that — *try* rather than relate. We're selling tea from an inner passion. Passion is something that everyone understands. To funnel that passion into slick messages intended to second-guess customers we can't relate to could have only one effect: Less respect for the customer, loss of dignity for ourselves.

By asking the wrong questions you will get the wrong answers. So it's not "Do our customers like to read, travel, cook, retreat, laugh, reflect, etc?" That is approaching it as if the customer is not you.

The question is "Does tea heighten my awareness and enhance the experience of whatever I like to do?"

— Leaves

THE MINISTER OF PROGRESS

22 May 90

Dear Leaves,

I'm afraid that I've not expressed my morning notions clearly with respect to CUSTOMERS THAT ARE NOT US. While wearing my practical hat I am ruminating on the HOW of engagement. I know what magazines I read. I know what kind of things you like in your home. I know that there are customers out there who our product is right for who need to be engaged in a different way than I do. It's not we *are not the customer;* it's *different approaches for different folks.* That is what I'm getting at and am trying to determine the different approaches to direct engagement for people who are not me.

My goal is to avoid the big marketing booby trap at all costs. It is clear that everyone is our customer, but everyone requires a personal touch. In your words, we must break form and out of this meaningless dehumanized mass market approach and reach out for the individual.

Anyhoo, thanks for your response. I got your point, and I concur. I have no intention of ever trying to sell something that people don't need.

— P

THE MINISTER OF PROGRESS

24 May 90

Good morning dear Ministers of Leaves and Enchantment:

First off, welcome back, Enchantment. I'm sure there were a couple of happy Ministers yesterday when you arrived back home. . . .

Getting into Business

I wanted to let you know that I'm thinking about creating a little tea stand in the Sedona Arts Center. Please contribute your thoughts and suggestions to this preliminary sketch of ideas:

My goal is to show them that tea will be an excellent way to:

a. raise money for the Arts Center in a steady way
b. draw more attention to the Arts Center in uptown Sedona
c. get more visitors to tour the exhibits

My secret ambition is to gradually make Sedona the tea capital of the world (or at least of this country). It will be the home of our tea movement. It will be here that the message of The Republic of Tea emanates from. I can imagine doing this is a very low key, grass roots, simple way to start.

I envision some kind of a roadside tea hut that sits in the front land of the Sedona Arts Center (SAC), just off the main road where 1000s of visitors walk and drive every week. We'll create a beautiful, exotic hand-made sign that advertises The Finest Iced Tea in the World. Then there will be a section where we can hang the names and flavors of the tea being served that day. During the summer we'll serve iced tea and if this is successful we'll continue with an afternoon tea in the fall, once a week or so.

This will be a fantastic place for us to:

a. test-market our products
b. gather names for our lists
c. begin to sell our product with little initial effort

Please rustle up those imaginations of yours and help me refine this one.

— Progress

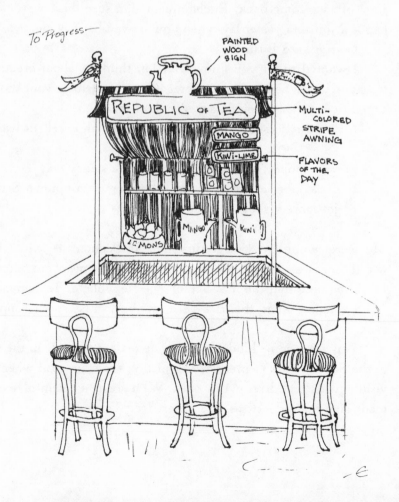

There are very few letters from me in this period because I was becoming more and more troubled by Bill's unwillingness to grapple with the real issue of whether he wanted to be an entrepreneur or not. And if he did want to be an entrepreneur, whether or not he wanted to start the tea company. In our conversations and letters he seemed to be shrinking from the big idea, growing a bit dispirited, running in circles looking for something he could do instead of doing what clearly needed to be done. I thought the idea of a little tea stand outside the Sedona Arts Center was absurd. One does not need to be a financial genius to reason that selling a few cups a day of tea at a dollar apiece to promote a business that does not yet exist was a quick way to dampen the necessary energy to truly get things under way.

*Bill wanted to trademark the name, incorporate the business, take care of all the formal and tangential details, but still he hadn't yet decided what business he was in, and how he was going to go about getting it into existence. He was waiting, and waiting, and waiting for something to happen, initiating nothing. The worst of it was that Patricia and I were beginning to feel his dependency on us, and clearly this is not what we wanted. We could see that if he set himself in the right direction by moving into the center of the gathering storm, not away from it, he had the necessary intelligence, stamina, and flexibility to succeed once the business began to impose its own agenda on him, as we knew it quickly would. We wanted to encourage him to realize his desire to get there, to empower him, to be of some practical help with contacts, money, a few ideas. But Bill was so wrapped up in the idea of a partnership with us that he seemed unable to face squarely the true nature of the relationship we were offering. I was pulling for him, but at the same time I was resolute that I would do nothing to influence him into a decision that we might both later live to regret. If he had it in him, he would do it. The process would reveal that to him in a much more true and lasting way than I would by playing God and telling him so. I decided not to acknowledge his ambivalence, but to continue addressing what I saw as his abundant potential to be a successful businessman. —**MZ***

THE MINISTER OF LEAVES

---

24 may 90

dear progress:

You will have to rely on your own instincts on the Lemonade Stand plan. The idea certainly has a powerful charm, but in terms of how it rates in energy = reward equation, it would not be for me to say. What's most important here is your own comfort level. You have to go into this business in the way it wants to take you. Keep in mind that numbers are the key to the door of a new business, no matter how good or sound the ideas. Money is the energy of business. Sooner or later if it doesn't start to flow, the idea is going to sputter and quit on you.

—leaves

THE MINISTER OF PROGRESS

---

25 May 1990

Dear Leaves and Enchantment,

It's been another turning-point Friday. Here's what we accomplished today:

1. Got our first wholesale customer
2. Got our first retail customer
3. Positioned TRoT at the center of an important actual tea *experience*

4. Entered the business in the bulk side of tea with minimal investment
5. Created a built-in test market for our product
6. Accomplished all this in an altruistic win-win partnership with the city's largest and classiest organization, the Sedona Arts Center.

Best yet is that we accomplished all of this on a shoestring and with lots of support and enthusiasm from our potential customers. I expect that after we buy our inventory, bags, and labels, we'll be turning a profit in a very short time.

I was amazed at how engaged the people became with the Art of Tea. I let *them* come up with the ideas: "Why don't we sell it in the store — we could do a whole special section about tea. Could you do gift baskets?" "We could commission some of our artists to do ceramic tea sets." "We could have artists do portraits and paintings during the teas." "Our board member could serve as a host and brewmaster at each tea." And on and on.

This also gives us a fantastic opportunity to roll out different teas steadily and get good instant feedback on them. We don't have to introduce a full line, just keep adding flavors (and refining them from the feedback). . . .

Basically, they are now committed to making "The Tea" their calling card . . . working toward becoming the social focal point of the week and of the community. We're right in the center of it.

I'm actually kind of shaky right now (with a nervous excitement) because this means WE ARE IN THE TEA BUSINESS and we are definitely on to something.

— Progress

THE MINISTER OF PROGRESS

26 May 1990 3:47 am

Dear Leaves and Enchantment,

It's fruitless to try and sleep tonight because my heart and mind are racing into the tea business. The night air is incredibly sweet; I can actually smell the Vanilla Through the Pines from the deck of my studio tonight.

I am starting to think very practically even at this wonderful hour of stars bright in the sky. To begin our bulk business we have three flavors right now:

> Metabolic Frolic Cinnamon Peach Tea
> Mango Pekoe Tea
> Passion Fruit Mint Tea

I think I'm also close on two herbals. I think I've got Deep Sleep down. I'm also working on this Well Within recipe that I liked so much. This, of course, is to be tested and agreed upon next week, when you are here. Aside: After drinking the real thing, the herbals are really wimpy. The only ones that are really flavorful are the ones with lots of artificial natural flavors like the CS Country Peach. They basically use the herbs as a carrier for the flavors. Natural herb teas are pretty bland/light, except for mint. . . .

MY COMMITMENT TO US.
I am committed to making this business profitable from day one. We will sell our products at a margin and quality level that allows us to make a profit from the beginning. We are going to start small but will always weigh the reward vs. time/effort issues.

It's now about 4:30 A.M. and my head is a bit heavy. I'm glad I seized this quiet moment to record some thoughts. I feel like I have much more to express and write down, but my eyes are falling fast. Please write when you have the chance. I want to know your thoughts and questions to this emerging path. We have much to brainstorm and much to be practical about.

— Progress.

THE MINISTER OF LEAVES

26 May 90

Progress:

How about

Romancer Enhancer
Passion Fruit Peppermint Tea

— leaves

P.S. My comment on the path you've chosen to launch the business: Your enthusiasm is its own confirmation. Listen to it.

In each leaf is its potential, its own unique flavor only to be realized when it meets the boiling water. The leaf and the water, what would one be without the other? As with tea so with life: only in union do we meet our fullest and truest essence.

— **The Minister of Leaves**

THE MINISTER OF PROGRESS

26 May 1990

Dear Leaves and Enchantment,

Back to Realitea

Ok, so I'm off my high of Friday and my little success of engaging a couple of local people in the sport of tea. I've got only one foot in the air now and at least one ear firmly planted to the ground. I was definitely turned on about making a sale, as insignificant as it now seems this morning. Here's what I'm starting to hear from The Republic of Tea: The Republic of Tea is a merchant specializing in the acquisition, creation, packaging, and sale of premium specialty teas. Central to our business is the idea of *tea experience* — that the act and art of making and taking tea has the potential for changing the world one person at a time.

OUR PRODUCT DEFINITION IS THREEFOLD:
1. We are a full-line tea company and offer only the finest teas and herb-based teas.
2. We *search* the world for the finest teas known to man and make them available to our customers.
3. We create spectacular blends and flavors of original teas and herbal teas that are available only from us.

WHAT WE BELIEVE:
1. That tea is about *balance* and the experience of enjoying life.
2. That there is a time for every tea and a tea for every time.
3. That tea is fun.

WHO IS OUR CUSTOMER:

1. Our customer is me, you, and everyperson.
    Of particular interest to us are:
2. People who presently drink coffee as their primary beverage who might be ready to discover the inherent health and taste benefits of tea.
3. People who think tea begins and ends with Lipton, Bigelow, or Celestial Seasonings.
4. People who appreciate quality and experience.

HOW OUR TEA IS PRESENTED:

Our teas are presented as a.) Premium Loose Tea or Premium Loose Herbal Tea; b.) Premium Tea Bags or Premium Herbal Tea Bags; c.) Premium blended tea and herbs available loose or in bags.

We believe fundamentally that *bulk is better*. It has a better taste, it is better for our world because it doesn't consume wasteful packaging, and, finally, it is more in the spirit of the tea experience.

We do feel, however, that tea bags have their place: they are portable and convenient, and it is impossible to deny that 80% of all tea that is consumed at home originates from a bag.

Therefore we have made it our goal to present the "finest teas ever placed in bags." We will offer a diverse line of premium tea and herbal teas in individually wrapped tea bags. (We also offer a "pocket pack" which makes it possible to take The Republic of Tea on the road.)

Our first step is to have the traditional tea bag customer discover our tea through tea bags, but our ultimate goal is to have them enjoy the spirit and flavor of our loose tea.

HOW OUR TEA IS SOLD:

Our long-term goal is that our products be as readily available as any of the world's most popular beverages. This would include grocery and food stores of all kinds and specialties, as well as restaurants and cafés. Initially our teas will be available direct from The Republic via a mail order catalogue and in selected retail and service establishments that recognize the virtues of our products.

HOW OUR PLAN UNFOLDS:
Our plan has four primary stages:

1. Startup and test market
2. Regional sales of loose tea to specialty retail stores and a small-scale mail order effort
3. Full-time product introduction (loose and bags), national catalogue business, and limited specialty retail distribution
4. Development of national distribution through mass market grocery and restaurant opportunities

Background and Review of Research

During our recent two-month research phase we have concluded the following about the tea market:

1. Tea is undervalued in the United States.
2. Selling tea has the potential of being a financially rewarding business.
3. There are opportunities to break form from existing competition and create a phenomenon around tea.
4. The time for tea in the '90s feels right.

With respect to The Republic of Tea we have resolved the following:

1. To start small and thrive.
2. To build the business as financially viable from the start by keeping our overhead expenses in balance with our revenues. We can do this by selling product as soon as we open the doors. We'll also maximize our use of contract resources for blending and packing to avoid heavy capital equipment and facilities expenditures. I'll try to involve

the most talented people I can in the business, mostly on a project basis, and keep full-time overhead to a minimum.

3. To learn the many dimensions of the business at an aggressive yet realistic pace.
4. To work from a plan that works.
5. To build the business along a personal path into a significant, thriving national endeavor.

The Ministers of the Republic have agreed to the following responsibilities at the outset:

The Minister of Progress will lead and operate the business on a day-to-day basis. He is responsible for assembling and implementing the business plan.

The Minister of Leaves is responsible for creating and directing the voice of the company. This Minister is also responsible for creating all copy as it relates to packages, promotions, and catalogues.

The Minister of Enchantment is responsible for creating and directing the "look" of the company and its products. This Minister is responsible for the art and creative direction of all packages, merchandise, and catalogues of The Republic.

These Three Ministers, in consort, are responsible for the creation, blending, and naming of all products, and for the creation and approval of the business plan.

The Ministers have agreed that the home for the operations of The Republic will be Sedona, Arizona.

Stage 1: Startup and Test Market

The first operating phase of the business will involve initial startup and the test-marketing of product.

In this stage, The Republic will formalize its legal form, file its trademark registrations, and acquire the necessary permits and licenses to conduct business. During this stage the operations of The Republic will be conducted from the existing office of The Minister of Progress.

Initially, The Republic will offer its products in loose form, packed in bags containing 3.5 oz. of tea. These bags will retail between $3.95 and $9.95 depending on the particular tea. A minimal inventory of tea and herbs will be acquired from two primary sources: GS Haly Co. and The Whole Herb Company. Packaging and labeling for the test-market phase will be done at the Sedona office.

The Republic has entered into a relationship with the Sedona Arts Center (as its first customer) whereby SAC will purchase product to be served at a weekly social tea and at other fund-raising activities. SAC will also sell TRoT tea and catalogue products in the SAC gallery gift shop. TRoT will be involved in supporting this endeavor (on a creative basis) in exchange for key information and feedback regarding the reception of its products.

When a tea blend has met the approval of the Cabinet Ministers, it will be made officially for sale to the general public.

At first we will build a small distribution of local Sedona stores including:

1. The Sedona Market
2. Elson's Kitchen and Gifts
3. The Atrium Cooking Store
4. The Pottery Store
5. The General Store Gift Shop

We will also try to place our loose tea at the Hidden Garden Restaurant which presently hosts an afternoon tea.

These outlets will be considered our local test market.

From the beginning we will use the printed word to convey our message. We will offer a minimal mail order catalogue (by request on the back of our bags) that will make available the *complete* line of TRoT products. It is anticipated that our retail outlets will carry a portion of our line. It is unlikely that they would stock the entire line from the onset, although this will be a goal. We will always make *all* of our teas available by mail.

During this phase it will be our goal to:

1. Develop and refine 15 names and flavors of tea, including 10 that will be suitable for bagging at a later time.
2. Fund the out-of-pocket costs of the startup phase through sales to our test market.
3. Develop and refine the voice and look of The Republic and its products through our packaging and communications.
4. Continue to explore the sources for products and co-packaging services and develop the details of Stage 3 of this plan.
5. Remain low key about the Zs' involvement in The Republic.

It is anticipated that the startup and test-market phase will require two to three months of effort.

Stage 2: Regional Sales, Catalogue Startup, and Specialized Marketing Tests

During this stage we will broaden the distribution of our loose teas to specialty retailers in the western United States. We will target specialty health food, cooking, and gourmet stores. We will also explore the potential of wholesaling our product to selected restaurants and cafés that have an interest in creating tea experience.

We will broaden our *by request only* mail order catalogue which will be used both as a sales tool to the retail trade and also to fulfill the orders of our customers who have difficulty finding our product on a regular basis. This catalogue will be self-produced. We will steadily build our database management and fulfillment capabilities during this phase.

We will also test several marketing ideas that we have defined including direct sale of product through neighborhood tea parties, and direct sale of product through the catering of business afternoon tea.

Our broad goals during this stage will be to:

1. Sell product and establish The Republic as a creative purveyor of exceptional teas (throughout the West Coast gourmet marketplace).
2. Generate cash flow to help fund future expansion.

3. Learn as much as we can about all aspects of the tea business.
4. Build a base of customers who enjoy our product and relate to our message.
5. Prepare for the national launch of our product, including co-packing, packaging, national promotion and distribution, as well as the creation of our first catalogue mail order effort. This will include the assembly of merchandise, creation of the catalogue, and testing of lists.
6. Obtain the funding necessary to continue with Stages 3 and 4 of the plan.

It is anticipated that the business will require a separate office/warehouse facility at this time.

Stage 2 of the plan will require 3 to 6 months of effort.

Stage 3: Full-Line Product Introduction, National Catalogue, Marketing, and Specialty Retail Distribution

This stage represents our national debut as a full-line tea company that sells loose and bagged teas. We will also launch our national mail order business and will begin to build specialty retail and restaurant distribution. We will look for strategic retail and restaurant marketing alliances where we can create the most visibility and impact.

It is at this point that we will maximize the advantage of the tea phenomena and the Zs' involvement. (At this point we have a successful business that has been around for about a year, if you include the research phase.)

During Stage 3 we will most likely be:

1. Exhibiting at various trade shows to build national retail distribution
2. Running an active catalogue and fulfillment effort
3. Creating unusual promotions and stories to maximize the influence of the media

It will require about 6 months to have bagged product once we make the commitment to proceed in this manner. We will initially use a co-packer to package our bagged product. Depending on volume, we may use a co-packer for loose product as well. The acquisition of catalogue merchandise and the creation of the mail order effort will take about the same length of time.

Stage 4: National Mass Market Distribution

Having successfully created a thriving mail order business with key specialty distribution, we will build our presence in the mass market through supermarkets and grocery stores. We will develop a strategy whereby we can move in steadily and assuredly first through specialty supermarkets and then on to the mass market shelves.

We will also address the specific needs of the restaurant industry through special packaging (sizes) and build our business in the office food service area as well.

If profitable, we will continue and expand our mail order business.

It is at this stage that we will also examine the need for our own packaging and bagging equipment.

THE MINISTER OF LEAVES

27 may 90

Dear Minister of Progress.

Magnificent.

— Leaves

. . . .

Finally! — **MZ**

. . . .

THE MINISTER OF PROGRESS

28 of May already 1990

Dear Leaves and Enchantment:

Not a whole lot of progress today, but I am starting on some financial projections that fit with the plan of several days ago.

    A couple of things to mention:

•   I found a husband and wife who import Yi Xing clay teapots from China. They are a unique handmade item, just starting to grow in popularity. They were recently featured in a home/design magazine and are collected by I. M. Pei and others. They are considered the finest teapot for Chinese tea. He's going to send me stuff on them. They wholesale for between $7–20 each. Could be a very interesting item for our catalogue. They are not sold in any other catalogues presently. He's doing all of this from his kitchen table too.

•   Am thinking that the first catalogue is on a big sheet of newsprint, printed in black ink with lots of copy and etching-type illustrations. Lots of story — a real feast of ideas and information. It's all Macintosh produced, but looks hand done. . . .

We're really looking forward to seeing you in Sedona.

                                         — Progress

Our visit to Sedona in the days that followed was a turning point for Patricia and me. I began to put things in a financial arena, setting some guidelines that would have to be met if Patricia and I were going to invest our funds. I knew this would expedite Bill to look at his plan in the cold light of day, particularly the ultimate dollar and cents value of his disproportionate fixation with wholesaling tea to a few local shops and the affiliation with the Sedona Arts Center. I was deeply concerned about him.

A few days after returning to Mill Valley, I sensed from our phone conversations that Bill, despite the good effort he had made at sorting things out in his business plan, was going into a tailspin. It was my hunch that he was foundering because he was feeling overwhelmed by the practical details, particularly the ins and outs of the tea business. This gave me an idea that what he might need to help him get TRoT launched was a nuts and bolts partner. — **MZ**

THE MINISTER OF LEAVES

9 June 1990

Dear Progress

Would it make sense to do TRoT with a distribution-oriented partner?

How about Lipton's? We've got the inspiration; they've got the distribution. We'll create the phenomenon that delivers the new concept for selling tea, and they'll get the tea on the shelves.

—leaves

Now I was losing it. Mel wanted me to contact Lipton, but in a phone conversation he told me he wouldn't meet with them if it meant leaving his family to get on an airplane to attend such a meeting. He wanted me to handle it. I didn't even have anything to show them but a slightly offbeat name for a company.

Impulsively, I wrote a pretty good letter to the president of Lipton anyway, expecting that it would be tossed out just after the Fed Ex envelope was opened.

To my surprise, I received a letter and a call back from their Sr. VP of New Business Development within a couple of weeks. They were interested and wanted to meet with us. I never followed up because I felt at the time I didn't have anything to sell.

I really felt like we were flying high again, pursuing completely impractical scenarios. I needed to get some objective, earthly input and I looked to Bruce Katz, our ad hoc minister of big ideas. I sent him this letter in hopes of involving him formally in the process. I wanted his brilliant, logical, and grounded approach to problem solving to help bring us all back from the clouds. I had just come up with yet another scenario, this one based in the housewares industry (selling tea-related and inspired housewares). This had come about unconsciously as a result of the unacceptable proforma forecasts for selling tea in Sedona. Another thing I observed at this time is that I was still looking to others, outside myself, for confirmation of the big idea. — **Bill**

Abba Eban once said "people of nations behave wisely once they've exhausted other alternatives." Having been exhausted by the arrogance of wine, rattled by the demons of coffee, and sickened by the rot of cola, the people of America, we are happy to predict, will soon find the wisdom in Tea.

— The Minister of Leaves

THE MINISTER OF PROGRESS

9 June 1990

To: The Minister of Big Ideas

Fr: The Minister of Progress

cc: The Minister of Leaves

Re: I could use your help thinking about this idea

I think that we have developed a very strong concept around tea. I think that the housewares design business as a core business around tea makes the concept very strong and gives it the opportunity to grow to a business of huge proportions. With housewares we can design a wide range of "lifestyle" products around a concept that reflects the philosophy of The Republic of Tea. We can apply our thoughts about enjoying life for what it is, slowing down, creating new rituals, and discovering traditions into products for use in the home.

In our thinking we have decided a couple of things:

1.)   We (Leaves, Enchantment, and I) want to focus our energies on the development of the TRoT concept and its implementation. I for one do not want to focus on manufacturing and distributing tea as the key use of my energies. Leaves and Enchantment want to contribute in the vision area, not the operating area.

2.)   In order for tea to be successful, we need to a.) have tea bags, which requires an investment in manufacturing, and b.) we need to have it on supermarket shelves, which is another dilemma.

3.)   You have to sell a lot of tea — it has to be available everywhere and the cost of distributing it has to be reasonable — for it to be profitable.

4.)   If we can get into tea, I think we can grow the housewares around it very naturally.

A solution that I see is to find the right partner to produce the tea product and use their distribution system to get it into the shelves.

From there we can build the housewares and catalogue business.

Questions for you:

How do we structure/negotiate with someone like Lipton or Traditional Medicinals who has manufacturing and distribution capabilities to get us into the tea business?

I would like to know how you might approach them with the idea (in the back of your mind) that a.) we want to control the overall integrity of the TRoT concept; b.) we want to do the housewares portion separately so that we can fund/own/license it independently yet in coordination with the tea.

I think our own primary obstacles to getting into business thus far have been:

a.) lack of desire to deal with the business of manufacturing and distributing tea through the existing supermarket system.

b.) recognition of the cost of entry into supermarkets without a proven track record.

We need to find our way, and it looks like a shortcut is what we're after. The tea is a path to the bigger concept in the housewares area.

I'm looking forward to some big ideas, Minister.

. . . .

A week or so passed without a response. Bruce called back a couple of weeks later, apologizing for not being able to respond, he'd been traveling in Europe. — **Bill**

. . . .

I was trying very hard to become partners with Mel and Patricia. I was consumed with accommodating their needs, and in the process was overlooking my own. I was trying to structure a business around personalities rather than products, and this kept me mired in organizational thinking as opposed to action. I was waiting for them to tell me what they wanted to do, and I was prepared to follow.

As my frustration grew, I generated eight different options for getting into the tea business. — **Bill**

THE MINISTER OF PROGRESS

Re: TRoT Development Scenarios

Dear Leaves, Enchantment, and Big Ideas:

I have outlined eight scenarios for getting into the tea business. After looking at them, it becomes clear that it is important for us to clarify our goal if we want to eventually be able to license the brand of TRoT into other product categories. If we look at the whole concept and recognize that the really "big" business is in housewares, then our initial goal should be to get into the tea business as quickly and as broadly as possible, while still retaining the licensing rights to our brand identity.

It seems unlikely that we will be successful in licensing if we don't have an asset to license. We need to create a national brand and then spin it off into the retail housewares business.

There is a certain inherent conflict between wanting to own and control the idea and wanting to leverage it or jump-start it with an existing company. We recognize the cost of launching a brand, so providing distribution is a major contribution to any business plan. It becomes difficult to put a hard dollar value (although we know it is of utmost importance) on the creative and managerial side.

I can't see (at this moment) a way that we can get around capitalizing our own creative group either from inside or outside. When we go to any of these potential joint venturers we're going to have to have something tangible to contribute to the equation. I don't realistically see any of them "sponsoring" or funding the whole thing.

Which of these scenarios appeals to you? And which would you be committed to pursuing? I look forward to your thoughts.

— Progress

1. Creative co-venture with Lipton

We provide brand concept, product definition, story, design, marketing, sales management. They provide product development, manufacturing, and existing distribution.

— Background:

Lipton was in the specialty tea business and pulled out about a year ago. Apparently they were in it for the prestige, but realized that the profits did not justify the cost of participating. Both Spillane and McMellville said Lipton is virtually impossible to crack and usually have no interest in this sort of thing. According to these guys, Lipton gets approached all the time from the outside. They were both very discouraging about this scenario, and about a co-venture with Celestial.

— Outlook:

Slim to none. We really bring nothing tangible to the table but the idea (and Z experience/credibility).

2. Invest in an existing company and spin off new line

This is Bruce's model to go to Celestial Seasonings or Stash, sit down with them to explore purchasing a portion of the company. Then spin off new brand with them. We would build a new brand marketing team within their organization to create the new product and get it to market.

— My View:

I'm confident that we could get a meeting with their CEO if we did want to sit down with CS to discuss this possibility. This would require some thinking about the investor group we would want to put together to acquire a portion of the company. We might be able to put together a limited partnership of investors (or investor) to purchase a portion of the company from the Vestar group.

Another scenario would be that CS and TRoT would invest together in a new company rather than us buying a portion of CS.

3. Co-venture with a packer who wants to have a brand

In this model we work with a tea packer who wants to have a brand. We develop brand and distribution through catalogue and whole food/specialty markets with the ultimate goal of getting it into the supermarket. There is a company in Southern California that Mike Spillane speaks highly of. He has spoken to them about us (at my request) and they are open to talking to us about this scenario. Here we would run the company, they would do manufacturing, warehousing. We would be starting from scratch but Spillane thinks these guys might venture something with us beyond a traditional co-packing agreement. This is a shortcut to getting into business with product, and could reduce the capital requirements at startup, allowing us to focus on the marketing and the distribution side.

— My View:

I think we could build a successful company this way, building distribution through the whole food/specialty market and catalogue first and then developing to a point where we can approach the supermarkets. OR, if we pursue this scenario we could later go to Lipton, now that we have a brand established and see if they would be interested in the co-venture at that point.

This scenario will require a good deal of capital to build the sales organization, but we would not have to worry so much about manufacturing.

4. Buy an established tea company

The only West Coast candidate might be Stash, but I haven't even checked into this preliminarily. A source says they are usually in some kind of a cash crunch, needing money. He said that their packer even might own part of the company now. I don't really see Stash and TRoT as brands coexisting in the same company. The approach is a little too similar. If we buy Stash, we would be buying a mail list and restaurant distribution and some supermarket distribution.

5. Start up a tea company and sell initially through catalogue and to the whole foods/specialty market

This would be the approach that Stash took. Here we would need to enter into a co-packing agreement and then hire a team to go out and sell the product. This would require substantial capital and the need for outside investors. We would own less of the company and it would take longer to get into business. This is the start-from-scratch scenario which would put us at a disadvantage if our goal was to build the brand and then cross-license it.

6. Go to a food company with good distribution and develop a tea line with them

Perhaps there is a successful company that would be a natural spinoff into the tea. Perhaps from the spice side or beverage side.

7. Go to a homewares (or other type of) retailer and develop a tea line with them

I can't really think of an existing company that this would work with. Initially it might be a company like Pottery Barn, where we would develop the whole look for the tea and housewares and offer it initially as an exclusive at the store and then spin off into broader distribution.

8. Go into the tea housewares retail business

Here we start up small stores of tea and housewares and create a model to grow them all over the country through a combination of company-owned and franchised stores. We create the next generation of Crate and Barrel around tea.

— Progress

THE MINISTER OF LEAVES

13 June 1990

Dear Progress:

Your development scenarios are well reasoned, but I'm beginning to get the sense we're swimming upstream when we might be more wise to find a way to go with the river.

In order to evaluate the scenarios, it's important that we all *see* our individual strengths and weaknesses, and that likewise we *see* our strengths and weaknesses as a group.

I can speak only for myself as an individual. While I love making money, I find it distracting to *think* about making money. That honestly limits my usefulness to any business startup. On the other hand, I get delight from creating things in the world. I love inventing the concept of TRoT, and seeing it to phenomenonhood, but I can't give a hoot about talking to the president of Lipton's or whoever. It's important that you factor this into the equation. It would be useful for Enchantment and you to more fully lay out your strengths and weaknesses.

As a group, we are a creative strategy team with visionary ideas and the experience and ability to implement these *creative* ideas. But we lack the dealmaker. BK could fill the role with élan, but he doesn't seem to resonate to the idea at this point.

Having said all this, I still feel that a co-venture with Lipton's is *the* way to go, but your scenario about co-venturing with a non-tea food manufacturer is also an interesting new possibility.

— Leaves

THE MINISTER OF PROGRESS

13 June 1990

Dear Leaves,

At this moment, I must admit I am a bit exasperated. I feel stuck and frustrated.

I am not confident in my ability to pursue the scenarios I described — being the person solely responsible for the business. I don't think I could sell Lipton the idea myself, based on my experience or related credibility. I would have to depend on you for some of that. But this is difficult, because you really don't have the interest or desire to participate in this part of the equation.

I guess in my ultimate scenario right now I would like to be involved in a business (a startup or existing business) that had the seed of a viable plan and I would be the guy responsible for making it happen. I would like to be part of a business structure where I could own or earn equity in the company. The key word is structure. We don't have a structure and it is structure that you are wanting to avoid in your life at this time. That's perfectly acceptable, but it does make it very difficult, if not impossible, to move ahead together in a business startup.

Structure is the thing that provides a framework to work within. We have discussed many possible structures, but I think the conclusion that we've reached recently is that you and Patricia would like to participate outside the structure and not have any real obligation to perform or commit your time within it.

The TRoT idea is so much *you* that it is difficult for me to see it succeeding without you in the structure. A housewares business would need Patricia's unique eye near the center of its structure. I love both of these ideas and can make them my own. I see myself as the guy that can make it all happen, run with it, lead it, grow it, manage it. But an idea like TRoT grew from your vision and center and it can't be handed off before it starts. I can't launch your idea without you in the structure. (Your idea includes your expectations about scale and return too.) I think I could manage it once it's going and relieve you of the day-to-day obligations, but initially, to get it going, it will require your commitment. It will require your commitment to participate emotionally and financially. Your (and my) financial commitment would be essential to attract the financial investment of other partners that would be necessary to start it in a significant and viable way.

I have been trying to get us to a structure. Any one of the scenarios I described could be created from a model that had at its core a group of talented, credible, financeable business people like us. But we have to share the commitment that we would do whatever it takes to make it happen initially. That's why it would be critically important for you to meet with the president of Lipton if I could get us the appointment. That's why it would be important for you to assist in contacting potential investors — because this is a strength (whether you want to rely on it or not) that you have more than I do. If we embark on a business endeavor we have to be willing to rely on all of our resources. I can't see how we can pick and choose the places we wish to play at the onset.

As I've told you, I want to do the tea business. I can see myself in it, successfully. I want to do it with you and Patricia. But I can't start it myself at the scale/dimension that you and Patricia want to participate in.

So, my dear Leaves, where does that leave us? I'm going to have to make some decisions for myself because my life and business are somewhat in flux. With a plan, I thrive and find fulfillment.

— Progress

THE MINISTER OF LEAVES

13 June 90

Dear Progress:

I understand your frustration. But if we look at the situation straight on, nothing really has changed except that illusion is lifting and we are all beginning to see exactly what is here, and what has been here all along.

Like you, I am easily enthused, perhaps too easily. I love the idea of TRoT. I love the idea of you taking it and running with it. I've enjoyed exploring it from every angle, and allowing myself to hang out with a lot of possible scenarios. It's been one of the more fascinating processes I've ever engaged in. I will feel let down if it doesn't get done. What I am willing to do, and if I can speak for her I think what Patricia is also willing to do, is invest in you to do it. Invest, and be here for you to bounce things off. I am willing to look at any plan you would regard as viable and do-able to get the thing launched if you made the commitment to see it through and had at least half as much money on the line initially as Patricia and I combined did.

You are most definitely underestimating yourself when you say the TRoT idea is mine. The TRoT idea is a dialogue, and you have been as significant a voice as I.

The housewares tributary took us off the map. It requires a commitment Patricia is simply not comfortable making.

I realize that at times in the last two months I showed, and expressed, an interest in involving myself in TRoT in a much more active and committed way, and I'm really sorry if I misled you. What I showed and expressed was *true* at the time, but as it became apparent that to launch something on the scale I was proposing was going to eat away chunks of my time, I had to take a much harder look at everything.

I guess I saw a situation where we brainstormed the ideas together, and then you went out and *implemented* them on your own. Those ideas might be in the business realm (joint venture with Lipton's), or creative (product development and marketing). What I was willing to offer was my support, my reputation, my money, and wherever I felt so inclined, my direct help — making introductions, writing some copy, sitting in on some meetings, etc. — but I'm clearly not comfortable with making any promises in the latter (direct help) area. But this doesn't seem to work out in the picture you had. Maybe that's partly because there were times during the process I raised your expectations, or, more likely, you really want a working partner.

One final point: You said that financial capability is "part" of being a good dealmaker. I agree with that, but in my mind it's the smaller part. The bigger part is imagination.

Bill, you're right about one thing when you say "When I'm without a plan, I get stuck." So I have two words of advice for you. **Write One.**

— Leaves

THE MINISTER OF PROGRESS

13 June 1990

Dear Leaves,

After I wrote all of that stuff out to you today, I went out for a ride with Sam and got a burst of an idea for A PLAN.

Sorry I had to dump all that stuff, but it was getting me stuck. I have a much better understanding of the way IT IS now and what I can do about it. I don't feel you misled me at all. I just feel that it has taken a good bit of time to arrive at the balance and practicality of our ideas. I think it has been a challenging process for you and Patricia too, to resolve your feelings about being involved in business at this point.

I am going to work on the new plan for a couple of days and then see how it sits. I can tell you one thing: this idea will not let go of me.

— Progress

· ·

Our interaction quieted and cooled. No letters, an occasional phone conversation. I thought it was just time for me to be alone with tea and stop talking about it. I had to stop trying so hard.

I turned my attention to more pressing matters (which concerned generating an income for my family). A wise friend suggested that maybe The Republic of Tea was better left as a fondly noodled idea, and was not meant to be a business, a notion that both troubled me and comforted me. I put the tea idea in my back pocket (it wouldn't go away), and concentrated on my consulting activities. During a trip to San Francisco in late June 1990 I met with a friend and business associate, Clement Mok, a very talented graphic designer who, at the time, had a two-year-old design service business that was growing like crazy. We used to trade stories about the challenges of running a small business. Clement had reached a point where he didn't want to build the business all by himself anymore and told me he was looking for a partner to help him. I told him that I was interested in figuring out how to take the skills I had learned in the design service business and transform them into a product business. We talked about our mutual desire to build a business with "equity," like a product or brand.

Within several weeks Clement and I were seriously discussing becoming business partners. On July 15 I began to help Clement better organize the design studio. We also planned to collaborate in making and marketing products. The Republic of Tea could be the first of those products.

I wanted to get Clement involved and bring the idea under the wing of our

new partnership. I envisioned a wonderful collaboration between Mel, Patricia,
Clement, and me. The next letter to Leaves came about a month later. I wanted
him to know that I hadn't given up. — **Bill**

. . . .

THE MINISTER OF PROGRESS

16 of July 1990

Dear Leaves,

This morning was one of those perfect starts: cool, clear, still air. A
flowery cloud bursting with pink sunrise. Birds, birds, and more birds
singing. I looked out our bedroom window and saw a huge yellow/green
balloon — coasting on hot air over the red rocks of Sedona.

I'm still working on a plan to get us into the tea business. I've also
been working on a *way of working* that invites your participation, but is
not dependent (on a day-to-day basis) on it.

I envision a way of working where you have the opportunity to
review everything at its key point of development and, most important,
to express the voice of the business as completely as your inspiration lets
you. I will carry the ball, make the progress, handle the day-to-day.

I want to apologize to you if some of my last letters have been abrupt.
I was reacting to my disappointment about your decision not to be a
working partner and my frustration about not finding a point of entry.

I think I have one now. The most basic way to begin is with sensational bulk tea. I mentioned 10 flavors initially, but my list is growing
and I see 20 or more initially. We will sell by mail, via an imaginative
catalogue that will be our story and design. Our initial package will be
an interesting box with some kind of natural handle (à la Chinese food

container) and a storybook attached to the handle. The storybook tells about the tea. One box for all teas; one storybook for each tea. The storybook is a version of the stuff that is in the catalogue, but more.

I have started to work with Clement to extend many of Enchantment's sketches and ideas into being. We are in the early comp stage on some of these things. In about ten days I want to show you our progress on the logo, package, and look for your and E's input and direction.

We will do a couple of test mailings of a small catalogue and some space ads in catalogue shopper sections of magazines like *Utne Reader* to begin to develop a list. The company will not be burdened with any operational overhead. We will fulfill orders when they come in. We will invest in a modest startup inventory. We will make money via our gross margin. We will let it grow slowly. We'll put our very best into it and do it right. That will create its own pace and course.

I will continue in my post as The Minister of Progress, overseeing the day-to-day operations. Fulfillment, mailing, etc. will be handled initially by making efficient use of existing resources (space, people, equipment) in the SF office. Only when TRoT can afford it will it have any people/overhead expense of its own.

As you can see, this is a bootstrap method. It is also the purest and simplest way of doing the TEA. I have realized that I must stop talking about it and just do it. So I am. I am willing to go for this seed stage with my own capital. I would like you to be involved in whatever way feels best to you. If you want to put your money in, that would be great. I envision sharing the company with you equally. I will share my part with the people that are going to assist me.

So, Leaves, you've put the idea in my hands. I want you to trust me. I am looking out for you and your interest in a lifestyle unburdened with day-to-day business commitments. I do feel that we can accomplish this and have a great deal of fun bringing The Republic of Tea into being. We have nothing to lose and the world has a lot to gain.

—Your friend Progress

When we pour Tea we must go with the flow.

If we pour too tentatively, the tea will dribble down the spout.

If we pour too hastily, much tea will be spilled and wasted.

THE MINISTER OF LEAVES

16 July 1990

Dear Progress:

So you have resolved to jump into tea and fall with the leaves, wherever they will.

So begins the odyssey of a young Zentrepreneur. May good fortune be with you. There will be many dragons to slay along the way. The mind will see to that.

You are entering a business in a way that very few do. You are entering a business because *you* need the business, and because it *needs* you. Your challenge will be to hold the course steady to *needs* — yours, the customers', the employees', the partners'. I can tell you only one thing about *needs*. They are not imagined. They are real. Imagined needs are disguised wants.

You are proposing for me to be of, but not in, the tea business. As you know, before my present unsayable existence, I was in, but not of, the clothing business. Life has a wonderful symmetry.

Enchantment and I will give careful consideration to whether, and how, we might join this most salutary enterprise, and would be happy to take a walk with you when you arrive here.

— Leaves

. . . .

Several weeks later my family and I moved to Mill Valley, California, and I began my new job in San Francisco as president of Clement Mok Designs. — **Bill**

. . . .

One Year Later

JULY 1991

A year had passed since my last letter to Leaves. I had spent a busy eleven months with Clement Mok Designs, developing marketing programs and materials for clients. Although Clement and I hoped to get the tea company going during this time, our casual efforts amounted to nothing. Neither of us had the time or the energy to make it a priority given our other responsibilities running the design firm. We tried to get some logo and packaging going for the tea, but the pressing needs of the studio always took precedence and we made little progress.

Yet even after a year of not doing much about The Republic, the idea was still very much alive in me. I grew discontented and unfulfilled producing marketing projects for other companies and began to spend more of my mental energy figuring out how to get into the tea business.

It was reassuring to me that I still had a strong desire to pursue tea. It was a confirmation — a test of myself to see if I could sustain interest in the idea. (It was important to me that this was no passing fancy.)

When I began my journey with the good Ministers many months earlier, I saw myself as their apprentice. I was looking to them to lead the way. I was comfortable being the "doer," the implementer of the ideas, but was not prepared to lead the idea into being.

In the course of that year I faced two personal obstacles: I never really felt like the idea was mine. I was still an outsider to it. Mel had told me many times that none of us owned the idea, but I needed to "own" it if I was going to lead it. And I was still looking to others to help me get the tea business going, if not with Mel and Patricia as full partners, then with Clement. These were slowing me down. But the real impediment, I slowly realized, was a formidable professional barrier I'd created between the business and me. It dawned on me that this business was much more than putting a better label on an existing product.

Most of what we had done during our correspondence the previous year was to invent the presentation of the tea product. We'd spent a lot of creative energy developing a new way to sell an old product. We knew that America could come to appreciate huge amounts of fine tea if we could provide the proper education. We dreamed up the product names, packages, and promotion. We defined the values and vision for the business and we invented a personality and position for the product, but I failed to look squarely at one key fact on which everything would ride: There was no product until I went out and found it.

As a marketing professional schooled in the media-blitzed business climate of the '80s, I had lost site of *content*. I had become a product of my own attention to presentation. I came to believe my own claims of "newer," "faster," and "better." Ironically, it was this very tendency toward the sensational and superficial that fueled my growing distaste for "marketing." After all, the heart of our new tea business was supposed to simply be about making finer quality tea (healthier, tastier) available and appreciated in America. Somehow I had lost sight of this primary purpose amid all of our creative "marketing" ideas. What I found appealing about selling fine tea was that it just was truly superior to what most people were used to drinking. It didn't need a gimmick.

So finally the missing piece exposed itself: my lack of product expertise. The only thing standing in the way of this idea becoming a business was that The Minister of Progress had failed to realize that it was he who must carry the portfolio of The Minister of Product.

In whatever time I could find I set out to acquire product knowledge. I learned to taste tea from an old-time tea broker. (We'd line up dozens of "pots and cups"—the utensils the tea trade uses to judge teas and sample ten China Keemuns or a dozen Indian Darjeeling's side by side.) I learned to taste the difference between a first flush and a second flush Darjeeling. (The first flush, harvested in the early spring, not unlike a Beaujolais wine, has a brighter, more flowery taste than the mellower, familiar second flush.) I began to understand how climate, geography, and cultivation came into play in the taste of a particular tea. I developed an appreciation for the complexity and medicinal properties of the leaf; I also learned how water quality and brewing time can affect the taste. Soon I started to understand the various buying seasons, the system of grading, and the way tea is priced.

Once I began my education into the product, I started writing to Leaves again, but my expectations of him were now different. I stopped waiting for him to lead the way into the tea business because it was finally clear that if I didn't start it, no one else would. And I really wanted the business started.

It had taken more than a year, but I finally began to see a complete picture of the tea business: the product, the need for the product (I saw a lot of gulp-by-gulping going on in the design office and my clients offices), and lastly, the presentation of the product.

My confidence was growing, but my fears lingered, as I moved back, closer to tea.

— **Bill**

The first cup moistens my lips and throat; the second cup breaks my loneliness; the third cup searches my inmost being . . . the fourth cup raises a slight perspiration—all the wrong of life passes away from my pores. At the fifth cup I am purified; the sixth cup calls me to the realms of the immortals. The seventh cup—ah, but I could take no more! I feel only the breath of cold wind that rises in my sleeves. . . .

— Chinese poet Lo-t'ung
(T'ang Dynasty)

THE MINISTER OF PROGRESS

July 16 1991

Dear Leaves,

I occasionally (almost daily) still feel the frustration of things not moving quickly enough, not being solid enough, not being "clear" enough. I wrestle between the plan and the flow. Doing and not-doing. It is here that I struggle for balance. Yet I'm gaining new confidence in understanding the nuances in taste and the properties of teas. My apprenticeship as a tea taster has begun.

I'm now going to work on the execution of some of our early ideas, trying to make them tangible and real, starting with the company logo. It's time to make decisions on directions and try to coax the very best work out of the most talented creative people I know.

I don't just want to "hire" someone to do this project. I want them to "get" the big idea for the business and understand it on a very personal level. I want them to identify with the message so that what comes out of their pen (or computer) is of the highest integrity.

This is an interesting predicament. The most talented illustrators and graphic designers that I know are mostly supertalented pros who do commercial work for hire. They do highly visible, recognizable work for big companies and brands. I want their talent and their experience, but in a way I don't want their experience. I want to inspire something that is completely fresh (and spontaneous) that *is* The Republic of Tea.

Here are my objectives for our packaging:

Usage:
- Keeps tea FRESH on the store shelf and in the customer's possession.

Workmanship:
- Clean, simple, high quality finish. Perceptible quality.

Materials:
- NO excess materials such as inner wrappers, seals, or anything that the customer needs to throw away after purchase.

- Reusable and recyclable container (with the potential for closed system recycling, i.e., customers bring containers back to us for credit, refill, etc.).

Graphics/Design:
- Informational, educational, beautiful, but not self-conscious of its own beauty.

THE MINISTER OF PROGRESS

30 July 1991

Dear Leaves,

I've begun to quietly come into the world with The Republic's message and concept. I'm beginning to "test" and describe the idea of the new tea business to a couple of close friends and collaborators in the marketing communications area. Today two talented people whom I respect (one an illustrator, the other a public relations master), were intrigued with the idea for a business but quickly asked, "How's that different from Celestial Seasonings?" Good question. So I went on to explain and I heard myself talking in a couple of voices. First, a philosophical tone:

"The Republic of Tea is a place of balance and awareness. It is a reminder about one's own pace in the world. Through every aspect of the business we want to entertain people with information and inspiration." I hear myself mention wanting to create a "new tea culture." I tried not to sound too off the wall or airy, but to explain that "it's a completely different and superior product." But that's not good enough for people who recognize the perils of selling things on grocery store shelves. Or maybe it is good enough?

Next I heard my marketer's voice:

"It's going to be *positioned* as a Celestial Seasonings' for the '90s, capturing today's social values and concerns that have to do with the massive reevaluation that is going on in the lifestyles of professionals and family members, about slowing down, placing more emphasis on family and home, and turning away from the acquisition of material possessions for fulfillment . . . Initially we'll be selling loose tea. . . . We're going to offer a higher quality and a variety of tastes of tea that Americans have never experienced before." I wondered to myself if it was more appropriate to describe this idea in terms of its competition or on its own. In business (and particularly to those people involved in marketing) a product is perceived almost wholly in terms of its competition. People seem to understand things in relationship to what they already know, so comparisons are helpful, but it's important to create clear distinctions.

I carried this question about "how is it different from" around with me all day, wrote it down in my notebook, and obviously took it to sleep with me, because here I am, sitting in the dark of 3 A.M. writing about it. Then I realized: The Republic of Tea: Tastier, Healthier, and more Whimsical.

Tastier because we use the freshest, highest quality teas and herbs found anywhere in the world. We seek out only the finest, and only market products that we *love* to drink ourselves. Healthier because tea and herbs have a rich history of medicinal and healthful use, and healthier because we use no flavorings or anything artificial in the preparation of the products. Whenever possible we use organically grown herbs in our blends. More whimsical because people need to giggle at something fresh and new, and conscious or not, most people are in search of balance and peace, always.

Still, these are comparative terms. There seems to be an inherent paradox in *describing* something that only our taste buds and body can experience. Any time we use words to talk about tea, we're moving away from the direct experience of sipping it.

Sometimes I feel like I've got to be careful of mission statement overkill.

I'll put my faith in what you once said to me: "The world is always waiting for a *truly great* product."

THE MINISTER OF PROGRESS

6 August

Dear Leaves,

(In rereading this letter, I find myself waxing slightly philosophical at 4 A.M.)

I must admit that I was a bit rattled by the news today that Mo Siegel was rejoining CS as chairman and CEO. It was clear that their company had lost its vision somewhere, locked up in a stale twenty-year-old identity. Now their visionary founder has returned and it seems that there was just too much opportunity in the tea business to stay away. I felt that sort of nervous rush of adrenaline. Although I've never met him, I know him as a dynamic marketeer and the king of tea. In my many conversations related to starting TRoT, many people have told me of the hallowed position that CS retains on the store shelves. I can still hear things like "many people have gone after their spot, but all have failed."

It's not really the competition that I fear, I just recognize now that CS will move aggressively to pursue some of the holes we recognized. I've learned that they are preparing to offer herbal iced teas as well as redesign their packaging and products. It's clear that they are going to take a position that is in sync with the environmentally conscious marketing trend that is sweeping the country.

This just forces me to be very clear about TRoT's own goals and identity. There's a tendency when starting out in business to want to be all over the map, but I want to concentrate on truly superior quality teas and herbs, the kind that can't go into a bag. I want to be conscious of environmental issues, but I don't want to build the company's position around that or call undue attention to the fact that we're environmentally conscious. I just want our products to come from a place of wholeness and consciousness of the needs of our customers. I want to focus on the experience of enjoying our products and I want to build the environments (stores) that people can discover them in.

As far as CS is concerned, TRoT is what you come to from CS. We're the next step in the appreciation of fine teas and herbal beverages. I want to also be sure that somehow we communicate the context for our products — a modern-day tea culture — that makes apparent the ultimate goal, which is to provide an enriching (entertaining, educational, and potentially enlightening) EXPERIENCE for our customers.

Bill Rosenzweig   FAX 4153814964

Bill
Wonderful!

M3

THE MINISTER OF PROGRESS

3 September 1991

Dear Leaves,

Well, you've done it again. Just when I thought I'd settled into a comfortable product plan you hit me with another big challenge: *Is the public really ready to be tempted into buying and brewing loose tea?*

Up until dinner last night, when you popped this question, I had built the product plan entirely on that risky assumption. I know that going the bulk-only route would greatly limit the size of our potential market (those who are just not going to brew loose tea) but I imagined not just selling tea, but selling the entire *context* for brewing and enjoying the tea. I want to sell the *tea experience*. (But do people buy *context* or do they buy *products*? I think they buy both. In your creation of Banana Republic, purchasing products certainly was an entertaining experience.)

I felt that our positioning was going to ride on the fact that loose tea is superior in every way to the traditional bagged tea found in the stores today. I devised an advertising campaign with a headline that said **WHY OUR TEA DOESN'T BELONG IN A BAG** which served to educate customers on several levels about the benefits of loose tea.

I'm still convinced that bulk is better and I want our customers to discover that too, along with the peaceful rhythm of preparing loose tea — the easy step-by-step motion of warming the pot, bringing the kettle to a rollicking boil, and savoring the smell of the leaves as the infusion takes place. . . . Brewing loose tea is about slowing down, it's about enjoying a pot with a friend, and enjoying the second cup (which I find is usually better than the first). Bags are traditionally about convenience, waste, and nominal quality. I guess it goes to another fundamental question: How much can we expect to change the habits of our customers?

But now you tell me your hunch is that we should really sell bags, too, from the start. Well, that blows the positioning of telling our customers our tea doesn't belong in bags. My gut tells me you're right.

No doubt, selling bags is safer. I still feel that I want to be in the loose tea business and I've got to understand how tea bags fit. (I'm sure wholesale buyers will have a much better comfort level with bags.)

I realized tonight how easy it is to fall in love with one's own ideas and get settled into a path based on self-imagined assumptions. I got hooked on the idea of selling the integrity and quality of superior loose tea and lost sight of the established market. Thanks again (sincerely) for pulling the rug out from under me yet another time.

— Yours truly, Progress

PS. The answer is clear, isn't it: We've got to figure out how to make the superior *bag* of tea too.

THE MINISTER OF LEAVES

3 September 1991

Dear Progress:

The question is not whether to bag or not to bag. Neither is the question, as you come to frame it by the fifth paragraph, *how much* we can change the habits of our customers. The true question is whether we can presume to change anybody or anything at all — other than our own habits, our own experiences.

In business, in life, there's no difference: We can change only ourselves, nobody else. That's the hardest thing I have come to understand.

By changing ourselves, it is possible to open others to the possibilities of change. If we change ourselves motivated by a hidden agenda, if we change ourselves driven by any sort of motive other than experiencing our own freedom and happiness, it's not the same. You can change. Yourself. Only. Period.

How does this apply to the business quandary at hand? I can answer that only with another question: Have you ever used a tea bag?

Progress, we can all come to *loose* tea only through our own journey. What we're offering is not loose tea, not bag tea, but the taste, the effect, and the full experience of tea. Every customer will meet us for tea on his own terms. What happens from there is up to him. One man will use tea as a metaphor to change his life; another will use it as a drink to quench his thirst. It is not for us to tell him what to use it for. It is our job to make the best tea available to him so that he can discover its possibilities for himself. We can lead a man to the leaf, and that's all. The alchemy the tea plays on him is between the tea and him, and it should make no difference to us whether he bags it, brews it, or chews it.

— Leaves

. . . .

I needed to learn more about tea, particularly how to taste it and differentiate it, so I decided to go to London, the center of the world's tea trade. There, during a month-long working vacation with my family, I had the good fortune of seeing the business practiced from the inside out. I spent time with tea brokers, tasters, blenders, packers, and growers. I met with a couple of real Ministers, representing the tea-producing nations of Sri Lanka and India, and had the good fortune of spending the day with gracious Samuel Twining, the ninth-generation representative of the legendary Twining Tea Company.

During these past several months of renewed activity, Mel and Patricia continued to express a genuine interest about seeing the business formed. I had told them of my plans to go to Britain and invited them to join us if they were interested. As was Mel's custom, he made no firm plans or commitments about coming, but when we arrived at our flat in London we were delighted to receive a fax that said "The Zieglers will see you on Friday." During their visit, Mel and Patricia accompanied me to a meeting here or there, but I was mostly on my own. I no longer felt as though I "needed" them to be with me (the way I did with the Lipton opportunity), and felt quite confident making my way in this foreign land as the sole emissary of The Republic of Tea.

While in England I experienced the tradition of tea and I saw it sold and consumed in inspiringly large quantities. I noticed a pleasant humbleness about the tea business; the men and women I met had come to tea because they loved it, or because it was part of their legacy. It was a charming, comfortably paced commodity business, perhaps more appealing to foreigners like myself, who didn't take it so much for granted. It felt a little stuffy and traditional in England — the British had a very specific (and I think limited) idea about what tea was to them. They drank good stuff all the time (mostly hearty, malty blends of Assam, Keemun, and Kenyan teas. This is what we know as English Breakfast Tea. There is no English Breakfast Tea in England. It's just tea). To my astonishment, more than 80% of all the tea now sold in Britain is in bags. My romantic notion of tea brewed loose in pots was becoming a lost art. England is now on the fast road with coffee. (Morning coffee, afternoon tea.)

Without being cocky or overconfident, I made it my mission to let my potential future suppliers and contacts know that the time was right for tea in America, and we were the guys that were going to get the US turned on to fine tea. (Everyone I spoke to knew how America has been getting gypped out of the better quality teas for many years. The English friends I have always complain that they can't find decent tea in America. This slight dates back to the way the British controlled the ports in Canton in the early 1800s. The captains would take all the best teas back to England [it was considered an aristocratic delicacy at that time], and leave the remainder for the other traders. The fledgling United States began its history as a second class tea buyer from the start.) I was sensitive about the *potentially cynical or skeptical response this bold mission might receive, but I must say I was inspired and encouraged by the genuine enthusiasm and support that was returned.*

I began to see that the big tea blenders were really ignoring the world's finest teas and hiding from their customers the fact that tea, like wine, is a product of its cultivation and varies from crop to crop and season to season. In an effort to maintain consistency in a "blend" (including its taste, color, texture, and price), a tea packer will choose lesser grade teas that they can always obtain throughout the year. In essence they have to ignore the finer quality teas in order to produce the consistency in the blends they market. There's not enough really fine tea grown in the world to fill the demand of the mass market. Part of my challenge was to find out how to get it.

After visiting with the manager of a number of Indian tea estates, I recognized the opportunity to market "unblended teas" — teas from a single estate (not unlike a specific vineyard). Imagine buying a Castleton Estate Darjeeling 1992 instead of a Bigelow tea bag? If the tea-is-like-wine analogy is accurate, the appreciation of fine tea is in its infancy — we're still at the point where most people recognize wine only in terms of red, white, and rosé. — **Bill**

. . . .

. . . .

I'd finally gained the confidence I needed to jump into the tea business. The difference now was that I was willing to jump in without counting on others to help me swim. I realized that it was completely up to me to create a plan and implement it — and it would have to be a plan that satisfied me first, then the others. I had arrived at the point where I was willing to trust myself completely with the idea for The Republic of Tea. This meant I was also ready to invest in myself, which included putting my own money squarely behind my efforts. I was now ready to go forward without the assurances of others. My confidence level had reached a critical point: I was now convinced that my own knowledge, expertise, and confidence would attract the confidence (and capital) of others.

Through a somewhat painful and lengthy process of getting comfortable with the concept of the business, thoroughly learning the product side, and coming to terms with the fact that being an entrepreneur is basically an individual pursuit, I finally became committed.

All my prior explorations led me to this point. As trivial as it may have seemed at the time, the Sedona tea stand was an early attempt to get my feet wet. I needed personal experience and proof that I could actually get people excited about tea. Each little move or inaction along the way contributed to my ultimate ability to take action.

Of course, losing your only client doesn't hurt either. — **Bill**

. . . .

THE MINISTER OF PROGRESS

October 13. 1991
Back from London

Dear Leaves,

Fate has given me a healthy shove off the board and into the pool. Before my trek to Britain, I had managed to redesign my agency job to focus on only one primary client, leaving the remainder of my time for tea. On my return I learned that a management coup at my sole client's firm has led to the installation of a new president, a new cabinet, and a new agency. And no job for me.

In a strange way I know this is the final push I needed. I can't imagine how long I could go on having one foot on the board and one in the pool, always hanging on to the security of the old, perpetually anticipating the fear of the new. I'm diving in now — hook, line, and sinker — and although I'm a little scared of the water, I know I can swim.

I have now become Enchantment's drawing for the Tea of Inquiry. The water feels fine.

THE MINISTER OF LEAVES

13 October 1991

Dear Progress:

It doesn't matter how long it took for you to get here. As the ancient Hindus were fond of saying, "The fruit on the tree ripens slowly but falls suddenly." Yes, you could have saved yourself a lot of soul-searching had you surrendered instantly to Tea Mind, and, throwing all resistance to the wind, recognized that you had no choice but to "do" this business once you saw the potential of it. But don't fret. The soul can always use a good searching. Nothing gained, nothing lost, I say. The news is you are, finally, *here*. Here in Tea Mind, and about to become, truly, The Minister of Progress.

Observing your odyssey brings me back to that "moment" when I myself became, truly, The Minister of Leaves. Many years before, I had been reading Lao Tzu, when suddenly he ambushed me with this stunning thought: *"Practice not-doing, and everything will fall into place."* I hadn't the slightest idea what it was, but something about those words rang deeply true. Imgine: Doing nothing. And everything falling into place. I was seduced by the notion of trying it. And so I set out with great determination to "do nothing."

It was not long before I found that my "not-doing" required quite a bit of doing. In trying to become "still," which seemed to me the prerequisite if not the very basis of "not-doing," I channeled my energies into projects that required me to make things with my hands, into writing and reading, into learning things in which I had long held an interest but never had the time to pursue, into playing with my son and puttering around the house. But I found myself *busier* than ever, and though a bit happier, I could not honestly say "everything was falling into place." And the irony did not escape me that I was "doing" all this "not-doing" so that I would not be tempted to "do" something like start a business. What was the difference? I wondered. It was clear that this "not-doing," whatever it was, was a very, very *subtle* thing.

"Not-doing," I discovered, was not at all about whether I worked or did not work, but it did have something to do with what is behind the work, the motive. If I worked for a selfish result, something that would benefit *me*, that was "doing." But if I worked for the work itself, totally absorbed myself in the means and gave no thought to the end, that was "not-doing." The tricky part, of course, was in getting clear about whether I was working for the work or for the result, the fruits of the work.

Day by day I fumbled my way through this mind-boggling territory. Confused as I was, I was lucky to have my heart in the right place. I truly did want to "not-do" — that is, do things for their own sake and not for mine. In other words, just "be." Interestingly, this put me *out there* in some very new place, where, floating free of the mental gravity that names and forms give to things, I began for the first time since being an infant to watch things happen objectively around without having to name them, judge them, categorize them, feel any particular way about them — in other words, *do* anything about them except let them "be." From the innocence of this perspective I began to see that there truly is "nothing to do," that if a person is alert and sensitive, he doesn't need any ideas about what to do — he just does things that need to be done, works for the sake of working, rests for the sake of resting. Experiencing this, I began to feel about two thousand years younger. Now, trusting that the necessary doing would take care of itself if I remained aware of all that was happening around me, when an *idea* "to do" something came along, it circled and circled but could rarely find a place in me to attach itself. Of course, being human, every once in a while my compulsions did manage to surface and I found myself doing a rash thing, like getting on an airplane to fly 3000 miles to attend a unique business conference where business people actually gathered for the purpose of finding ways to hold businesses responsible for more than enriching their owners, one of the few close-to-the-heart ideas that I found hard to shake in my new state. But if I did go, I did not stay long, maybe two nights out of a four-day conference, before I came again to my senses and left on an early flight home.

On one such early flight home I met a young man. He reminded me of myself, fifteen years younger. It was in that meeting that finally I came to understand what "not-doing" truly was, and it has been since then that "everything has fallen into place." "Not-doing," I learned, was listening to what wants to happen of itself, not forcing it, not attempting to control, but only *serving* it by helping to remove the obstacles that are keeping it from happening. In other words, Progress, tea wanted you and you wanted tea. And I saw that it was my "work" to serve you both by staying out of the way. Now through your "work" in bringing TRoT to life, many do-ers will be lured into stopping and sipping the leaves, and if they are lucky enough to get a taste of "not-doing" in their cups too, who knows what wonders might soon fall into place.

— Leaves

. . . .

One day while walking down Fulham Road during our trip to London, the idea for our own retail store vividly materialized. We had been inspired by the successful Whittard's chain of tea shops with their fine catalogue and broad selection. We three recognized the importance of creating a "context" for enjoying fine tea in America. We wanted to sell tea and create a new tea experience, and the most dramatic way to do this was clearly in a retail environment. (The potential of this hunch was also reinforced by Mel and Patricia's personal legacy with Banana Republic, which in some people's opinion was the ultimate in experiential, theatrical retailing — a direction which transformed the traditional shopping experience during the '80s.) Since our return, Patricia and I had been concentrating on a retail approach to the tea business. — **Bill**

Restaurant Tea Service

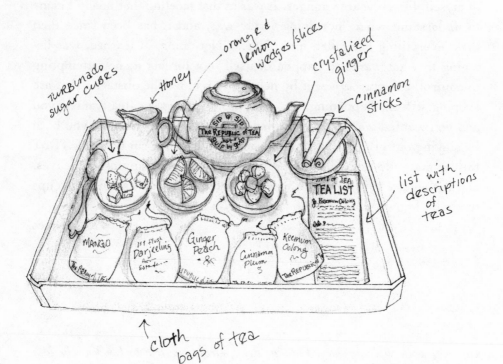

turbinado sugar cubes

Honey

orange d lemon wedges/slices

crystalized ginger

cinnamon sticks

MANGO

1st Flush Darjeeling from Estate

Ginger Peach

Cinnamon Plum

Keemum Oolong

TEA LIST

list with descriptions of teas

cloth bags of tea

• patron can make his/her tea selection from assortment of Teas & condiments

• waiter will then brew selection for them

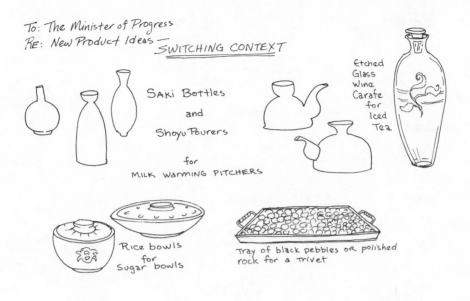

SAKi Bottles
and
Shoyu Pourers

for
MILK warming PITCHERS

Etched
Glass
Wine
Carafe
for
Iced
Tea

Rice bowls
for
Sugar bowls

Tray of black pebbles or polished
rock for a Trivet

THE MINISTER OF PROGRESS

14 October 1991

My dear Minister of Enchantment:

There is a market for "tea life," as you say, based on an aesthetic of simplicity and a sense of awareness. How can we take this notion and translate it into a product line that clearly conveys tea life?

The actual tea we sell is the key to our business. It is a consumable product that grounds our metaphor in the moment-to-moment enjoyment of preparation and sipping. But well beyond the English tea shop model we experienced, with its many teas and pots, we need to build a business around a lifestyle, a lifestyle in which the enjoyment of tea is central.

I think it is critical that our first store and catalogue convey a clear expression of this lifestyle. What simple, functional products will enable people to reach this aesthetic and state of peacefulness and grasp immediately (perhaps in an intuitive sense) what business we're in?

PRODUCT Ideas for CATALOG One

A broad bottom copper or stainless steel kettle

Traditional cherry wood cannisters to store tea

A Tea Scoop

A thermal "hot pot" to hold tea that is not served immediately after brewing

A tea mitt

TEA TOWEL

REPUBLIC of TEA

An Iron Tea Pot...

... and Trivet.

Several special types of honey

HONEY

REP of TEA

A Tea strainer & holding dish

A Yixing clay pot and SET of...

...cups for Green Tea

A bamboo strainer

A Tea Tray

A TEA Infuser

A warming pitcher for milk that can be used safely in a microwave oven.

A ceramic or glass tea pot, maybe both

A Tea timer

A set of porcelain "paper" cups

New and Wonderful Tea cups.

MOST OF THESE PRODUCTS COULD BE exclusively designed for TROT, or private labeled.

THE MINISTER OF PROGRESS

Thursday 16 October

Dear Leaves,

Yesterday I felt motivated to write it all down — a new draft of the whole business plan. The latest one — that has been brewing in my head, in our conversations, and in my conversations with others — has been expressed in about fourteen pages of specific actions and details.

The plan sounds good to me. (A wise lawyer/venture capitalist once said to me, *"I've never seen a business plan that didn't work."*) Maybe that's why something else nags at me. The key now is to really test the validity of the ideas with numbers.

I've begun to make numeric assumptions about the conceptual ideas in the plan. This is hard for me to express, but there's something very strange about the relationship between words and numbers. On one hand, you'd think that numbers were concrete, definable terms, empirical in nature. 2 + 2 always equals 4. But in the business plan of a startup company, the numbers become abstract, because for the most part they're all guesses. What if 2 doesn't really become 2?

Not all the numbers are guesses, but the ones that count are: the sales forecast. How many people will come into our store each day? How much will they spend? The success of the business rides on my ability to guess accurately the answers to those two questions.

I'm back to the spreadsheets, turning them inside out, stripping them to the essential so that I can really understand the relationships of all the numbers involved. I need to know how many people I *need* to come into the store to *spend* "x" to break even. I must confess: the numbers always scare me a little because I fear they will call my intuition a liar.

This is a lonely part of the game.

— Progress

THE MINISTER OF LEAVES

October 17, 1991

Dear Progress,

If by intuition what you mean is *your imagination*, then you have good reason to be wary of it. On the other hand, if by intuition what you mean is your inborn nature, free of all the knowledge you've filled yourself up with over the last thirtysome years, then you have good reason to listen to it . . . carefully. *That* intuition can see that numbers and words, by their very nature, lie. Place your ultimate trust in what cannot be reduced to numbers or words, and you will always know what to do, or not do.

And your process need not be *lonely*, only *alone*. Understand the difference. It's an important one.

—Leaves

THE MINISTER OF PROGRESS

October 21, 1991

Dear Enchantment,

Woke up with a couple more ideas about catalogue #1.

1.   Tea-of-the-month club (hate the name), but the idea is good. We brainstormed on this one long ago, and it still seems like a strong,

Dear Progress,

Your fax w/ the tea carafe reminded me of the cup of tea served to me on the train from Helsinki to Leningrad. The "cup" was actually a tall glass in a silver holder w/ an ebony (?) handle.

This was a wonderful breakfast cup. Maybe you can find the cups sold to the russian RR, or maybe this is a standard Eastern European way to serve tea. These would be wonderful for the catalog.

E—

viable idea. It's going to need to be enticing — great copy — focusing, I think, on the surprises of life, rambling without destination, etc. If we want to get promotional about it, we could offer our customers the opportunity to sign their friends up for it as a birthday or holiday gift. Every first shipment could come with a personally signed "green card" (you get it) from The Minister of Leaves, authorizing their welcome to citizenship in The Republic.

2. Those little no-fat cookies we found that everyone loves . . . could they sell by mail?

3. A small pitcher for your milk. I found a lovely terra-cotta one, crafted

with hand care, when we were in Ireland. I'd like to show it to you. It's got a very nice story behind it too.

4. Sweeteners? like honey or those neat European brown sugar cubes. I'm not into them myself, but I guess a lot of people like that breakfast tea with a spot of sweetener. Also the herb teas benefit from honey once in a while. All available easily and easy to private-label.

5. A little handmade book called *How to Make a Perfect Cup of Tea*.

— Progress

Progress —
    We need simple brewing instructions on every package, maybe on hangtags. a condensed version of the book?

HOW TO MAKE A PERFECT CUP OF TEA

Scald the milk.

(microwave works well, prevents burnt pots)

Warm the pot and cups.

Bring water to a full boil for black teas...

...to a rolling boil for green teas.

Measure the tea.

Bring the pot to the kettle.

Watch the clock or use a timer. Each tea has its perfect brewing time.

Sip by Sip Not Gulp by Gulp

— E

CATALOG Nº1

- 8 pages w/ stiched in order blank
- digest size
- duotone on recycled stock – pencil sketches

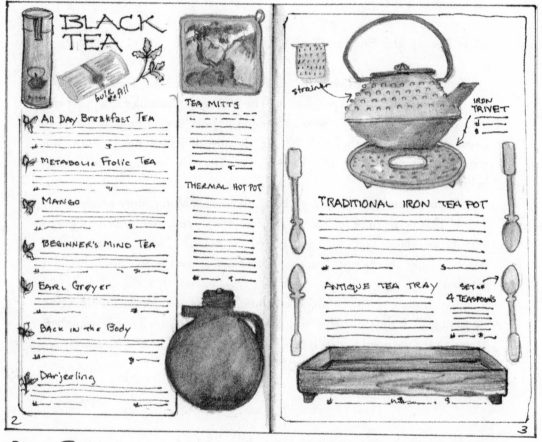

BLACK TEA

bulk refill

- All Day Breakfast Tea
- METABOLIC Frolic Tea
- MANGO
- BEGINNER'S MIND TEA
- EARL Greyer
- BACK in the Body
- DArjeeling

TEA MITTS

THERMAL HOT POT

strainer

IRON TRIVET

TRADITIONAL IRON TEA POT

ANTIQUE TEA TRAY

SET OF 4 TEASPOONS

2   3

- Black Teas
  - Thermos
    - Hot Mitts w/ Chinese landscapes

- IRON Tea pot & Trivet
- set of 4 teaspoons
- Tea Tray.

THE MINISTER OF PROGRESS

22 October 1991

Dear Leaves and Enchantment,

It seems that in recent days when I open the *New York Times* the pages are filled with gloom and pessimism. The recession (feels like a depression) isn't coming and going the way people expect everything to do these days. It seems like this will be the decade of emotional growth, not economic growth. And The Republic of Tea will be the business that helps foster this growth.

Your recent words to me about time are making more sense every day. ("This is the time for tea. . . .") The '80s were a race fueled by greed and status. "How fast can I get where I'm going?" Now, instead of how fast can I get there, perhaps the question will evolve to "how should I get there."

My hunch is that things are much worse economically than the "indicators" indicate. The numbers are all politically manipulated. Through tea we need to reach people on an emotional level with a message that is true, modest, and contagious.

What might that be?

— Progress

PS. Very positive meeting with Bruce Katz yesterday. I reviewed a basic business plan with him, and he helped me define an ownership structure that encompasses our individual and mutual interests. I'm still striving to include you and Patricia as "founding" partners with me as the "working" partner. Finding the right balance between percentage ownership, amount of capital contribution, and managerial responsibility is challenging, particularly when each partner has something different to contribute. The goal is to create two tiers of stock offering. First will be the founders' stock for the three of us, and then (at a higher price) we'll issue investor stock. I will be meeting with a couple of other people in his office this week to sort out details and the proper way to express this ownership structure. By the beginning of next week (or this weekend) I would like to get together with you two to review this business structure and financing proposal.

— Progress

. . . .

Bruce Katz, former owner of Rockport shoes and our illustrious Minister of Big Ideas, reentered the picture. One night Mel called me up and said, "Bruce wants to fund the company. He offered $250,000 for 25% of the business, but you better make sure that fits with your plan. You want to be sure you have enough money to fund the plan." Bruce had been over at Mel and Patricia's home and had seen some of the early catalogue sketches and packaging ideas that we had been working on. Seeing the potential for the company (as opposed to just hearing about it) compelled Bruce to want to participate formally. Mel made it clear that the follow-up on this was entirely up to me. — **Bill**

. . . .

THE MINISTER OF LEAVES

October 22, 1991

Dear Progress,

Let's forget the *shoulds*. If, as you say, the '80s were about getting where we want at any cost, we really haven't come very far if the '90s are about getting where we want but (as you put it) "peacefully." The fact is that there is nowhere to get, and until people get *that*, nothing will change. The peace is here! The happiness is here!

The work at hand is to use the metaphor of tea to get people to turn on their headlamps. Life is the *tea*cher. That's why I feel that you should put your entire advertising budget into T-shirts. *Philoso-tea* shirts, if you will. Let's emblazon chests everywhere with slogans like

Happiness Needs No Cause
I Want What I Have
I'm Taking Life Sip by Sip, Not Gulp by Gulp

As far as I'm concerned, our only dangerous competition are drugs and alcohol, and I've even got a Philoso-tea shirt to vanquish them:

Sobriety Is Higher

Or let's just *say* it:

Life Is a Teaching
Tea Is the Teacher

And my single favorite would be a map of the US with this inscription:

Great Nation Forced to Drink Swill
I'm Defecting to The Republic of Tea

— Leaves

THE MINISTER OF PROGRESS

22 October 1991

Dear Leaves,

When is the right time to start a new business?

— Progress

THE MINISTER OF LEAVES

22 October 1991

Dear Progress,

Never and always.

— Leaves

Life is impossible and so what. It is in its very impossibility that we find our joy. Tea Mind allows life to live us. It frees us from the hubris of trying to control what cannot be controlled. The life of tea is the life of the moment. We have only Now, and we each sip it in our own cups.

— The Minister of Leaves

THE MINISTER OF PROGRESS

23 October 1991

To: Minister of Enchantment

Fr: Progress

Re: More thoughts on catalogue 1 merchandise

1. Been thinking about product mix and would like to offer two types of cups. The crinkled-paper-style porcelain cups and the basic handleless Chinese style. The more I think about it, the more I want to concentrate on primary tea drinking pieces rather than the more esoteric ones.

2. We may also want to explore a second type of caddy or canister that is less expensive, like a tin. Perhaps a set of three tins for $20. This is probably a good price point.

3. The two-cup iron teapot will probably be more like $35–40.

4. If the tray is really beautiful, it could be about $65. Also I've found these really nice, very simple wood stacking trays (3) that have this wonderful Japanese aesthetic to them. Those three trays together, one larger one for the pot, smaller ones for each cup of tea and slice of bread, etc., would probably retail for about $50–60.

5. I don't have a clear idea on the coasters yet. The ones I was thinking of were very inexpensive cardboard . . . I'd like to hear what you have in mind for the look for those.

6. Green tea spread. Let's really be the green tea experts. I think we should leave plenty of editorial room for background on recent positive medicinal qualities of green tea. If we show our emphasis and

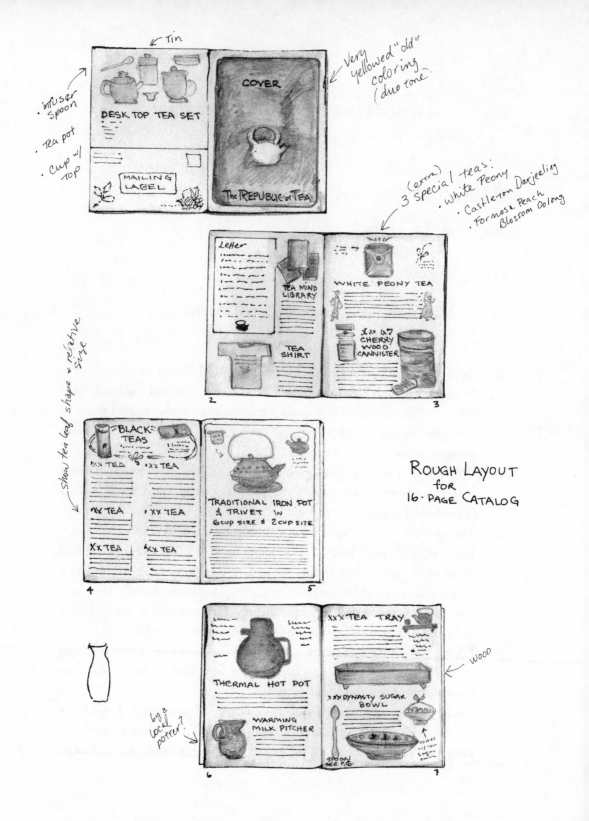

Tin

COVER

DESK TOP TEA SET

MAILING LABEL

The REPUBLIC of TEA

Very yellowed "old" coloring (duo tone)

• infuser spoon
• Tea pot
• cup w/ top

3 (extra) special teas:
• White Peony
• Castleton Darjeeling
• Formosa Peach Blossom Oolong

Letter

TEA MIND LIBRARY

TEA SHIRT

WHITE PEONY TEA

X in 67 CHERRY WOOD CANNISTER

2   3

Show tea leaf shape + relative size

BLACK TEAS

XX TEA   XX TEA

XX TEA   XX TEA

XX TEA   XX TEA

TRADITIONAL IRON POT & TRIVET in 6 cup size & 2 cup size

4   5

ROUGH LAYOUT
for
16·PAGE CATALOG

THERMAL HOT POT

WARMING MILK PITCHER

by a local potter?

XXX TEA TRAY

XXX DYNASTY SUGAR BOWL

SPOON SEE P.6

WOOD

6   7

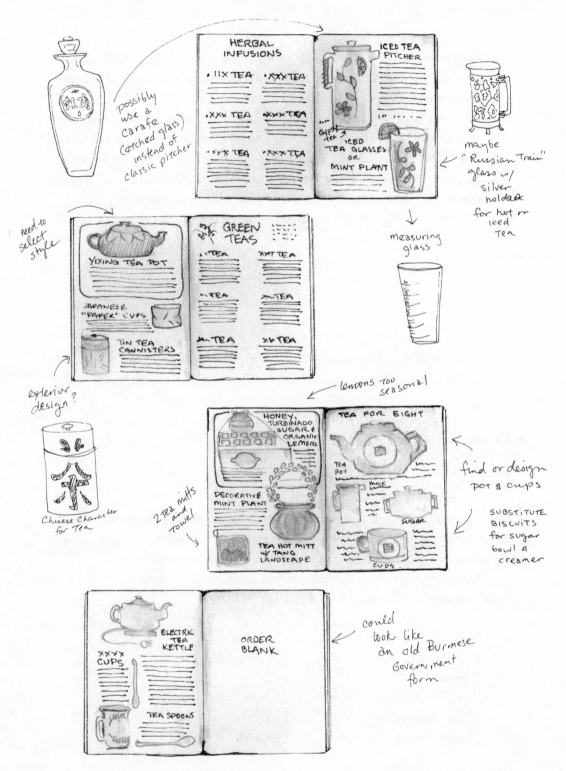

expertise in this area, it will give us one more thing to talk about that shows our differences from others already out there. We have to be the first people to really emphasize a non-Oriental approach to green tea (do you know what I mean?). The only green tea that is really out there is packaged and presented for the Asian market. We have to be the ones to make it mainstream. I'd like to be able to refer to the *NY Times* article about the health benefits of green tea in the copy section of this spread if it's appropriate.

7. Tea timer. What shape might it be?

—Progress

THE MINISTER OF PROGRESS

October 23, 1991

Dear E:

We really enjoyed receiving the thumbnails. Your style is charming and endearing. Faye said everything feels alive, animated. I've got some thoughts, suggestions, and questions to toss back to you.

Here's my latest pricing breakdown per your page roughs. Pls feedback comments, changes. Are the prices too low?

Page 2	
Tea Mind Library	$35 (3 books?)
T-Shirt	$15
Page 3	
White Peony Tea	$15
Cherry Wood Canisters	$35 each

•   You're showing the very rare White Peony tea from China as our super special choice. I've got to be sure we can get this. I don't know much about where to get white tea, so I'll delve in and see what we can find. I can see that you're showing it presented in the box with the coin . . . very nice. My question really is, should this be white tea or an incredible first-flush Darjeeling that is perhaps a bit more respected and more widely known?

Page 5

Large Iron Teapot	$50
Small Iron Teapot	$40
Trivet	$15

Page 6

Thermal Hot Pot	$45
Warming Pitcher	$12 seems unlikely, low ticket item

Page 7

Tea Tray	$55
Sugar Bowl?	$15 not crazy about this yet

Page 9

Iced Tea Pitcher	$35 need help here with look
Glasses (6)	$24

Page 10

Yixing Teapot	$39
Japanese Paper Cups (4)	$28
Tin Tea Canisters (3)	$12

Page 12

Honey, sugar, lemons	$18
Mint Plant	$14 nice with topiary
Hot Pad and Towel	$17 add towel to increase price?

Page 13

Ceramic Teapot	$30
Chinese raku cups (4)	$36
don't know others?	please explain other products

Page 14

Electric Tea Kettle	$60
Morning Mugs (2)	$18
Teaspoons (4)	$16

Page 16

Desktop Tea Set pot, trivet, kettle, canisters?	$99 let's discuss

THE MINISTER OF PROGRESS

27 October 1991

Dear Leaves,

Welcome back from Bolinas! (Are you back?)

Conversations are continuing positively with BK. I also spent a good deal of time this week with Claudia at Rosewood. She's helped me to identify key board-related issues and open items to nail down between the partners.

Key issues include what legal form the entity should take and how to protect founding investors from being diluted of their percentage ownership in the event of second-round financing which might occur if we were forced to offer stock at less than what Bruce will pay for it. Given that the four of us have different financial resources (and tax situations) and different financial needs, we need to work through this very carefully.

The attorneys are encouraging us to have an odd number of seats on our board to avoid any deadlocks, but I know that we are all in favor of an even number to encourage consensus decision making. Bruce wants to have two votes due to the amount of capital he's contributing, which means the four of us would elect the sixth member by unanimous consent. It would be nice to bring someone to the board who has some contacts in the specialty food distribution business. Know anyone?

We need to discuss how to structure our shareholders' agreement to determine what type of decisions require unanimous or majority approval and what decisions can be made by me as CEO. The initial areas that will require unanimous approval include incurring debt, opening a store, any contract where a director has an interest, issuance of stock, payments of dividends, capital expenditures, loans by the company. These matters would be decided by majority vote: annual budget of the company, hiring of executive officers, employee bonus arrangements, profit sharing, leases for equipment, any merger, consolidation, liquidation, or sale of the company, any acquisition by the company of any business. Everything else will be the decision of the CEO.

I am aiming to get the business incorporated by November 15.

— Progress

Do Not bleed – use rounded square border (like Chinese stamp – 示)

Catalog cover sets tone – mood – stillness

unbleached, recycled stock

The REPUBLIC of TEA

CATALOGUE NUMBER ONE

blue & black or olive & " – duotone –

evocative scene & time of day

Larger logo

THE MINISTER OF PROGRESS

Dear E,

We love the cover sketch. Thanks for sending it over.

How about putting Leaves's first letter to the People of Tea on all of page 3 in the primo spot? I realize that this goes against all good mail order logic since this is the prime catalogue real estate, but for our first catalogue I think it's important to set up the context of The Republic. We need to provide our customers with some entertaining reading to convey that this is more than just a catalogue of products. This is a lifestyle.

I've put together our total printing, production, and mailing budget and have divided it by our projected 16-page length. This gives us the base cost (rent) for each page in the catalogue. That number is then divided into the number of products on each page in proportion to the amount of space they consume. Then we calculate the gross profit margin dollars for each product. (The retail price minus our cost including fulfillment.) Now we can determine how many of each product we need to sell to break even for this catalogue. We'll test these assumptions to see if we think they're realistic. This will also help to determine how many of each product we should order from the start. We'll need to invest in enough inventory to pay back "the rent" on the space in the catalogue, but not too much to risk overbuying something that won't move. I'm inclined to buy on the cautious side for the first catalogue.

I'll be sure our sources are in place to rapidly reorder when necessary.

Leaves also had an idea about increasing the size to 20 pages and dedicating a little more space to descriptions of our teas and a lot more on children's teas (perhaps a whole page). I think we have a big opportunity to set ourselves apart by emphasizing the herbal children's teas and a page on green teas. I've requested more background on the green tea health research that could add valuable information to this coverage. (At the same time, I've found an exciting, more direct source to tea in China. More on that later.)

I'll calculate the added expense of going to 20 pages. I know that it will be incrementally minuscule at this point (because we're basically paying only for paper) and it might make a lot of sense. It will actually probably decrease the rent per page so it might make some sense. Let's explore.

— Progress

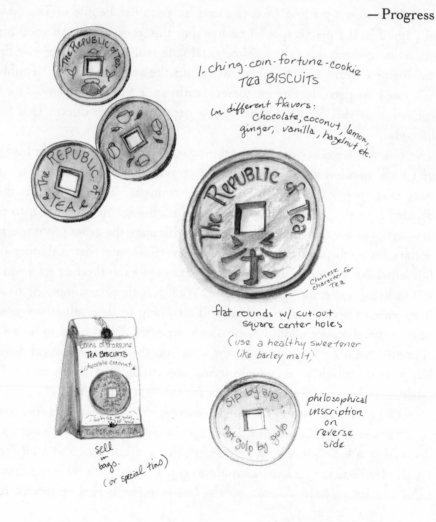

I.ching.coin.fortune.cookie
Tea BISCUITS

in different flavors:
Chocolate, coconut, lemon, ginger, vanilla, hazelnut etc.

Chinese character for Tea

flat rounds w/ cut.out square center holes

(use a healthy sweetener like barley malt)

Coins of Fortune
TEA BISCUITS
chocolate coconut
The Republic of Tea

sell in bags.
(or special tins)

SIP by SIP
not gulp by gulp

philosophical inscription on reverse side

THE MINISTER OF PROGRESS

---

29 October

Dear L & E,

"Today everybody can get everything" lamented your friend Richard Walker, the European buying agent. It seems that the world has gotten so much smaller that it's hard to find those special, unique products. The catalogue business is an extremely competitive area where there are very few proprietary products anymore. Popular designs are quickly knocked off and inexpensive and instant access to international markets is possible thanks to the ubiquitous fax machine.

The opportunity, then, is to assemble existing products in a new context and present them in ways that are new and fresh. I can see that by bringing a Japanese iron teapot together with a Chinese cup on an African wood tray with some black-gold river rock serving as a trivet we can create a new sense of place and lifestyle that is enticing and exotic but not foreign.

The search for great product has begun. The scope of my search right now is defined as products that support the preparation and enjoyment of full leaf teas.

— Progress

THE MINISTER OF PROGRESS

31 October 1991

Dear Leaves and Enchantment,

Sometimes starting a business feels like a connect-the-dots treasure hunt.

I'm in the "search" phase now, trying to bring innovation and distinction to our product line in every conceivable way. I'm just out there every day "looking." Two thirds of the time I don't even know what I'm looking for.

Today, for instance, I found an importing company in our Marin County backyard that is small and was a secret to me. It's taken me eighteen months to accidentally discover them (and you know how thoroughly I've combed even the least obvious resources). I noticed the name of this firm in an old trade show directory under "coffee merchandise" and called them up cold, looking for a particular tea kettle. What I discovered was that they work with one of the key tea suppliers that I need to import from in Germany. This is nice because when just starting out, minimum orders always kill you. They are a traditional barrier to entry. With tea, a great deal of cost is related to shipping the product. So, here's a company I can split a container of product with and have it delivered right to San Raphael. That's nice, but here's the fun part.

After telling my newfound friend and neighbor at this local company a little bit about what we're going to do (and having her respond "I want to be your customer." [What more could I ask?]), she says, "You should call Gail Clemat at Bowker Marketing because she's a sales rep that would probably want to sell a product like that."

When I call up Gail and tell her that her friend suggested I phone, I'm met with warmth and an open ear.

So, in the course of a couple of unintentional phone calls, not only do I end up with an accidental shipping companion but a potential distributor as well. I'm amazed at how a little enthusiasm can open people up to share priceless information. Just in the last several weeks, people I've never met have volunteered knowledge and insight about the tea market, distributors, and specific sales figures that even the highest-priced research firm couldn't procure.

It's rewarding working person-to-person. I think people in general miss personal contact in business. Right now I'll continue recruiting one citizen at a time to The Republic of Tea.

THE MINISTER OF PROGRESS

No leaf falls in an inappropriate place.

3 November 1991

Dear Mel and Patricia,

Despite Bruce's ambivalence about going into this business with his friends, I think the Friday meeting to look at a business scenario was very positive. From the discussion, I feel the four of us now have a clearer sense of how we could structure a business and how an investor might or might not fit in.

I'm planning to proceed this week with the basic incorporation of the business. I would like to appoint a corporate attorney who would represent the mutual interests of the founding partners and the corporation and then have us as individuals retain our personal representatives to take a look at what the corporate attorney prepares on our behalf.

I see us setting up a Sub-S corp which allows losses to pass through to the shareholders (an incentive for some wealthy investors). This also gives us the added benefit of not incurring a double tax (corporate and personal) in the event of a sale of the company. The scenario that BK proposed the other day, of his being a "preferred shareholder," doesn't exactly work in this context because Sub-S corps have a single class of stock. He likes the preferred-shareholder status because it enables us to assign different rights to different shareholders. For instance, he would like to request a liquidation preference for his stock (in the event of bankruptcy, his capital is treated like a loan, and receives the same preference in liquidation that debt does). In a Sub-S corporation there is only one class of stock allowed. There are other ways of accommodating some of his requests (seats on the board, etc.) through the formation of a limited partnership, which is the most flexible business structure in terms of assigning specific benefits, restrictions, and liabilities. The limited partnership would work for us, but it doesn't offer the benefits of a Sub-S corp when it comes to the sale or merger of the company. I'm going to spend some time with Bruce and during the next two weeks determine if he's in or out. At that point we'll incorporate with or without him. Our shareholders' agreement and the corporate form we choose will obviously be influenced by his decision. My sense from Bruce was that he was testing everything on Friday. It came as a surprise to me when he said he hadn't made up his mind because he had been so enthusiastic, even initiating progress in a bold way. I understand his hesitation over not wanting to jeopardize his friendships in any way, and, honestly, I'm glad I saw how tough he was at the meeting.

In any case, I think it will be easier and cleaner to attract an outside investor if the three of us are set up as founders in an S corp. That way it is clear to a potential investor how they can participate. Of course it's harder for us because it takes away our flexibility in terms of setting up the entity to accommodate the specific needs of an investor. After all, it's extremely difficult to place a dollar value on the potential of an idea. We don't have an operating business yet with any track record. All we have is our own abilities, experience, and the work we've done to date.

Mel, I wanted to tell you how much I appreciated the support and confidence you expressed in me. I know that this is my deal to sell, but your consistent and clear participation at the meeting was a great help. I know that you were exasperated by his attempt to clarify your commitment. Thanks for hanging in there.

— Bill

. . . .

At first I, too, was a little troubled by Bruce at the meeting. He came with a list of "shoulds," presenting his ideas in monologue form without fully informing himself as to what had already transpired between Bill and Patricia and me. Was he testing whether our friendship could weather a business relationship? If so, I thought, "What do I need this for?" Business relationships are easy to come by. Friends, true friends, are hard won.

In the few years after selling our companies, Bruce and I had very different experiences. He regretted his decision. I was happy with mine. He wanted to build another empire. I had no interest in going around the same track twice. He created a venture capital company and went out looking for a business he could take over and run up. I stayed home, played with my son, read books, wrote, gardened, hiked. I enjoyed hearing about Bruce's business adventures, and he was an eager listener when I talked about what life felt like to me from outside the business loop. I made no secret that I considered "avoiding obligations" a key to happiness, so, knowing this about me, it mystified me that Bruce (and for that matter, Bill) would want me as a business partner. Perhaps it was this very thing that Bruce was trying to find his comfort level with, but there was little I could do to help him. It would not have disturbed me if Bill went ahead with the business on his own without me, or went ahead with Bruce. I wanted to see TRoT started, and I was not at all proprietary about the idea.

Looking at our meeting as objectively as I could that evening, I saw the problem in a new light. Bruce was doing what the lawyers have trained all astute businessmen to do these days: having the fight before The Fight. He was poking and probing, probing and poking, to see how things might come unmoored when they got rough (as they always do in business). It is a confrontational approach that has it benefits, I suppose, but when you believe, as I do, that thoughts have a life of their own and a way of becoming real, the wisdom of this approach is limited. In any event, Bruce saw quickly that I had no intention of getting actively involved in the day-to-day business, and we were soon on to other things.

It was, however, clear to me that the brief sparks between us did shake Bill up a bit. He feared it was an expression of a "business is business" mentality that he, admirably, was doing all he could to avoid in his life. The idea that I can be a perfectly decent, warm, loving, and generous human being one minute, but the next minute, when we're conducting business, I license myself to be a wolf so I can get the better of you is very much a part of our culture. The specter of this socially condoned hypocrisy infecting young TRoT alarmed Bill, with good reason. But Bruce is a pussycat, not a wolf, and this is not what he was up to. Rather, he was deliberately picking an argument with me to play out a scenario that he feared might one day happen, wanting to get it over with before it did. It was his way of being cautious, in business and friendship.

Yet it did raise an interesting point that seemed relevant to TRoT's new way of business. To me there are no boundaries. Life is everything, including business. Therefore, life is business, and business is life. In being a businessman, I find no license to do or be things I could not do or be as a man. It's that simple. The "business is business" mentality is a social sickness that chokes off the higher nature of human beings. It elevates being in business to a station higher than being human, and therefore is in its own time ultimately counterproductive if not to the business itself, then certainly to the businessman (or woman) who spreads the infection.

The little bit of friction with Bruce aside, the meeting left me heartened: Bill, like it or not, was getting something from Bruce he sorely needed that I could not bring myself to give him. Bruce was questioning the launch concept from every *angle, forcing Bill to be accountable for some of the bottom-line business problems he had still managed to avoid looking at. Bruce also made many challenges on financial and control issues (what Bill could decide by himself as opposed to what the board would decide etc.), which were designed to save Bill from a common entrepreneurial disaster — paddling up a tributary and then finding out he's lost the river. I thought Bruce's suggestions here to be quite wise. After all, my money was in the deal too, and I liked the prospect of having a partner as capable as Bruce who would be looking out for these things.*

For me, the most interesting part of the meeting was observing the tug that was going on between Bruce's heart and his mind. I believed he knew our friendship could survive any business problem, and yet there was something almost compulsive about his need to test it. His logical mind was trashing his deep intuition, a problem endemic to many businessmen.

In any event, we both let it drop. It had been Bruce's idea to invest in the first place, so I said only, "Make your decision based on your confidence in Bill's ability to create a successful tea business, not on the basis of our friendship." Other than that, I decided to let Bill and Bruce work things out for themselves. It was Bruce's call. But if he was in the deal, one thing Bruce was going to have to find comfort with was the fact that The Republic of Tea would, in its deepest soul, remain (as far as Bill and I were concerned) business not as usual.

Knowing Bruce, however, that was only going to intrigue him more. — **MZ**

I gave Bruce a copy of my latest business plan that involved opening three specialty tea and tea wares stores in two years. A couple of days later he called me from Holland (it was 4 A.M. his time — he was up all night thinking about this) to tell me that the retail approach was the wrong way to launch the business. He felt that we'd have much greater success as a wholesale business, but was somehow concerned that this approach might offend Mel and Patricia.

Bruce's reasoning was clear: tea is a beverage, a consumable, replacement commodity. Most people buy their tea in a grocery store, not in a specialty tea store. And besides, said Bruce, "I can't see putting $300,000 into a tea store in San Francisco." He made his point. After I digested his input, I wrote him this fax. — **Bill**

THE MINISTER OF PROGRESS

Fax Memo
7 November 1991

To: Bruce Katz

Fr: Bill Rosenzweig

2 pages total
_____

Dear Bruce,

I wanted to tell you that everything you said last night made a great deal of sense to me. Thank you for calling and thanks for putting your mind to work on the business. I've had the chance to sleep on your suggestions and woke up this morning to take on recasting the business plan with a core wholesale focus from the launch.

The key challenge that I see for selling our products through other people's stores will be to bring it out of a context that includes the tea experience, as opposed to it just being perceived as another nicely packaged gourmet food product. We'll have to create that context through powerful promotional campaigns that include the preparation and serving of tea (as you did with walking) at Rockport. I feel comfortable that we can carve out some specific product niches by providing better quality tea than is commonly available, and by being innovative in the flavors and presentation area. Specialty and loose tea continues to grow at 15% a year, so we've got to get in and ride this wave.

I realize that the store is fun (and perhaps easier to do at first) but if we look at the cost of the store as a marketing expense designed ultimately to support and promote a wholesale brand business, there are much better ways to apply that capital in the startup. In a way, I think I saw the store as the physical thing that could easily establish the lifestyle context (look, feel, environment) for the business, but a single store (or a couple of stores) is so limited in its reach that it won't do much more than create publicity for a while. Bottom line, stores today rarely make money.

(If we want to create publicity, we can open a tea room in our warehouse and get the Marinites in there for afternoon tea, tea tastings, workshops, etc. The outlet concept makes sense, particularly if it's part of our home base.)

Going wholesale from the start (with a simple retail/gift catalogue) simplifies the start and makes sense in terms of the scale that I feel comfortable launching the business. I want it to grow from natural roots. I don't want to force it into the market and into places that it doesn't fit.

I don't think Mel and Patricia are overly attached to a retail focus for the business; that's where they're comfortable and experienced. The benefit of the store is that it gives us firsthand experience with our customers and enables us to learn directly from them. I think my recent experience in England, seeing a chain of successful tea stores, influenced me to start with one, but I must keep in mind that at present the US doesn't consume tea like the Brits or Europeans.

Patricia naturally gravitates to the catalogue (which I feel is an important supporting tool for the wholesale business) and Mel gravitates to the *context and expression* because this is what they enjoy most. They are both extremely fluid in their thinking, and this issue of how we *best enter* (retail, wholesale, catalogue, direct selling, etc.) the business has been our ongoing discussion. The last plan I offered wasn't really intended to settle it; it was designed to get input like you're generating. I've always seen the business ultimately as a wholesale *brand* that would ultimately transcend the tea category into a broader lifestyle context. Creating the context for the "tea lifestyle" right from the start is where the challenge is. I think a hard look at the numbers will reveal the truth, and you've intuitively identified the short-term and mid-term needs and obstacles associated with taking a road that's initially retail focused.

This wholesale with catalogue model is very similar to Stash tea, which is doing very well. The challenge will be to step up a notch in quality from them without narrowing the market considerably. Many of their customers could easily become our customers with the right marketing and exposure.

I've got a wholesale plan outlined now with proformas. If you're up for it, I'd like to get together with you on Sunday or Monday for a short time to go over it and refine it with you one more time.

Thanks again for calling. It was a great surprise to hear from you. I certainly appreciate your advice and input. See you soon.

— Bill

THE MINISTER OF PROGRESS

Dear Leaves,

The attorney I'm considering retaining to do our incorporation is perceptive and opinionated, and someone I would consider a target customer.

I shared the plan with her and the current state of who's who and what's what. She was delighted with the idea for the business, but she had some strong suggestions about execution.

She liked the idea of a store or environment, but did not at all like the idea of it being on an "in" street. She thought that would force something on the concept that it didn't need. She thought it was critical that we have tea tastings and samplings in order to educate people about fine tea.

She very quickly suggested that she doesn't want to pay for excess packaging of a good thing. The thing she likes about Peet's tins is their simplicity. She doesn't want a lot of hype, she wants information, but she wants to be paying for what's inside, not what's outside.

She didn't like our TRoT names at all. She thought we should just name the tea what it was. She said that Metabolic Frolic, All-Day Breakfast sounded cute and clever, just like Celestical Seasonings. She thought we should be the serious tea company that people graduate to from CS and Bigelow, Stash, etc. She liked Anhwei Keemun Tea and Mango Ceylon Tea. She made a lot of sense. I could imagine using our clever ideas as part of the package copy. For instance Keemun Oolong Tea. "The Minister of Leaves thinks of this Keemun Oolong as his all-day breakfast tea because he drinks it morning, noon, and night. . . ."

— Progress

THE MINISTER OF LEAVES

10 November 1991

Dear Progress:

Bruce makes a lot of sense. I agree with him — wholesaling is the way to go. The attorney makes a lot of sense too — although I'd be careful with some of her suggestions. What the world most certainly does not need is another *serious* tea company. Maybe you should slip a little Metabolic Frolic into her tea next time.

— Leaves.

THE MINISTER OF PROGRESS

22 November 1991

Here's a copy of our working charter that hangs in front of me as I work (all alone) at the Embassy:

Charter of The Republic of Tea

1. We will sell only the best teas we can find.
2. We will be driven by *our own curiosity* to discover new products and insights about our lives and business.
3. For the citizens of The Republic, the process of preparing and enjoying tea is as important as the quality of the tea itself. There is a tea for every time and a time for every tea.

4. We will work diligently to educate our customers and potential customers about the health benefits of tea and the extraordinary variety, quality, and flavors of fine loose tea. We will always present our message with humility, free of zealousness and pressure.

— Progress

THE MINISTER OF PROGRESS

23 November 1991

Dear Leaves,

Sometimes I go to the store and stand for hours in the tea aisle, staring, studying, and soaking it in. The other day I watched people pick up one box of tea, only to put it back on the shelf and pick up another. I saw people stop and reflect on the packages, almost "feeling" the product's presence as part of their decision-making process. Others walked up, predetermined and efficient, and grabbed their old favorite.

At Cost Plus I watched a man pick up a pack of tea bags, only to return it to the shelf in favor of a tin of loose tea. Another gentleman started with a tin of Twinings Earl Grey, but returned it to the shelf in exchange for bags. I saw a professionally dressed woman go for the exotically packaged Chinese herbal teas and an older gentleman go right for the Ridgeways.

Here's some observations (as limited and subjective as they are sure to be):

1. People are drinking a lot of tea after meals and before bedtime. Sleepytime, camomile, and mint teas seem to lead the pack consistently in sales.
2. Lemon seems to be popular, particularly Bigelow's Lemon Lift and

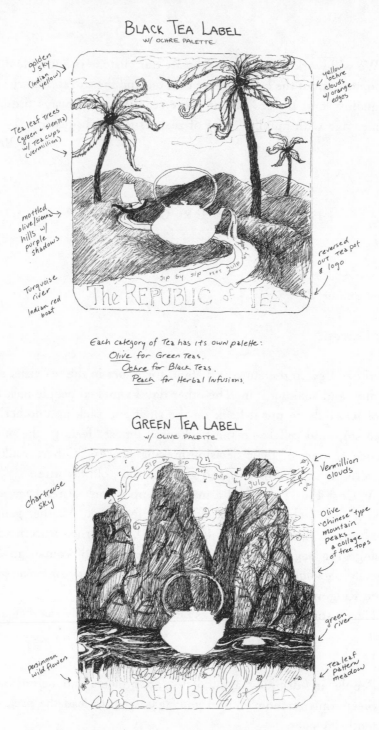

BLACK TEA LABEL
w/ OCHRE PALETTE

golden sky (Indian yellow)

yellow ochre clouds w/ orange edges

Tea leaf trees (green + sienna) w/ tea cups (vermillion)

mottled olive/sienna hills w/ purple shadows

Turquoise river

Indian red boat

reversed out teapot & logo

sip by sip not gulp by

The REPUBLIC of TEA

Each category of Tea has its own palette:
   Olive for Green Teas.
   Ochre for Black Teas.
   Peach for Herbal Infusions.

GREEN TEA LABEL
w/ OLIVE PALETTE

Chartreuse sky

Vermillion clouds

Olive "chinese" type mountain peaks — a collage of tree tops

green river

Tea leaf pattern meadow

persimmon wild flowers

sip by sip not gulp by gulp

The REPUBLIC of TEA

Generic labels for each category of Tea.
Combination of collage, black line illustration
& hand tinting.

CS Lemon Zinger. Also Bigelow sells a lot of Constant Comment, which is really Orange Pekoe with a little cinnamon (I think).

3. There is no green tea on the shelf that looks appealing at this point. It still looks "foreign" (as opposed to exotic) or cheap à la Chinese restaurant tea.

4. The American palate in tea must be "flavorized." People drink lots of "flavored" tea. So for the most part they're not tasting tea, but the flavor that covers it up.

5. There's a ton of tea out there, but there's still room for us. No one is connecting it to societal trends, slowing down, and the tea experience. It's still principally a commodity business, even in the specialty area.

More questions about context:

•   We've got to be able to emphasize the process of preparing and drinking tea in our packaging and communication.

•   We've got to be perceived as serious about tea and light on life. (Leaves: you're The Minister of Serious Mischief, ok.)

•   We've got to awaken people to the idea of "rare," "original," and special teas without making them exclusive or snooty. There's already so much hype out there. Stash: *specialty* and *gourmet*. CS: *distinctive*, Twinings: *traditional*, etc.

We've got to get The Republic on the shelf. And soon.

— Progress

The Minister of Progress

26 November 1991

Dear Leaves and Enchantment

Every day it becomes a little clearer to me how to distinguish our products:

All tea that is put into bags is processed by the mechanized CTC (Cut, Torn, Crushed) method. The majority of our teas are hand picked. Some are even hand rolled.

Tea-bag tea is dust (bottom of the barrel) or fannings (tea trade lingo for the very small, crushed leaf). Ours is full leaf or large leaf tea.

Most teas sold in packages today, even the finer ones, are blends of many different teas. The components of these blends vary from week to week, but the goal is to keep a consistent look and taste to the tea. In a way, this approach nullifies the natural wonder of the plant and the fact that tea is truly a product of its unique cultivation. Blending tea to a standard in some ways denies the exceptional and transient characteristics that might be unique to one harvest or another. I understand from my reading that the tea trade intentionally went to marketing blends to avoid difficulty in years when the crop was not so good. In a way, then, we've been marketed into accepting consistently ok product (or poor product) instead of learning to appreciate outstanding and exceptional products.

Unlike Blends, some of our teas are original or orthodox that come direct from a specific estate.

Our teas will be known as rare teas because they are available in limited quantities.

Our gift to the customer will be our ability and commitment to find and distribute the rare, original, and great teas on an ongoing basis. We will build our credibility by selling only the finest teas we can find.

We will no doubt be vulnerable to competition once this high-end

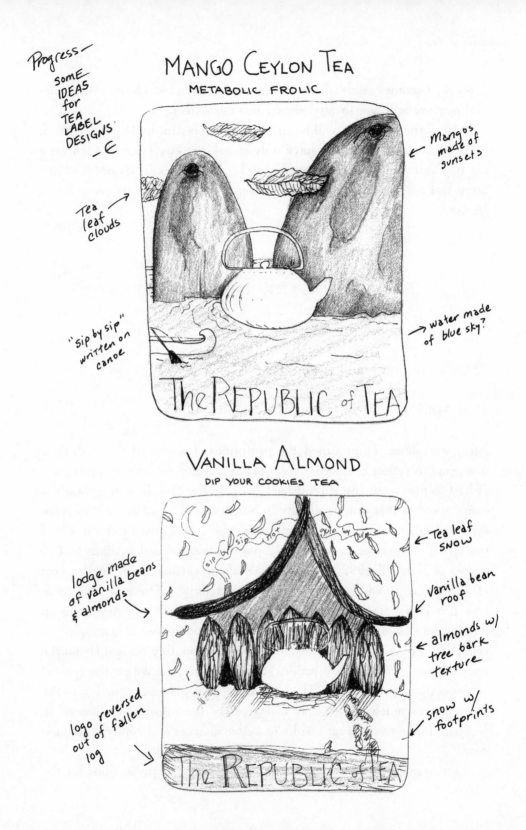

category becomes established, but hopefully the brand identity we create and nurture will win loyalty among our customers.

Now the challenge will be in the education. But on the other hand, it's as plain as can be. We have only to ask the customer to open up a tea bag and pour out the dust, then take a look at a teaspoonful of our large leaf tea. And of course the difference cannot only be seen, it can be *tasted*.

— Progress

THE MINISTER OF PROGRESS

---

12 December 1991

Dear Mel,

After we talked, I fine-tuned the proformas. I amended the cash flow proforma to reflect the actual costs of purchasing the startup inventory. (I had to play with the spreadsheet because the cash flow template I'm using assumes that you're already in business and I had to fix it to work for a startup.) I also clarified and made specific the goal (and integrated the specific costs) of creating a 12-page catalogue and mailing 60,000 copies of it in fall 1992. (For the sake of forecasting, I assumed a cost of 75¢ per copy and a 2% return on the mailing.) The cash flow plan now provides a more accurate depiction of how much money we end up with at the end of year one. The first version you looked at last night did not. Also, I plan to create a detailed company monthly budget (from the rough annual proforma projections) to work from once we get the general business plan agreed upon. This will make management reporting to the shareholders much easier, and will give me the information I need to compare budget vs. actual results to better manage and control the business.

I also eased back just a hair on my overall sales projections for the third year to $2.1 million. This represents a doubling of sales between years 2 and 3, which is aggressive enough a forecast. (My actual hope and hunch is that I will exceed my sales forecast during the first year.) I also beefed up the marketing/travel budget a bit in anticipation of some early year travel. And I changed Payroll Burden to read Payroll Taxes and Benefits, as you suggested.

Thanks again for the input.

— Progress

The Minister of Progress

14 December 1991

Dear Leaves,

I just got off the phone following a one-hour grilling by Bruce's father. It came as a surprise to me that our conversation took on this dimension, because when Bruce suggested that I speak to him it was in the context of someone who could offer me some sage experience and advice about quality control and overseas business dealings. I thought *I* would be asking *him* the questions. Not so. I faced a most challenging and almost confrontational questioner.

I wasn't expecting this onslaught of tough issues, but I rallied my knowledge and confidence to address them. I also didn't realize that he had already reviewed a copy of my business plan when he zinged me with one about why two numbers on the balance sheet didn't jive. He caught me with a quick jab and pushed me off guard. I was a bit jittery, but I charged back. He told me he was looking at the plan with the scrutiny of a "banker." I could sense that this was going to be an important test for me.

Some of the questions he posed with a hard-edge challenge:

"How are you going to secure and insure the quality of the product from door to door?" (I described the terms and conditions of our purchase orders and shipping instructions.)

"What mechanism do you have with your vendor for resolving disputes that have to do with quality, consistency, and delivery?" (We discussed the possibility of holding back 20% of the invoice to be paid 30 days after receipt to accommodate this possibility.)

"What vulnerabilities does your product have with respect to weather and contamination?" "How are you going to manage against those in transit and in storage?" (We talked about the need to ship it in its own container so it wouldn't get contaminated by foreign cargo.)

"How are you going to convince the bank that they should loan money against inventory?" (By providing examples and references of other businesses that do exactly that. We can get these examples and references from other fast-growing wholesale businesses that import products from other countries.)

"How are you going to clearly tell the market that this is not a "me-too" product?" (By doing tastings and developing third-party endorsements.)

"How are you going to obtain third-party endorsements?" (Very carefully.) And many others . . .

After forty-five minutes the tone of our conversation warmed up considerably as he came to see that I had done my homework. Soon our discussion became relaxed and cordial and he wished me the best of luck. The tone transformed from difficult to supportive as he became more comfortable with my knowledge of the business and how I thought about it. He ended the conversation by offering his expertise and assistance at any turn.

He'd made me question my own thinking in a way I hadn't, and forced me to think (and talk) on my feet. I had to justify anew every premise I was working on. Whew! There's nothing like having one's personal, fragile ideas raked over the coals by a tough-minded, return-on-investment-minded business person.

— Progress

THE MINISTER OF PROGRESS

17 December 1991

Dear Leaves,

These are long, dark wintry days in the canyon. I'm struggling each day to finalize my arrangement with Bruce — who seems so close to committing but also strangely elusive at the same time. It's probably just a matter of being a "lower" priority for him than it is for me. This emotional imbalance creates a nervous mood for me: There is nothing more crucial to me than to get him signed, sealed, and his money delivered, yet to him it is just one of many things in a busy life to get to. This is the story of a startup. To everyone I contact I am a small potential customer. As far as they're concerned, I may as well be just another wild-assed speculating guy playing with an idea. Yet to make serious progress, I need all of my potential suppliers and collaborators to take me seriously.

I spoke with our corporate attorney today about where we were with our investor, and she remarked, "Boy this feels like it's taking a long time." I felt a little defensive about that comment because every day I make this turning point (getting the money in the bank) my highest priority. I'm inching toward it, fulfilling each request in their due-diligence process with blazing responsiveness, asking questions to uncover any potential objections or concerns, and continually putting the ball back in his court. This Friday is my day. I'm going for the close.

It seems like I'm concentrating on nothing but product (and funding) now. I started the day talking to brokers in Europe. I'm working on acquiring (or acquiring access to) a new tea-bagging machine which really produces a better bag (pillow). (Nothing "me-too" about any of our product.) I'm also doing cost analysis on contract packaging vs. leasing our own equipment to determine the break-even points. And I'm analyzing the shipping and customs charges of importation and figuring out my strategy with respect to developing aggressive terms and credit with our vendors.

I reread some of my earlier letters to you this afternoon and I'm almost embarrassed by them now. How could I be so oblivious to the fact that there is no way to start a business without having a tangible product? or a full-time commitment? or a workable business structure between partners? My letters were all dreams about marketing and positioning. No wonder I was stuck. I understood the concept for the business, but I guess I was waiting for someone (from somewhere?) to *give* me the product.

Tea has changed the tempo of my life. Although I still get wrapped up in the frenetic pace of a startup at times, tea anchors me and reminds me of my own limitations. I prepare each pot consciously, aware that this process, like my life, has its own unique time: *The tea comes out of the teapot at its own pace. If I pour too fast, I make a mess; If I pour too slowly, it dribbles and I make a mess.* I've learned to pay better attention to what I'm doing while I'm doing it. In the past I often was thinking about something other than what I was doing. Now I try to be completely involved with what I'm doing at the moment. I guess I've got to master doing before I get to the not-doing, right?

As for becoming a tea merchant, now I touch, taste, drink, and differentiate the product every day. I'm now talking the language of tea with growers, blenders, packers, shipping agents, customs brokers, the FDA. I'm an outsider becoming an insider. This process takes time, persistence, commitment, and especially a deep belief in the company's purpose. I'm receiving samples to cup weekly. Just today two samples of organic tea arrived from a broker I met in London: an exceptional organic Darjeeling, good enough to stand on its own as an original tea, and a good-caliber Malawai tea which would be useful as a base for future organic-based flavored teas.

I have learned so much in the past twenty months. Business isn't just about an idea for a business. It's fundamentally about a product that has an intrinsic value to a customer. I finally understand: the *name* of the tea doesn't really matter — (it's not going to get the customer to buy the tea more than once). It's the tea itself that is going to motivate a second buy. How simple.

It's taken me a long time to get here and I'm still only at the beginning.

— Progress

Tea opens the place beyond words. With the first sip I am only a visitor, but by the time I have drained the last drop from the cup it is my home. The tea inhabits me, and I the tea; there is no longer a distinction between us. What is named "me" and what is named "tea" are passing clouds. Together as one, we are the ineffable buoyancy of being.

— The Minister of Leaves

The Republic of Tea was incorporated on January 22, 1992, by Mel, Bill, and Patricia. The company's first product shipped in May 1992.

Epilogue

The Birth of a Business

AND SO A BUSINESS IS BORN.

Like all birth, it began with a gathering of the energies of conception, then a fusion, and growth — growth in Bill, in the universe as Bill experienced it, in Bill's relationship to himself, in Bill's relationship to Patricia and me, in Bill's relationship to Bruce, and in Bill's relationship to the *camellia sinensis* leaf known as tea. As a gestation it was exactly as long as it needed to be. Recognizing that true creation takes place outside time, The Republic of Tea came to life when it was ready to be born. It was, to be sure, Bill who carried it in him for the twenty up-and-down, all-around months documented in these pages, and it was Bill who, in accepting his first dollar for a tin of tea in May 1992 delivered the baby to the world.

As for my role, I got him pregnant.

In compiling these letters for publication, a keystone of ancient Hindu philosophy comes to mind: "Everything happens as it does because the universe is as it is."

There is no formula for starting a business. It is an exercise as unique as the individuals who undertake it. Starting TRoT was an exercise in allowing things to happen. Yes, the business could have started sooner; yes, I could have taken a more active role; yes, I could have saved Bill a lot of "wasted" effort by helping to straighten out some of his loopier ideas; yes, yes, yes, to every possibility that was floated. But the underlying truth, the ultimate reality, is that had we *forced* anything, that very forcing would today be part of the business itself, and latent though it might be, it would surely one day be the beginning of the undoing of the business. What is put together by force will sooner or later come apart, if not by force then merely by itself. In conceiving and brainstorming and imagining TRoT, none of us ultimately wanted to force something that did not want to be — concepts, structures, relationships. Difficult as it was for us at times, we learned to listen to it. This is our proudest achievement. Whether it translates to a huge business success remains to be seen. Only time will tell if there were lapses in our awareness that also resulted in an *unwillingness to listen to, or an unwillingness to see* something about the business, about ourselves, about the relationships. If there were, these, too, will be part of the business, and we will pay the consequences for them later.

So starting a business is no different from starting anything else — a marriage, a painting, a new life. The opportunity it presents as a path to self-realization is the one most often overlooked, and yet I feel this is ultimately its greatest benefit. On this score, Bill is already a billionaire. He had the earnestness and the courage to look at things squarely, to accept that the "problems" were only a projection of his own limited thinking, and to "correct" his course and move ever onward. So it is. If the process is organic, if the impulse is true, if things can be seen in their own nature and let be, nothing will go wrong. Ultimately it is only our willingness to *yield* that makes the business thrive for the long run. Though it might seem at first anathema to the aggressive and preemptive nature of today's business practices, *yielding*, is the surest course for success. It is having the grace to be friendly with the inevitable, to make the universe your partner (i.e., *"Everything happens as it does because the universe is as it is"*). To master the art of yielding, the business person must open himself in awareness to the forces at play that are focalizing around him. You cannot bully reality. To yield, the business person's ego must be set aside. Yielding means listening to what is truly inside ourselves buried under the weight of our so-called "knowledge," as well as to what is in the hearts and minds of customers, vendors, employees. It means *letting in* what's in the air we breathe. If a thing is useful and relevant, it will live, and all to whom it is of use and relevance will share in its life. If it is of no use, it is of no use, and forcing it will make it no more useful.

A word or two needs to be registered here about practicality and business. Practicality is the Master. No good thing can come from fighting with practicality. That is not the problem of most businesses, however.

Where business tends to go astray is that their executives seem to *worship* practicality, and do not dare allow themselves to look beyond it. Practicality, of course, is born in chaos. Practicing practicality as if it were divinely conceived is to deny oneself access to the inexhaustible source of all inspiration. Yielding means yielding, first and foremost, to chaos. Order is a construct made from chaos, and the business person who resists chaos, which is at the heart of the creative process, will find that in time his business will only grow brittle and irrelevant. A business that is conceived in practicality will be congenitally dry. Bill and Patricia and I may have been a little wacky in some of our early ideas, but this is because we knew the day of practicality would come. Because we dared to be impractical at the outset, however, TRoT will likely carry with it a legacy of free, unmoored thinking, which is really the only true insurance policy a business can have.

So now we have The Republic of Tea. It happened because Bill is as he is, Patricia is as she is, Bruce is as he is, I am as I am, and the universe is as it is. How long it will live, whether or not it will realize its limitless potential, the destiny it will shape for itself—these are the things that cannot be foretold. TRoT is no longer a dialogue among the four of us anymore. It is a dialogue between itself and customers. And if we correctly heard the winds whispering to us all those months that TRoT lived inside our heads, it will soon have people everywhere pausing for a sip, and a little peace of Tea Mind.

— MZ

Who draws the water and boils it? Who spoons the leaves from the tin, and places them in the pot? Who lifts the kettle and pours? Who waits? Who fills the cup?

Who drinks the tea?

— **The Minister of Leaves**

BUSINESS PLAN AND PROFORMA PROJECTIONS

19 DECEMBER 1991

Confidential
(For Internal Use Only. Not For Distribution)
Prepared for the Executive Council of
The Republic of Tea
for the purpose of defining and clarifying
the direction and plans of the company.

Business Summary

Fine, full leaf teas (black, green, and herbal) are an undervalued and underappreciated product in the United States. Our initial goal is to build a company and a specialty brand that creates and captures the market for superior quality teas and ushers in a new "tea experience" in America.

The Republic of Tea is a purveyor of exquisite teas and tea-related products that support the preparation and enjoyment of tea. The Republic offers teas and herbs superior to anything that is presently (widely) available on the market, as well as a fresh and welcome philosophy to life that is conveyed by the personality of the business.

America knows tea through the tea bag, a product that is dull and tasteless when compared to the rich and diverse leaves that are brewed whole in virtually every other nation on Earth. In recent years America's specialty coffee retailers have begun to offer loose tea in bulk, but to date no one has claimed a leadership position as a recognizable packaged brand in this category. This is the opportunity we will pursue.

The Republic of Tea distinguishes itself by offering only the finest grades and tastes of teas and herbs, many of which have been previously unavailable (or difficult to find) in this country. We continue to search for superior products with broad potential appeal that are not readily known about or available. Many of these beverages are successful in other parts of the world and have never been popularly marketed in the US. Our charter insists that we will sell only a tea that we love to drink ourselves.

Drawing on the rich history of tea, recent scientific discoveries, and the growing trends toward moderation in American society, The Republic of Tea is a business that not only sells tea and related products but interesting and inspiring information as well. Through its packaging and extensive company communications, TRoT presents a whimsical metaphor for a life that is attentive, balanced, and happy. The company's philosophy is best summed up as "Life . . . sip by sip, not gulp by gulp."

While tea represents a healthier alternative to coffee, a drink representative of the fast-paced 1980s, it also represents a history of ritual and ceremony that America is desperately in search of. Tea is about time and noticing the moment. Indeed, for thousands of years, many diverse cultures have used tea as a focal point for social interaction and personal reflection. Despite some existing preconceptions, fine tea is no more difficult to prepare than fresh roasted coffee beans. TRoT will endeavor to design and market the delightful tools that make the preparation of fine tea easy and enjoyable.

The present state of tea has been compared to the wine business in the '70s and the specialty coffee business of the '80s. Indeed, there are many parallels with wine and coffee that the public will relate to. While the commodity tea business (Lipton, Tetley) has remained flat over the last decade, specialty tea sales (Twinings, Celestial Seasonings, Bigelow) have continued to grow at about 15% a year. Some experts expect that tea has the potential to explode in a similar way that specialty coffee did during the past ten years. There is clearly an opportunity to establish a quality position and expectation beyond Twinings, Celestial, Stash, and Bigelow. TRoT intends to dominate that niche.

Specialty tea sales in the United States are estimated to be in excess of $300 million per year. We expect this category to grow significantly during the decade as more customers discover better tea, move toward increasing moderation and temperance in society, move away from coffee and alcohol, and learn to appreciate the health and medicinal benefits of tea.

TRoT's packaged full leaf and bagged tea will be marketed through wholesale distribution to specialty gourmet, coffee and tea, department, natural food, and gift stores; to special restaurants, and targeted mail order catalogues; and through our own small response-based mail order operation. The company will maintain a central warehouse facility for storage, blending, packing, and shipping, complete with a public "tasting room" facility, designed to reinforce the "tea experience" we are promoting.

The target customer for The Republic is primarily a female professional, educated baby-boomer aged 25 to 50. Initial customers will probably already be tea drinkers, but others, like health-conscious coffee drinkers, will be drawn to TRoT through hard-hitting health-oriented communication and enchanting promotion.

Although the primary product focus of the business is on tea and the enjoyment of tea, the company ultimately is in the lifestyle business. The long-term goal is to create a powerful brand identity that is representative of a market and a lifestyle with numerous expansion opportunities into areas like food, housewares, clothing, and furnishings.

Short-term goals (first 18 months):

During the first 18 months of operation, our goal is to establish prominent national distribution and create a highly visible product and brand identity that exemplifies the quality and aesthetic of the business.

1. Open a central **business facility** for the importation, storage, blending, packaging, and shipping of tea. Create a (adjoining if possible) tasting room to be used for education and promotion of the tea experience. Build a small, dedicated, and talented **team of employees** to grow the business.
2. Establish **wholesale distribution** of the product in specialty gourmet (including department stores), natural foods, and gift stores, as well as in several catalogues and trend-setting restaurants and hotels. Will account for 80% of sales.
3. Publish **two simple, low-cost mail order catalogues.** The first catalogue will be available on a request-only basis; the second will involve a test of lists. Catalogue sales will account for approximately 15% of the business but a higher percentage of the profits.
4. Explore **line extension of the brand** to include tea cookies and honeys in conjunction with a contract manufacturer/private labeler. These products will then be sold through our developing and existing specialty distribution.
5. Generate substantial **publicity and recognition** for the brand.

Longer-term goal (18 months to 3 years):

1. **Expand** the company's proprietary **product line**, exploring specialty food extensions such as cookies, cakes, bottled beverages. Also explore further extensions of the brand to include lifestyle opportunities like clothing, furnishings, and housewares. Explore the potential to license designs and the TRoT brand identity to other leading manufacturers.
2. Define and evaluate a **retail store plan** that may include franchising, company-owned stores, co-ventures (store within a store), and mall kiosks.
3. Evaluate the **profitability of the catalogue** to determine if it is a viable and useful component of the business in the long term. Develop a roll-out plan if desired.
4. **Expand distribution** on national and international levels.

Product

TRoT's initial packaged product line will be comprised of full leaf black, green, and herbal teas. The catalogue will offer a small variety of tea-related products like pots, cups, kettles, and cookies, as well as a much richer selection of teas.

Tea: Our emphasis is on fine *loose* tea because it is clearly superior in taste and quality to tea found in tea bags. Loose tea is also best suited to the ritual of preparation that is key to TRoT's message. Our teas come from the finest gardens in China, Japan, India, and Sri Lanka. Initial tea offerings include limited-edition products (first flush Darjeeling from the Castleton Estate) and special blends (All-Day Breakfast Tea, Ginger Peach, etc.). Herb teas are blended from exotic, hand-crafted, organically grown herbs. We avoid any artificial additives and flavors. In general we will position our teas as healthier,° tastier, and of higher quality than the competition. (We will be upscale from Celestial Seasonings. *"Graduate to the Republic of Tea."*) Our teas are named for actual ingredients and for their philosophic spirit and their flavors (Metabolic Frolic, Surrender to Sleep, Wake Up Dancing, etc.). Some teas are blended with a specific medicinally oriented purpose in mind such as a sleep inducer,

---

°Recent published studies indicate that tea (green tea in particular) may prevent cancer and cavities.

digestive aid, etc. The herbal and medicinal qualities of tea and herbs will be woven into the overall voice of the business. The tea product line is a mix of real teas, healing herbs and botanicals, and Chinese medicinals. Whenever possible we will push the boundaries of the existing tea business into the distribution of higher quality products, organically grown products, as well as new blends and flavors.

Product Development

Status as of 12/1/91

Tea products sourced, priced, tested:
>   Mango Ceylon (loose and fannings)
>   Ginger Peach Ceylon (loose and fannings)
>   Keemun-Oolong All-Day Breakfast
>   Rare Wuyi Mountain Oolong
>   Hojicha Roasted Organically Grown
>   Yin Hao Jasmine

Products in testing, negotiation, or development:
>   Cinnamon Plum
>   Insomniac's Tea (herbal)
>   Orange Blossom Oolong
>   Digestive Tea (herbal)
>   Castleton Darjeeling (first and second flushes)
>   Lemon Ginseng Tea
>   Ma Huang Licorice Herbal Tea
>   Children's Fruit and Herb Tea
>   Vanilla Spice

Catalog products sourced and priced:
>   Iron teapots
>   Cherrywood canisters
>   Hot pot carafe
>   Teacups
>   Ceramic teapots
>   Yixing teapots

Proposed Product Plan for Launch
(to be discussed at council meeting)

3.5 oz tins packaged 12 to a case

Name GM SRP Margin		COGS		Whsle	
Mango Ceylon Metabolic Frolic Tea	1.98	3.95	50%	7.50	45%
Ginger Peach Longevity Tea	1.78	3.95	54%	7.50	45%
Orange Blossom Oolong or Mao Jian Green°	1.95	3.95	50%	7.50	45%
Keemun Oolong All-Day Breakfast Tea	1.95	3.95	50%	7.50	45%
Insomniac's Bedtime Herb Tea°	1.75	3.95	55%	7.50	45%
After Meal Cleansing Digestion Tea°	1.85	3.95	54%	7.50	45%

40 tea bags in tins packaged 12 to a case

Name GM SRP Margin		COGS		Whsle	
Mango Ceylon Metabolic Frolic Tea	1.50	3.00	50%	6.00	50%
Ginger Peach Longevity Tea	1.50	3.00	50%	6.00	50%
Keemun Oolong All-Day Breakfast Tea	1.50	3.00	50%	6.00	50%
Restaurant table caddy w/6 tins (each)	15.00	45.00	75%	$300	85%
Restaurant refill 1/2 lb of 6 flavors	24.00	60.00	50%	$600	90%
Gift sets with 3 tins of tea	6.50	13.00	46%	25.00	48%
Gift set with pot (fall 1992)	11.00	20.00	45%	29.95	44%

Custom designed and produced for specific customers who can meet minimum order

°Still in formulation

Product Launch Sales Plan

FIRST FOUR MONTHS: (March–June)
- Develop attractive opening promotional order
- Target: Major metropolitan areas of the US
- Multistore businesses (2 or more locations) (specialty grocery, specialty coffee, specialty gift, department, natural food, bookstores, restaurants, and hotels)
- Market Leaders who will support the total TRoT concept through merchandising, tastings, and promotion
- Personal presentations by WBR for direct sale

NEXT FOUR MONTHS: (July–October)
- Develop key regional distribution through existing channels and contacts
- Concentrate on national catalogues and retail chains such as Williams-Sonoma, Smith and Hawken, Nature Company, Gloria Jeans, Crate and Barrel, B. Dalton, Waldenbooks, Rizzoli, Brentano's
- Personal sales presentations and custom promotion support
- Coordinate with book publication for in-store signings and promotions
- Publish and distribute 12-page catalogue from Republic of Tea (fall 1992)
- Test 60,000–100,000 names in conjunction with book promotion

NEXT FOUR MONTHS: (November–February)
- Expand distribution in metropolitan markets and begin regional distribution
- Target: High quality specialty food and coffee representatives
- Create wholesale selling kit with press clippings and story
- Interview rep companies, select and train, and set sales targets
- Provide business-to-business direct mail campaign direct from home office and through rep firms to service accounts

ACCOUNTS PENDING: (I have met with the principals of all of these companies and they have agreed to purchase and support the product as soon as it becomes available.)

Just Desserts (7 stores in Bay Area) will serve tea and sell packaged tea

Zona (2 stores NYC, Aspen) will sell packaged tea and support program

Terra Verde (2 stores) will sell packaged tea

Packaging and Presentation

Initially, we will define our niche as Exquisite Full Leaf Teas. We will package six types/flavors of tea for wholesale distribution in 100g (3.5 oz. tins). Three teas (Mango, Peach, and All-Day Breakfast) will be available in tea bags. In addition, we will offer gift samplers and packages that will be customized for large special accounts like catalogues and department stores. (It is conceivable that Smith and Hawken would have a specialized package that would be different from one sold to Norm Thompson.) SRP of the tea will be between $6.00 and $15.00 per tin. Gift packs from $15–25.00.

After six months of successful distribution and acceptance we will introduce six more flavors of tea and refine the original six packages if necessary.

Our restaurant service will include a special table caddy containing six teas, special logoed brewing pots (with ceramic infusers and customized with the TRoT logo), a tea menu, and an informational booklet that explains tea. We will work with specific restaurants to develop a special service program, offering on-site training and video training support. We will offer a startup package and a fulfillment package that will offer the restaurateur exciting profit potential as well as an opportunity to distinguish their institution.

Although our emphasis will be on loose teas, we will offer our best-selling products in pillow-style tea bags, free of unnecessary wrapping, tags, string, and staples. (We will market an environmentally friendly, unbleached tea bag only.) All packaged products will be presented in attractive, natural, and environmentally conscious resealable and reusable containers that keep the tea fresh. All labeling will convey educational information and the whimsy and spirit of the business.

The Republic of Tea is a progressive, environmentally and socially conscious business that will work to elevate consumers' consciousness of wasteful packaging and the opportunities for reuse and recycling. Our own approach will exemplify our commitment to simplicity and the elimination of excess and harmful packaging and the encouragement of recycling and reuse. Whenever possible we will look to develop mutually beneficial relationships with community growing and sustainable agricultural projects to help supply ingredients for our tea.

Margin

Wholesale packaged goods will carry a 50% gross margin from manufacturer to wholesaler with another 45% to suggested retail. (Our cost $1.50–2.00 per unit; wholesale cost $3–4.00 per unit; SRP $6–7.50 per unit.) Tins of tea will be sold in cases of 12 units for $48.00.

Teas sold at retail through the tasting room and our catalogue will carry at least a 75% gross margin.

Tea-related products sold in the catalogue will carry a 40–70% gross margin.

Operations

PERSONNEL

The business will be a small, tightly run operation. Bill Rosenzweig will be responsible for overall business management as well as sales and marketing. An operations manager (see job description) with responsibility for inside sales support including manufacturing and customer service will be hired in April. Part-time warehouse personnel will be hired on an as-needed basis. A full-time office assistant (hired in February) will provide customer service support and general office services. As distribution and sales grow we will add a shipping manager and additional customer service support.

We will leverage our resources by using as much contract labor as possible, particularly in the creative services, bookkeeping, and contract packaging areas. Our goal will be to stay as lean and flexible as possible without compromising the health and well-being of our employees or the company.

Full-time personnel summary:

Bill Rosenzweig, President and CEO. Start date December 1, 1991.

Operations Manager. Start date April 1, 1992.

Office Assistant (Customer Service). Start date February 1, 1992.

When sales reach $500,000 on an annual basis, add warehouse manager and additional customer service assistant. When sales reach $1 million, add controller.

FACILITIES

The company will begin shipping product in April 1992. A 3000-square-foot warehouse set up for storage, packing, and shipping of product will be procured by March 1992. Ideally, the warehouse will be in a location and have a facility that can serve as a public tasting room that will offer a small retail presence. The warehouse will also have a small area for three offices.

COMPUTERIZATION

We will use computers extensively for order entry and processing, inventory management, financial management and bookkeeping, and creative tasks. Our goal is to leverage our human resources as efficiently as possible by establishing a small in-house computer network.

PACKING

Packing of tins will be done on premises with a simple form-and-fill machine that will be acquired for the business. Tea bagging will be done on a contract basis off premises. Tin labeling and sealing, and case packing will also be done on premises. We will utilize contract packing labor to do production runs of product. This will be managed on a just-in-time basis. We will design the warehouse to be set up for packing shifts that will coordinate with sales.

INVENTORY MANAGEMENT

Importation and shipping costs dictate that tea be imported in full container-load shipments. A container is approximately 200 chests of tea. (Each chest contains 66 lbs.) 200 chests of tea will yield approximately 3770 finished tins or 314 cases of product.

A container of product takes approximately twelve weeks to arrive from Europe or Asia to San Francisco. The FDA regulates the importation of tea, so all tea must be inspected before being released. We will work with an experienced and reputable customs broker to be sure we comply with all necessary requirements. We are working with our vendors to negotiate favorable pricing and terms not less than 90 days from receipt.

Our tins will be coming from Japan, where the minimum order is 10,000 units. Manufacturing lead time is four weeks and shipping time is eight weeks. We need to place an order in late January to be able to ship product in April.

The paper label system for the tins will be modular and will allow for maximum flexibility in the development of finished inventory to match orders. This way we don't get stuck with obsolete packages. As we develop some sales history and customer feedback we will fine-tune our inventory management system for greatest efficiency and customer satisfaction.

Sales, Marketing, and Promotion

Our goal is to generate $500,000 in sales during our first year, $1 million in our second, and $2.1 million or more in our third year.

Initially, the company will be a sales-driven organization. During the first year the CEO will spend 75% of his time selling: opening distribution, evangelizing, and promoting the enjoyment of TRoT products.

The Republic of Tea is dedicated to informational, truthful marketing. We will continually educate our customers about our products: their intrinsic value as well as the story behind them. The collective efforts of the entire business will be to create a consistent and highly attractive image of the company and its products. We will emphasize imagination and coordination in all of our communications and promotional efforts, working to leverage our resources to the fullest extent possible.

Wholesale Sales Strategy

Our strategy will be to build success stories within the businesses of established (and perceived) market leaders and leverage this toward further distribution. We will explore as many "direct" and large-size clients as possible but may also develop relationships with reps, distributors, and food brokers. During this phase we will be primarily a sales-driven organization looking to build strong, long-term relationships with our customers. We will develop a quality and service-oriented organization that understands sales from the inside out.

We will launch the business in the Bay Area in conjunction with several specialty retailers, restaurateurs, and hotels. We are already involved in discussions with Just Desserts, a wholesale/retail business with seven dessert retail stores in the Bay Area. They have agreed to serve and sell our tea and we will work closely with them to create an early success story. We will offer training and support to assure the successful creation of a new tea experience in the Bay Area. This resource will serve as a great launching pad for publicity as well. (The Good Earth restaurants launched a highly successful retail brand from their restaurant identity.)

We will proceed to open as many local direct accounts as possible and then work through our network of contacts in the specialty food business to create national distribution. We will affiliate ourselves with those businesses that have a special affinity for our message and product. We will try to create special events and in-store promotions with these customers. Whenever possible, we will deal as personally as possible.

Next, we will open some representative relationships with specialty tea, coffee, and food reps who have an affinity for TRoT. We have already identified many of these in key markets in the country through our research.

Finally, we will participate in the appropriate gourmet and specialty food trade shows.

We will develop a variety of sales tools, including a wholesale sell sheet, business-to-business direct mail program geared for specific niche customers (restaurants, coffee/tea stores), retail shelf talkers and POP displays, coop advertising ad slicks, promotional training videos (brewing, serving tea), background fact sheets on caffeine, health, and other related topics, T-shirts and other specialty ad items, and a trade show display.

Christmas 1992 target catalogues:

Smith and Hawken, Fortune's Almanac, Williams-Sonoma, and Judy Frank need to be introduced to the product no later than April 1992.

TRoT Catalogue Sales Strategy

We will generate our own customer list by offering the catalogue on our wholesale packages. (This has been very successful for Stash tea.) We may also do limited, highly targeted advertising to generate leads. The catalogues help to establish the total context of The Republic of Tea, conveying the spirit, distinct identity, and philosophy of the business well beyond the confines of wholesale distribution.

The catalogue allows us to develop direct relationships with our customers and will enable us to help expand their enjoyment of tea through a much broader product offering than will be available via wholesale. The catalogue business also provides a venue for research and product testing and facilitates word-of-mouth dissemination of the company's products and concept. The TRoT catalogue will also be key in the development of wholesale distribution (serving as a sales brochure). Catalogue fulfillment will initially be kept simple and low key.

We will plan to test a simple 12-page catalogue in fall 1992. We will mail to 50,000 to 100,000 target customers to coincide with the introduction of the book and the publicity generated around it. We will initially utilize a fulfillment resource to assist with the test to evaluate its potential as an in-house activity.

Financial Information and Proforma Projections

Contents:

Milestone Calendar
Financial Highlights (chart)
Break-even Analysis (chart)
First Year Sales by Month (chart)
3 Year Sales by Year (chart)
First Year Personnel Count (chart)
3 Year Personnel Count (chart)
Proforma Sales Forecast (2 pgs)
Proforma Income Statement (2 pgs)
Proforma Cash Flow (2 pgs)
Proforma Balance Sheet (2 pgs)

Notes and Highlights to Projected Financial Information

(in 000's)

	1992	1993	1994
Gross Sales	$330	$1,000	$2,100
Net Profit (loss)°	$(74)	$3	$315
Net Profit	(8.5)%	3%	14.5%

Assumptions to Proformas:

1. Reflects capital contributions of $430,000 during first three months of 1992 from Katz, Ziegler, Ziegler, and Rosenzweig.
2. Assumes initial shipment of product to customers in April 1992 and orders for inventory placed in January 1992. Assumes a startup order for inventory of $150,000 (which has been booked in the proforma as preexisting).

°After tax, assuming Sub-S status

3. Assumes capital expenditures of $35,000 during first quarter of operation for startup, legal, package design, warehouse equipment, and computer software. Assumes monthly lease of computer equipment and car of approximately $750 +. Capital depreciation has not been factored into the proforma as of this point.

4. Cash flow projection is not adjusted to reflect actual inventory purchasing cycles. This will be impacted by minimum orders, shipping times, and terms negotiated with vendors. Actual negative cash flow will be higher for certain periods due to the necessity to purchase 3 to 4 months worth of inventory at one time.

5. Assumes revolving line of credit in years two and three of 150K and 100K against inventory to stabilize cash flow management.

6. Assumes 50% per year increase in facilities (and related) costs to accommodate expansion of business.

7. Assumes net 7% decrease in cost of goods over 3 years due to volume purchases.

8. Assumes net 10% increase in sales price of goods over 3 years.

9. Assumes that we negotiate 60-day (minimum) terms on purchase of inventory and that we receive payment from our accounts within 45 days.

10. Assumes that the majority of first year sales are made direct without commissionable sales people. Years 2 and 3 reflect sales commissions paid to reps and brokers of 5%.

11. Third year sales of $2.1 million assumes extension of product line into related food product like cookies.

Excerpts from the First Catalog

Dear Fellow People of Tea:

I came to The Republic of Tea through a journey of many cups:

I had served nearly ten years as Prime Minister in another Republic where the beverage of choice was brewed from roasted coffee beans. Fueled by the coffee, life moved very rapidly in that other Republic, so fast that I began to sense I was missing something quite grand along the way. The sensation grew until I could bear it no longer. I was compelled to defect. Fleeing the race-to-nowhere that had been my life, I tasted the joys of existence in a new way – sip by sip rather than gulp by gulp.

I switched to tea.

With all due respect to Sir Thomas Lipton, be he apocryphal or real, I sadly realized that to drink the beverage served under his name for the rest of my life would be a sentence too bleak to bear. A new mission had finally found me. I set out in search of true tea.

It was with supreme good fortune that the Minister of Progress appeared one fine day and graciously offered his services. He declared it his own personal charge to canvass the most prized tea gardens of the world for their worthiest leaves, and said he would not rest until he saw these teas steaming in the cups of men, women and children everywhere. Inspired by his dedication, I too vowed I would stand beside him and serve Tea, as its humble Minister of Leaves. I took upon myself the task of easing the worried, the frustrated, the stressed, and the obsessed into the tranquil spell of the divine little camellia sinensis bush, where they would find themselves in the company of the immortal who, sipping himself into eternity, wrote, "Steam billows, the teapot fragrant. I enter a state of desires diminishing. Within the stillness, a further pleasure. Nothing coarse or superficial. This is drinking tea."

THE MINISTER OF LEAVES

TABLE OF CONTENTS

Day of Tea.................3
Our Full Leaf Teas.......4
Black Teas.................6
Brewing Tea.................8
Black Blended Teas......10
Yixing Teapots.............12
Green Teas.................14
A Year of Tea.............16
Herbal Infusions..........18
Teaware.....................20
Defect Now Kits..........22
Teabags.....................23
Tea Mind Library.........24
Rare Teas...................26
Tea Gifts..................28
Gift Certificates...........30
Teashirts...................31

YIXING TEAPOTS

In many parts of the world, tea is more than a drink for quenching thirst or delighting the pallette. In China, Japan, the Middle East, Britain there are great traditions of tea—from formal ceremonies to relaxed social occasions. In The Republic of Tea, we think of tea as a whimsical, modern-day metaphor for health, balance and awareness.

In China, over the centuries, preparing and drinking tea became an artform—and in the art of tea, there are three cherished ingredients: the leaves, the water, and the teapot. Without question, the finest teapots for brewing fine green and oolong tea leaves are made from the unglazed purple clay of Jiangsu (100 miles west of Shanghai).

Our special selection of Yixing teapots are not only authentic and beautiful, but practical as well. On the outside, their artful exterior expresses a special individuality. On the inside, their porous interior begins to absorb a small bit of tea with each brewing, and after some time, develops a special patina that retains the taste, scent, and color of the tea. We recommend choosing a favorite tea—such as Wuyi Oolong, or Sky Between The Branches and dedicating a Yixing teapot to its brewing.

Each handmade pot comes with a descriptive historical booklet, and instructions for tea brewing and care.

Teapot of round leaf shape, polished Shouzen mark. $46.00 with a tin of Sky Between the Branches $50.00

Teapot of compressed round shape and bulging sides $42.00 with a tin of Wuyi Oolong $52.00

Teapot of bamboo tree trunk shape, polished "Shouzen" mark. $46.00
with a tin of **Dragonwell** $50.00

Teapot of gourd shape $42.00
with a tin of **Wuyi Oolong** $52.00

Teapot of round shape with four cups $65.00
with a tin of **Lapsang Souchong** $75.00

Order Toll-Free 1-800-354-5530

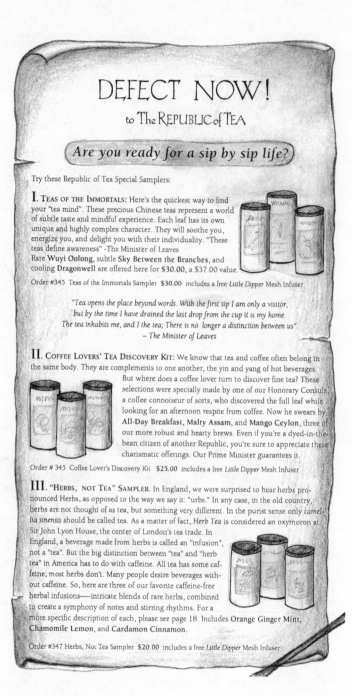

DEFECT NOW!

to The REPUBLIC of TEA

Are you ready for a sip by sip life?

Try these Republic of Tea Special Samplers:

I. TEAS OF THE IMMORTALS: Here's the quickest way to find your "tea mind". These precious Chinese teas represent a world of subtle taste and mindful experience. Each leaf has its own unique and highly complex character. They will soothe you, energize you, and delight you with their individuality. "These teas define awareness" -The Minister of Leaves
Rare **Wuyi Oolong**, subtle **Sky Between the Branches**, and cooling **Dragonwell** are offered here for $30.00, a $37.00 value.

Order #345 Teas of the Immortals Sampler $30.00 includes a free *Little Dipper* Mesh Infuser

"Tea opens the place beyond words. With the first sip I am only a visitor,
but by the time I have drained the last drop from the cup it is my home.
The tea inhabits me, and I the tea; There is no longer a distinction between us".
– The Minister of Leaves

II. COFFEE LOVERS' TEA DISCOVERY KIT: We know that tea and coffee often belong in the same body. They are complements to one another, the yin and yang of hot beverages. But where does a coffee lover turn to discover fine tea? These selections were specially made by one of our Honorary Consuls, a coffee connoisseur of sorts, who discovered the full leaf while looking for an afternoon respite from coffee. Now he swears by **All-Day Breakfast**, **Malty Assam**, and **Mango Ceylon**, three of our more robust and hearty brews. Even if you're a dyed-in-the-bean citizen of another Republic, you're sure to appreciate these charismatic offerings. Our Prime Minister guarantees it.

Order # 345 Coffee Lover's Discovery Kit $25.00 includes a free *Little Dipper* Mesh Infuser

III. "HERBS, NOT TEA" SAMPLER. In England, we were surprised to hear herbs pronounced Herbs, as opposed to the way we say it: "urbs." In any case, in the old country, herbs are not thought of as tea, but something very different. In the purist sense only *camellia sinensis* should be called tea. As a matter of fact, *Herb Tea* is considered an oxymoron at Sir John Lyon House, the center of London's tea trade. In England, a beverage made from herbs is called an "infusion", not a "tea". But the big distinction between "tea" and "herb tea" in America has to do with caffeine. All tea has some caffeine; most herbs don't. Many people desire beverages without caffeine. So, here are three of our favorite caffeine-free herbal infusions—intricate blends of rare herbs, combined to create a symphony of notes and stirring rhythms. For a more specific description of each, please see page 18. Includes **Orange Ginger Mint**, **Chamomile Lemon**, and **Cardamon Cinnamon**.

Order #347 Herbs, Not Tea Sampler $20.00 includes a free *Little Dipper* Mesh Infuser

OUR FULL LEAF TEA IS UNLIKE THE "TEA" FOUND
IN MASS MARKET TEA BAGS. It is tea in its pure,
simple, natural form: hand picked leaves direct
from the world's finest tea gardens. Tea leaves
grow on the evergreen *camellia sinensis* bush which
produces nearly 2000 varieties of leaves. Like
wine, fine tea is rare and is a product of how
it is cultivated – where it is grown, elevation,
and climate. The Republic
of Tea offers only teas of
exceptional character. All
selections are limited in
availability and represent the
best of a particular harvest.

OUR CAFFEINE-FREE HERB
GARDEN TEAS ARE MADE with
exotic, often non-commer-
cially grown full-leaf herbs
and blossoms. Whenever
available we use organically
grown botanicals. We blend
these infusions to achieve
superb and uncommon
tastes combined with the
underlying attributes and
properties of the herbs.

MADAME OOLONG'S TEA LEAF READINGS

.."you are independent, and will travel far & wide."

..."you have many diverse interests and relationships"...

..."you are not yet living life to its fullest."

Order Toll-Free
1-800-354-5530

MY DAY OF TEA

by Bill Rosenzweig
Minister of Progress, The Republic of Tea

7:00 am

My day begins with a hearty pot of **All-Day Breakfast Tea** (see p.6). This small, tightly rolled black leaf, called Keemun, only grows in the Anhui province of southern China. Its distinct reddish cup, deep, yet cheerful flavor and light orchid aroma warms me, waking me gently and setting up my day. It tastes great with a slice of fresh bread and almond butter.

8:30 am

When I get to work, I put the kettle on and brew up some **Sky Between the Branches** (p.14) – a very subtle, rare Chinese green tea with a peaceful chestnut taste. This tea helps me focus and think clearly. It is so delicate in character, it makes me pay attention to it. It keeps me balanced before (and during) my morning staff meeting – which, with all the energy in the room, can sometimes turn chaotic. I share this tea with my companions to achieve a calm, yet alert state that helps keep the meeting humming.

10:30 am

By mid morning, my first appointment arrives and I prepare a pot of **Mango Ceylon** (p.10). I do this because it's a winner: I've yet to meet anyone who didn't love its buoyant, tropical taste and head-spinning aroma. Sometimes I serve our clean, flowery special **Glenburn Darjeeling** (p.7) because its bright, fresh flavor is also easy to appreciate.

Noon

At lunch I treat myself to several small cups of estate-direct **Wuyi Oolong** (p.6), a very rare, large silver-tipped leaf from Formosa – my absolute favorite tea. It always inspires me. When I go out to lunch (and eat that heavy meal that begs a nap), I lift my spirits with a cup of tingly, head-clearing **Cardamon Cinnamon Herb Tea** (p.18).

3:00 pm

Early in the afternoon when I'm ready for a snack (and some letter writing)., I turn to the **Tea of Inquiry** – traditional Japanese Genmaicha – a wonderful, flat green leaf blended with toasted rice (p.14). This cup is so refreshing, and so filling, that I often forget about the craving I was having for a York Peppermint Patty a half an hour earlier.

4:00 pm

This is the time of tea tradition in Britain. We celebrate it a little differently in the Republic, but we try to stop what we're doing to take stock of our lives and our progress for the day. We usually mark the moment with **Malty Assam** (p.7).

5:15 pm

On occasion, when I work late and need a bit of an end-of-the-day push, I like **Big Green Hojicha** (p.14) for its sturdy roasted flavor, noticeable effect, and miniscule caffeine content.

7:00 pm

Back at home – with dinner, especially during a meal of spicy vegetable stir-fry, my wife and I enjoy **Jasmine Jazz** (p.15). Its heavenly scent and crystal clear taste complement many foods. After eating we turn to **Orange Ginger Mint** (p.18), our favorite herbal infusion, for its healthful, flavorful notes and slightly spicy finish. When we have guests over, we usually serve **Coconut Carob Herb Tea** (p.18) or **Vanilla Almond** (p.10) with dessert.

10:45 pm

Before bed, I calm down sipping **Chamomile Lemon Herb Tea** (p.18). This relaxing, honest blend, with its soothing, yet potent botanicals, helps me rest and surrender to sleep at the close of a full day.

A Day of Tea: *One 3.5 oz tin each of my Eight Favorite Teas* including All Day Breakfast, Sky Between the Branches, Mango Ceylon, Wuyi Oolong, Tea of Inquiry, Malty Assam, Vanilla Almond, and Chamomile Lemon. A $76 value for $49.00.

A Day of Tea Sampler: One sampler bag (15 cups or more) of each of the eight teas. $12.00

Send us your Day of Tea. If we select your letter to include in our next catalog, we'll send you a tea-bill gift certificate good for ten different tins of tea of your choice.

Order Toll-Free 1-800-354-5530

Tea is contentment, and contentment is love of content. Drinking tea, desires diminish and I come to see the ancient secret of happiness: wanting what I already have, inhabiting the life that is already mine.

— The Minister of Leaves

CURRENCY

DOUBLEDAY